# Dogs that Bite and Fight

## A Guide for Owners and Trainers

**David Ryan** PG Dip (CABC), CCAB

ISBN 978-1-291-56232-3

# Dogs that Bite and Fight

## A Guide for Owners and Trainers

# Contents

## Part One
## The Principles of Biting and Fighting

## Part Two
## The Practice of Changing Biting and Fighting

Chapter 10 (continued)

# The Author

I was a police dog handler and Home Office accredited instructor for twenty six years, handling and instructing general purpose, public disorder, firearms support, cash/drug/firearms detection and explosives search dogs, originally hunting thieves and burglars in the back streets of Carlisle before being elevated to the dizzy heights of explaining to others how to do it. It was a relief to get off night-shifts and call-outs.

Realising there was more to know about dog training, but not what it was, I took myself off to Southampton University's post graduate diploma in Companion Animal Behaviour Counselling, where I not only found out what some of it was, but also where to go to find out more. Putting the theory to the practice I had so many light-bulb moments I still retain a slight halo to this day (it helps hide my horns).

I passed Southampton with distinction, and consequently reduced training time and costs for police dogs. It's amazing the insights you get when you learn the principles behind what you've already been doing. You start to understand why it doesn't always work and what to do to make it better or put it right. I'm still waiting for the police to thank me.

Southampton led me into behaviour counselling, seeing clients with problem pets on veterinary referral, and when I retired from the police I spent a few years in a James Herriot-esque existence, trundling around the countryside visiting all creatures great and small, and their equally interesting pets.

Because I like to do things properly, I joined the UK's leading organisation for behaviourists, the Association of Pet Behaviour Counsellors, and served as Chairman for three hectic years. I still sit on the committee and help out when I can.

Again aiming for the best, I applied for and was granted accreditation as a Clinical Animal Behaviourist by the Association for the Study of Animal Behaviour in 2008 and have had the privilege to be able to talk about dogs to a pool of the world's best behaviourists.

Amongst others, I've worked with and for the Animal Behaviour and Training Council, the RSPCA at local and national level, and the PDSA. With other APBC members I helped the Scottish Government prepare for the introduction of the Control of Dogs (Scotland) Act.

I don't have time to see private clients any more, which saves on trundling, but continue to help local and national charities with dog assessment and re-homing to keep me on my toes, but mostly because I quite like dogs.

My main work now is divided between lecturing and providing legal expert witness advice, so I guess I'm still plugging away at pulling practice and theory together. I still do some travelling around, assessing pit bull types and other dogs that are alleged to be dangerous, and presenting seminars on my work in the UK and abroad.

I enjoy the balance of hands-on working with dogs and the opportunity to discuss their behaviour with students as diverse as those on Newcastle University's MSc in Applied Animal Behaviour and Welfare and Police Dog Legislation Officer's Courses. I do see some different viewpoints.

This is my solo third book, although I'm proud to have also contributed Chapter 2 *Our Relationship with Dogs* to the joint APBC Book of Companion Animal Behaviour, edited by David Appleby. If you'd like to read the other two, they are:

"*Stop!*" How to control predatory chasing in dogs - looks at the reasons for inappropriate predatory chasing, the more effective solutions and how to go about changing the behaviour.

Dog Secrets - Ironically titled because there are no "secrets", just things you haven't yet learned, this is a common-sense training book about understanding dogs and teaching methods that work.

# Acknowledgements

This book is the culmination of over thirty years of considerable practice and learning, and I'm grateful to all the people with whom I have had the privilege to work and learn from along the way. They are far too many to mention, but all the instructors, handlers, teachers and people to whom I addressed all the questions, and were patient enough to talk through the answers, know who they are. Thank you for your forbearance, but don't think I'm finished yet.

To Sue, Stuart and Claire, my long-suffering family, who I regularly neglected whilst I was handling, learning and asking questions, I owe an enormous debt of gratitude. Without your support, patience and tolerance I'd never have learned anything. Oh, and I'm probably not finished yet.

Finally, I am grateful to all the dogs down the years who taught me more than the academic journals, papers and books put together. I know I shouldn't have favourites, but some just etched their presence, their essence, on me. Every dog is extraordinary in their own way, but some deserve special mention. So here goes...

To Cindy, our first pet and the sweetest Cocker Spaniel you ever met. To Kaiser, my first GSD, who was far too sensitive to be a police dog, and to Major, who was his exact opposite and the first dog I handled that regularly tried to kill me. To Ava who failed as a guide dog, but excelled as my police dog, and Belle, who had more energy per pound than any dog I ever met. To Dan, the Lab who searched for explosives and shared my distress at being away from home, and Moss the Border Collie who helped with his, and my, training.

Come to think of it, I have a growing debt to all the dogs that have helped train me, and to the ones who continue to train me still, because they're not finished yet.

# Introduction

## The problem

Man's best friend can sometimes be our worst enemy. The huge benefits of dog ownership, such as a healthier lifestyle, lower incidence of heart disease and reduced stress have to be weighed against the harm they cause when they bite and fight. The majority of dogs kept as pets fall into the first category – best friends – but a significant minority are our worst enemies.

In the western world dog ownership increased throughout the 20th and the 21st Centuries, with a quarter of households now owning a dog in the UK (over 8 million pets). There are similar percentage numbers in most European countries, over a third of Australian households own a dog and there are almost 80 million dogs (39% of households) in the USA and Canada.

Likewise, the incidence of dog aggression has risen dramatically. In the USA an average of thirty people are killed by dogs each year, double the average during the 1980s, and every year 4.7million Americans are bitten by dogs. The vast majority are children under ten and older people over sixty-one. In the UK deaths are thankfully still relatively rare, but recorded hospital admissions for dog bites more than doubled in the thirteen years between 1998 and 2011 (2,915 to 6,118); the figures are continuing to rise at about 5% per year – far faster than the increase in pet ownership.

You can contrast this with statistics released by the Institute for Economics and Peace which show that in the UK human to human violent crime has decreased by a quarter between 2003 and 2012.

I should emphasise that the UK dog-bite figures are for people who have to spend 24 hours or more in hospital as a result of a dog bite or strike, because these are the only figures recorded, and do not include treatments at accident departments or doctors' surgeries, or those bitten who did not receive official medical treatment. The walking wounded, those stitched up and sent home, simply aren't counted.

In the UK in 2012 nearly six and a half thousand people were admitted to hospital for more than a day as a result of a dog bite or strike. One in six was a child under ten years old – again, as in the US fatality figures, the biggest age group to be represented. Over one thousand UK children were kept in hospital for at least a day due to being bitten by a dog. Almost half needed plastic surgery and two hundred and seventy-eight young children needed speciality oral/facial surgery (plastic surgery to the face) after being bitten by their "best friend".

All studies of dog bites on humans agree that you are far more likely to be bitten by a dog you know than a random dog in the street (usually a ratio of about ¾ to ¼) and that children suffer disproportionately. The family/stranger figures are even more skewed than might be thought because the huge number of postal and other delivery people bitten falls into the "stranger" category. I strongly suspect that if we were able to adjust the figures accordingly they would show that most dog bites are on people known to the dog or visiting the home in some capacity.

Dog bites cost the UK National Health Service in excess of £3 million per year and the USA an estimated $1billion, and attempts by governments in many countries to legislate preventative breed specific bans (where it has been made illegal to own so-called dangerous breeds or types of dog) have also failed to stem the tide, largely through a lack of understanding of where the danger lies.

Behaviourists can be extremely effective but the nature of dog aggression is such that they are only called after the event – after the dog has shown a significant level of aggression, quite often for some time. Whilst they continue to help individual cases they are merely a sticking plaster on the wound. They cannot address the underlying cause.

Nobody records the exact number of people who are bitten, or how many dogs or other animals are attacked by our pets, but the two most significant problem behaviours for which people seek help from behaviourists are aggression towards other dogs and aggression towards people.

Dogs that fight other dogs are a significant category of those relinquished to charities for re-homing (most charities won't re-home dogs that have bitten people) and also a significant source of people being bitten as they intervene.

Our dogs are biting us and fighting other dogs. They are supposed to be our cherished pets. So where is it all going wrong?

In the past century, as humans have become more urban, we have lost our connection with the natural world, and this is no more reflected than in our relationship with dogs. We have lost our feeling for what dogs are, what they value and how to treat them. The population seems polarised between thinking dogs are cuddly little people, teddy-bear substitutes, and alternatively that they are barely-tamed wolves that have to be intimidated into submission lest they seek domination over us. One camp showers them in treats and unconditional affection whilst the other bullies them.

This lack of understanding of the nature of dogs, of what they are, of what they need - this lack of connection - is driving our pets to aggression. And there's no need for it.

Pet dogs depend on us. We breed them for our purposes, we bring them up, we keep them in our homes. There is no need for any pet dog to bite a person or fight another dog. Every time it happens we have let them down. But the numbers of dogs that bite and fight continues to escalate disproportionately.

11

In the following chapters I am going to examine what dog aggression is, what it is for, why it surfaces and what can be done both to prevent and address it. Many of you will recognise your own dog in some of the descriptions and you will find some basic solutions that will reduce or eliminate episodes of biting and fighting.

Nowhere in this book will I suggest anything that the average owner isn't capable of. However, if you have a dog that bites or fights you may have gone beyond the point at which you can correct it yourself. If that is the case, or you simply don't have the confidence to take this on, I urge you to seek qualified professional help rather than continuing to struggle on your own. A tip for when seeking help is to avoid like the plague advice from anyone who says, "*Don't try this at home*". If you can't do it at home, it isn't worth trying.

What I or any other professional can't do though, is provide a cure, because it is not a disease. If it is any single thing it is a misunderstanding; a misunderstanding of a whole species by humans and a misunderstanding by dogs of how to cope with situations into which we force them.

Only by addressing both of these misunderstandings can we hope to make any progress with preventing and changing dogs that bite and fight.

# Part One
# The Principles of
# Biting and Fighting

In which we examine all the whys and wherefores:

the reasons some dogs feel the need to bite and fight,

the role of communication, emotion and learning,

development, breed, sex and individual differences,

and how to prevent and assess the problem behaviour.

## Chapter 1
## Aggression – What Is It?

### Defining aggression

As a concept, aggression can be difficult to pin down. It is far from easy to describe the communication of often complex emotions in terms of a single word, but we all know it when we see it in action, don't we?

Dictionaries use words like "*pugnacious, combative, argumentative, confrontational, violent, hostile, belligerent, agonistic, threatening…*" but it can be very difficult to know where it starts and stops.

Think of two dogs: Meg is chewing a bone that Dan wants.

* If Dan intimidates Meg into leaving the bone by leaping towards her, snarling and showing his teeth, is he being aggressive?

* What if Dan intimidates Meg into leaving the bone by showing his teeth without any noise whilst walking stiffly and slowly towards her?

* What if Meg leaves the bone because Dan is sitting next to her, staring at her without moving?

* How about if Dan lies down next to Meg and invades her personal space, making her feel uncomfortable enough to walk away from the bone?

Most people would agree that the first and probably the second examples were aggression in action, but maybe not the third and fourth. However, the end result is the same in every case – ownership of the bone changes. The emotions of Meg, the intimidated dog, are the same – happiness at having a bone followed by a sense of sadness on losing it. The emotions of Dan, the aggressive dog, are the same – frustration at not having the bone followed by happiness at acquiring it. So where do we draw the line?

There are many definitions of canine aggression (including but not exclusively "territorial", "possessive", "maternal", "competitive", "food-guarding" "defensive" and the ephemeral "dominant"), and many ways of illustrating what it is and isn't, but the only thing that really matters is what the dog feels, the emotional state of the dog, because that is what drives the behaviour.

Obviously we cannot see into the mind of a dog to check on his emotions, but fortunately we can infer emotional states through interpreting actions.

If a dog can be seen through his actions to attempt to proactively control a situation (try to make another dog or person do something or stop doing something) through the use or display of force, then we can infer that he has an aggressive intent.

In all four examples above Dan is displaying a degree of aggression because we can see each time that his intent was to dispossess Meg of the bone (attempting to proactively control a situation) through the use or display of force. The type and degree of force was different on each occasion, and was considerably less in the last two cases, but the emotion driving the behaviour was an aggressive one nonetheless.

Take a moment to visualise all the "types" of aggression in which dogs are involved and you will find that each one fits the above definition. In every case the dog will be attempting to control a situation, not by moving away, or by deferring or submitting, but by using or showing that they are prepared to use force.

All aggression is at the same time communication. The dog is communicating his intent and will use the communication that he thinks most fits the circumstances. However, communication is also simply a reflection of the dog's emotion, which is why we must separate out the proactive element of aggression. A dog can growl because he is afraid, but this is not necessarily an aggressive action. It only becomes aggressive when he attempts to proactively (as opposed to reactively) control the situation that is making him afraid.

Exam time. Ah-ha! You didn't know there was going to be an exam did you? Let's revisit our two dogs: Meg, who is chewing a bone that Dan wants. We can expand the scenario to see if you've been paying attention. Meg still has the bone and is approached by Dan, walking stiffly towards her growling. I think we can agree that he is acting with aggressive intent, but what about Meg's actions?

* If she whimpers and scurries away, leaving the bone, is she being aggressive?

* What if she walks away, leaving the bone, growling and showing her teeth, with the hair on her neck and back standing to attention?

* What if she places her foot on the bone, stands up squarely and silently curls a lip?

15

* How about if she leaves the bone and lunges at Dan's throat, growling?

Go to the top of the class if you said that the last two had aggressive intent, but the first two didn't. The difference of course is in what happens next. In the first two examples Meg does not want to compete, but is upset enough to express her fear and frustration using some of the ways dogs communicate. In the second two she is signalling her intent to stop Dan taking the bone from her by engaging him in a fight, if he wants to take it that far.

If she growls and walks away she is communicating her fear and trying to avoid becoming involved in any conflict. If she growls and walks towards you she is communicating her fear and trying to make you walk away. Her intention is to engage you in conflict and it is up to you to back down, or escalate to fighting.

All dogs are entitled to growl and walk away. Growling and walking towards you is where communication crosses the line into aggression.

In some situations we may agree that dogs are forced into it by circumstances, misunderstanding or conflict imposed upon them by another, and we will address the conditions in which biting and fighting arises in due course, but at least we now know how to recognise aggression when we see it. Next we need to have a look at what aggression is for and why pet dogs seem to becoming more aggressive.

## Why are dogs ever aggressive?

Why do dogs ever feel the need to be aggressive? Why is aggression in their make-up? What's the point of biting and fighting?

All behaviours are *for* something, and the reason is wrapped up in the neo-Darwinian Selfish Gene. Behaviours naturally evolve because they allow the animal to be better at surviving to reproduce than animals that do not show the behaviour, passing the tendency to behave in a successful way to their offspring. So aggression must have a genetic benefit, or it wouldn't exist.

It is easy to see that aggression is part of the survival strategy of many species. It is of huge benefit if you can defend yourself from predation by tooth, claw, hoof or horns, or if you can secure access to the important resources that keep you and your genes alive by fighting for them. The latter includes fighting for the right to mate; beating other members of your own species for the privilege of passing on your fighting ability.

It might seem at first glance that the best strategy for a species to adopt would be to fight for everything and go all-out in attack all the time. Surely this must have the best chance of winning? Unfortunately, any behaviour has trade-offs, the costs of performing the behaviour set against its benefits, and fighting can be costly for survival.

The future is of very little importance if you must fight to prevent being eaten today. If you are defending yourself, then all-out is the only way to go if you have no other options for getting away but, if you are trying to gain a small advantage, all-out fighting may not be your best option.

If you are injured in a fight you may not be able to find food tomorrow. So, even if you are not directly killed in the fight, you may die eventually through sustaining an injury that makes you less able to look after yourself. "*He who fights and runs away, lives to fight another day*" is a natural survival strategy. If the consequence of *not* fighting is that you are a bit less warm, or a little hungrier, you may prefer that to the risk of being so injured through fighting that you cannot walk. There is therefore a balance to be struck.

Dogs' cousin, the wolf, will use extreme aggression when defending their home territory from other unrelated wolves, but moderates to posturing and inhibited bites during disagreements within

17

their own pack. This is because the pack is invariably their family and it would be nonsensical to breed, bring up pups and then kill them in a quarrel over a single meal. Even inflicting a minor injury could result in the sufferer being less able to hunt and therefore less able to help support the pack as a unit to survive.

Because the risks associated with fighting can be so high, most social species have developed a range of behaviours designed to prevent aggression between members of the same group. Canine proactive behaviours, used by individuals to threaten, include forward movements, forward inclined postures, making themselves look bigger, facial grimaces, direct staring, showing teeth and snarling. More passive, defensive behaviours, used by an individual that feels threatened, are usually the opposite: retreating away, backward inclined postures, making themselves look smaller by crouching, passive faces, looking away, and whimpering. We will return to these behaviours later, but here we should note that it is only when this system of posturing breaks down that overt biting and fighting breaks out.

Dogs therefore have a system of aggressive behaviours that can be very useful in defending themselves or their family but should inhibit them, as wolves do, when quarrelling in-house.

Unfortunately (or for them, fortunately) our pet dogs no longer exist in a natural state where survival and reproduction regulates the use of behavioural strategies. *We* now decide which dogs pass on their genes and we have significantly shifted the costs and benefits of individuals using aggression.

In removing the direct survival pressures from our pet dogs we have also removed the need for them to be behaviourally balanced. Dogs no longer have the usual selection pressures that determine which ones survive to reproduce their genes, and consequently their behaviour, in subsequent generations.

Our decisions made in choosing which pet dogs reproduce often have nothing to do with balancing their behaviour, but how they perform in selected tasks or, more recently, how they look in a show ring. We have removed the selection pressure that inhibits aggressive behaviour. Worse than that we have actually increased the tendency for some dogs to use aggression by breeding them for purposes for which it suits us to have dogs that bite and fight, such as dog-fighting, vermin control or guarding.

In a natural state a dog that started too many fights, because he can't or won't use the posturing communication that prevents it, would suffer the consequences of too many wounds and infections, or eventually come up against a bad-assed mother he couldn't beat. He would not live long enough to reproduce the behaviour in many offspring. Likewise a dog that fought for every resource at every opportunity may be resource-rich in the short term (have a lot of bones) but is unlikely to secure many mating opportunities because he is impossible to live with. Any potential mother wouldn't tolerate his bad-ass attitude.

In the unnatural state in which we keep pet dogs there is little cost to fighting in social encounters. If they are injured we take them to the vet who patches them up and doses them with antibiotics. We keep him on a lead to "*keep him out of trouble*". We explain, "*She doesn't like other dogs*" and smile resignedly. When dogs bite people we apologise it away and give them another chance. We make a joke of it, "*Ha-ha, dogs are supposed to bite postmen – that's what they do!*" The use of aggression only has a cost for dogs when it is at its most extreme. Only when they have inflicted so many or such damaging injuries do we apply the ultimate sanction and permanently remove them from the gene pool.

But lots of lower level bites by dogs are tolerated, especially from the smaller breeds that do not inflict massive injuries. We tread

19

carefully around the bigger ones, bred for guarding and fighting, lest we provoke them: *"Don't step over him." "Don't come in until I've put her in another room to calm down." "Don't touch him there." "We can't show you their Mum, she gets defensive around her pups."*

There is an underlying pool of potential aggressive behaviour in our pet dogs. It should be a small puddle, kept small through the use of posturing communication, driven by the genetic costs of biting and fighting.

By removing the consequences of not inhibiting aggression, in both frequency and degree, we have encouraged an ocean of potential aggressive behaviour in our pets. The selection pressures we apply reduce the costs of aggressive behaviour so that the benefits appear more attractive. Even when the benefits are quite low, if the cost is even lower the behaviour won't be inhibited.

In any population there is a tendency to inherit and indulge in aggressive behaviour on a scale. At the very bottom end of the scale are the individuals who never behave in that way. They are very few and tend to die away because they are not indulging in a behaviour that has a benefit. Towards the middle lie the majority of individuals who exist in the Goldilocks zone, they are performing the behaviour at just the right level. At the top end of the scale are the individuals who are doing too much of it and they too have a tendency to die out because the costs are too great to sustain the benefit. Natural selection pressures keep the Goldilocks zone where it is by lopping off the extremes.

However, removing some of the costs pushes the bulk of the population towards an over-use of the behaviour. Now there are more individuals indulging in the behaviour, none at the lower levels and far more at the higher levels.

This graph shows the population of pet dogs' use of aggression as a strategy.

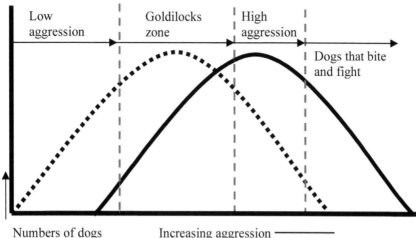

The left hand (dotted) line shows what happens under natural selection pressures: some under-use aggression (and probably get bullied), most individuals use it appropriately, that is in the circumstances and degree which most benefits the species, fewer over-use aggression, and fewer still bite and fight. But if costs are removed, as exemplified by the right-hand (dashed) distribution line, although there are still quite a large number of dogs in the Goldilocks Zone there is an enormous shift in the percentage of the general population using a high level of aggression, and the proportion of dogs that bite and fight increases significantly.

In the current domestic pet dog population there is a bias in the tendency to use aggression. The bias is in favour of aggressive behaviour because the costs are so low. If the costs are low, more of the population will indulge in aggressive behaviour, pushing the centre point towards a general increase and more individuals over the unacceptable point (biting and fighting). But why is this happening now?

It might seem strange to us but the concept of pet-dogs-for-all is relatively new in terms of canine evolution. Dogs have been with us for about twenty thousand years and there are skeletons that have been identified as dogs of different shapes and sizes dating back to about eight thousand years ago. We know pretty much as a certainty that dogs were used for particular purposes at least six thousand years ago because identifiably different dog types appear on pottery and cave art.

The UK Kennel Club is recognised as the world's first and was founded less than one hundred and fifty years ago (1873). There were stud books (records of breeding) for dogs in existence before then, but most of these were breeding for a type of "work", such as foxhounds. The Foxhound Kennel Studbook was officially founded in 1844, but the first official pack (the Bilsdale hunt) had been around since 1688.

Anyway, therein lies the reality of pet dog breeding. All modern pedigree dogs have, in terms of canine history, been recently bred as pets from dogs that were workers. "Recently" means the last 150 years or so. Even our companion dogs were originally guards, Spaniels and Terriers.

Breed differences will be examined in Chapter 4, but for now we simply need to know that only tolerable aggression was bred in to working dogs - that is the degree of biting and fighting that was necessary for their work. Any dog that bit their owner or fought with other dogs to the detriment of their work would not be bred from and in many cases would be knocked on the head to make permanently sure they couldn't do it again. Those that were purposely bred to be aggressive certainly didn't find their way into the pet population.

In practical terms our failure to do the modern equivalent of this now means we end up with a population of dogs that is generally more aggressive, and a significant proportion that are too aggressive.

This is not something that can be addressed at the level of individual dogs and owners, but must be dealt with by society, starting with the breeding of dogs for temperament.

I know that many responsible breeders will throw up their hands and shout, "*But I DO breed for good temperament!*" and that is commendable. Well done. Smiley face. But a larger number will protest that taking any temperament traits away will harm "their" breed. This of course is nonsense of the highest order. Taking away aspects of temperament that encourage a dog to fight other dogs, or be overly defensive or territorial, may be detrimental to the original purpose of the breed, but how many breeds fulfil their original function today? There is no need to be breeding pet dogs that have a tendency towards using aggression in any way, shape or form.

Look at some of the words used in breed standards and descriptions: courageous, bold, fearless, suspicious, independent, protective, one-man-dog, aloof… all are euphemisms for _not friendly enough_. The Kennel Club description of a breed standard is that it "_ensures that the breed is fit for function_", but functions change. The function of most breeds now is that of pet and family companion.

More worrying are the majority of hobbyists who are breeding dogs, because they have no idea what we're talking about. Sadly, dog breeding is considered to be a thing that anyone and everyone can do, requiring no expertise at all. Unfortunately, good dog breeding is a skill, not something that everyone can do, and the huge rise in the numbers of hospital admissions for dog bites is testament to that.

Anyone who breeds a litter of pups has to shoulder responsibility for the temperament of their dogs. Every aggressive incident is a combination of nature and nurture, but until breeders get over their vested interest in breeding from a, "_good specimen_" regardless of its temperament rather than because of its temperament, or just to make a few quid, we will continue to have a less than optimum raw material.

And don't think we can get away with just blaming breeders either. All of us who love dogs have a responsibility to lobby for better standards for breeding, and to educate those who are breeding dogs. Everybody who buys a puppy contributes to the current poor state of dog breeding unless they consciously take a stand against it. When I say it is a "society problem", that means us. Me and you.

Dogs need to be able to use some aggression because aggression is part and parcel of the canine make-up. Trying to breed it out completely would probably be impossible, but reducing it should be an aim. I have lost count of the number of times I have been told that the snarling monster on the end of the lead before me is "*really well bred*" and has "*several champions in his pedigree*".

The problem isn't that dogs can use aggression when they need to – all animals do that. The problem arises with the degree of aggression that dogs use and the contexts in which they feel the need to use it. Overall, the current population of pet dogs uses it too soon and too severely. Breeding can address that by compensating for the loss of natural costs. Take the more aggressive dogs out of the gene pool, regardless of how good a specimen they are, how many trophies their granddad won, or how much you love them (and the money they generate) and aggression in the general pet population will reduce.

But although this goes some way to explaining why too many pet dogs bite and fight, it is a long term problem rather than something that can help current dogs and owners.

For even the most temperamentally aggressive dogs there are alternatives to biting and fighting available in any given circumstance and the first, as already mentioned, is the social communication that in most canines serves to reduce it. Why is it failing in pet dogs?

# Chapter 2

# Communication – *"What's that you say?"*

Having noticed that aggression is all wrapped up in communication, we should examine what dogs are trying to tell us when they bite and fight.

Biting and fighting are extreme manifestations of communication that should only be necessary in the most extreme of circumstances. Even lower forms of aggression, such as such as grumbling, growling, snarling, teeth-baring and snapping should only be necessary occasionally.

If they are occurring frequently we can assume that other forms of communication have broken down, like humans declaring war only after diplomatic channels have ceased to be effective.

Because there is a cost to biting and fighting, even if it is artificially low and boils down to just the expenditure of energy, dogs too will only bite and fight if they believe that diplomatic relations are ineffective.

There are two parties in every communication: the sender and the receiver. The sender transmits the information in a form that she expects it to be understood. Only if the receiver takes delivery of the information in a form that he can understand will he be able to act on it appropriately.

If the sender transmits information in a form that no one understands, it cannot be acted upon. If the sender transmits information in a standard form of communication but the receiver fails to understand, it cannot be acted upon.

What is needed therefore is a common language that can be sent, received and understood by all dogs and understood by all humans. Unfortunately we don't have one. We have the makings of one in the canine postural communication of dogs, but there's a problem with it. The problem arises precisely because it *is* postural and involves subtle changes in positions of different parts of the body. You've probably noticed that not all dogs look the same. It would be easier for them to communicate with each other and with us if they did, but they don't; they come in all shapes and sizes. This causes them huge problems when it comes to sending intelligible messages and in interpreting the messages sent by other dogs.

## Dog to dog

As a simplified example let's consider two dogs, a German Shepherd Dog (GSD) and an English Springer Spaniel (ESS) meeting for the first time. Neither has met another of that breed before but both are adept at the postural communication of their own breed. Both know that pricked ears are a sign of alarm in a dog.

As they meet, the GSD is fairly relaxed but the ESS is worried by the approach of this bigger dog. Therefore the GSD's ears are not actually pricked in communication, but the ESS's ears, though hardly showing anything but their usual floppy droop, are very pricked indeed.

Remember, the template of communication they are each working from starts with how they themselves look. They each consider their own static posture to be the norm for a relaxed dog. The conversation goes something like:

**ESS**: *Good grief, look at your ears! They are hyper-pricked! How do you get your ears up there? You must be in a massively high state of arousal!*

**GSD**: *Wassup man? You look relaxed. I'm coming over to sniff hello.*

**ESS**: *Stay back! My ears are mightily pricked, or at least as mightily pricked I can get them. I'm telling you to get back! I'm scared half to death by your "enormous ear approach"!*

**GSD**: *Cool man. Ears still down – happy to see me eh?*

26

**ESS**: *Aaaargh! GET BACK!*

That's when he launches at the throat of the unsuspecting GSD. All caused by the difference in ear carriage between two breeds. And that's only one small aspect of posturing communication. A few years ago (before tail-docking for cosmetic reasons was banned) we could have gone through the same introduction using the tail as a guide – up and wavy for the GSD and docked short for the ESS. The result could well have been the same. What then of dogs with permanently high or curled tails?

Dogs are usually adept at learning their own breed body language from their dam and siblings, but how are they going to learn that of every single breed? The best they are going to do is learn the general principles and try to extrapolate them to every dog they meet. Dogs that are similar in shape to them might be easier to understand, but the ones that are dissimilar could be very difficult indeed. The opportunities for mistakes and conflict are huge.

GSDs speak GSD and ESSs speak ESS, but they are two different dialects of the same language. The same goes for every other breed – they all have common canine components but they are hampered by the convoluted shapes into which we have bred them. What chance has a Hungarian Puli got? Half the people who see one for the first time mistake it for a sheep! But don't think that it is only the exotic breeds that have problems, what about a Boxer, or a Pekinese, Shih Tzu, Old English Sheepdog, Poodle, Bearded Collie, Lhasa Apso, Pug, Afghan Hound, Bichon Frise, Chow Chow and Maltese?

I could go on… there are only about another three hundred breeds to go… but right through the A to Z from Affenpinscher to Yorkshire Terrier, dogs' communication is hampered by their looks; by the way we have bred them to look. Dogs failing to understand other dogs' body postural communication is common, as are fights that start through miscommunication.

## Dog to people

Dogs are remarkably adept at learning human communication. In fact they seem to have a special relationship with humans that other animals do not, for example they are the only animal that follows the direction of a pointing human finger without being taught (other animals, including wolves, look at the finger). They are the only animal that investigates where we look when we have signalled it might be pertinent to them. Try it – call your dog, make eye contact with them, then look towards the door – your dog will look too. Now try it with your cat. See the difference?

These kinds of glances and looks are the level of communication that dogs work on all the time. They are very subtle and most people don't take the time and effort to watch and learn from them. Dogs learn to understand human communication but only a few humans bother to learn "dog" as a language. If you want to change a dog that bites and fights, you have to learn the more subtle levels of communication.

There are shelf-loads of books with lovely pictures and explanations of what the dogs are showing, but there is no substitute for going to the park and observing dogs. Watch them, try to interpret them and you will eventually be able to predict what is about to happen. This is a skill, much like learning any other language. The more you practice the better you become.

By the way, barking, the sound we most associate with canine communication, seems to be the dog equivalent of shouting in a *"Look stupid! I'm trying to tell you something!"* way. There are about six types of bark, depending on how you categorise them, that reflect the emotion of the dog:

Fear - Anger - Frustration - Loneliness - Pleasure - Excitement

The average human isn't particularly adept at telling them apart. It seems we only get it right about 40% of the time. So, if they don't have the function of conveying meaning, maybe they have the function of emphasis. Maybe dogs evolved to bark because we don't pay their quieter body language any attention. Maybe if we paid more attention to what they're expressing, dogs wouldn't need to bark.

Of course dogs make other noises such as whines, whimpers, sighs, groans and grumbles, but as communication they are always a poor second to the body language.

Because dogs regard us as part of the family, they use their body postural communication towards people, so far as their breed body type will allow, and they expect us to understand and act on what they are communicating.

This isn't the "*woof-woof-woof*" that Lassie used to convey that little Jimmy had fallen down the old mine shaft, breaking his leg, and the flood waters were rising so fast that if the rescue helicopter didn't follow her right away he could well drown. Canine communication is the reflection of their emotions.

As I get up from my chair, our Collie dog, "Fox", lying on her bed off to one side of me, lifts her head, slightly pricks her ears and looks at the door. As I turn away from the door, towards the kettle, she deflates a little, her head droops back down, ears flatten and she lets out a little sigh – her whole being reflecting her disappointment. I smile at her and we both understand each other.

If that had been a human conversation, with words, it would have gone:

Fox - *Time for a walk?!*

Me - *Not yet, maybe after this brew.*

Fox - *Aw, blimey, I'm bored and fed up…*

Me - *I know. We'll go soon, just relax for now.*

Dogs express what they are feeling through their body language. Read it and we can communicate with them. They read ours all the time. Failing to read theirs causes us all manner of difficulties.

Aggression over food can be one of the most difficult behaviours to change. The reason is that is has usually been practiced for a long time before it is seen as a problem. It often arises from a lack of our understanding of canine communication.

Bobby's case illustrates how confusion can arise. Bobby was a placid Labrador, just over two years old. He'd always been fed in the corner of the kitchen, bowl nestling in the crux of the two walls as he greedily shoved his head into it. He liked his food. The children were told not to bother him while he ate, but one or other would occasionally walk past him on their way between the door, the fridge and the sink, as they did their homework at the kitchen table.

They didn't pay him any attention when he had his head stuck in the bowl, but if they had they would have seen him tense-up every time they went past, stopping eating and giving them a sideways glare. He had always been tense when eating because he'd been from a big litter and had to defend his portion of the communal dish as a puppy. He'd learned that eating was to be done in a hurry if he was to get his share, or another pup would take it.

The tense glare reflected his emotion every time one of the children walked past. Bobby was communicating his fear of someone taking his food from him, and that he was not going to let that happen. From his point of view it worked really well; the children always walked away from him. The family had no idea there was any communication happening at all.

On the occasions when one of the children lingered by him for slightly longer, or walked a little closer than usual, he would turn his shoulder towards them, stiffen, glare sideways and flick his lips into a half-snarl, increasing the, "*Don't try to take my food*" communication. But he was facing the wall and all the family saw was a brief pause in him eating.

It came as a huge shock to them the day the eight-year-old dropped her pencil from the kitchen table and ran after it as it rolled towards the corner of the room. As she got closer to Bobby and his food-bowl he stiffened, then glared and flicked his half-snarl. As she bent down to pick up the pencil from where it had come to rest against his bowl he snapped and bit her cheek. Just a front-tooth snap, a quite inhibited bite really, but enough to take a chunk of skin and leave her scarred for life. As her parents said afterwards, they simply didn't believe he would ever do a thing like that. It was completely out of character and out of the blue. From Bobby's perspective he'd been telling them for two years; they'd always listened before; why had they forced him to be really assertive?

The communication started as a slight tensing of posture, developing into glares and half-snarls when that wasn't working, and then to the bite. At what point did communication become aggression? It was always aggression. Bobby was always proactively controlling access to his food through a display of force. He was making the children go away by using a threat gesture. The family never knew because they hadn't bothered to watch what he was telling them. Had they done so they could have intervened before he bitten their daughter's face.

We will look at to how to change aggression in Part Two, but I should tell you about changing Bobby's attitude whilst we're here. We could have done lots of stuff, moving the bowl, training a "leave-it", doing some lifestyle changes, but we didn't. Bobby ate dried kibble food and was a good eater; most Labradors are. All we did was place a pot of tiny sausage-pieces on the table and the children picked one out and threw it at him every time they walked past him at teatime, calling his name at the same time.

Pretty soon Bobby would look up from his bowl in expectation when the children called his name and it was only a short step from there to ask him to come away from his half-full bowl for a sausage-piece. Eventually we phased out the sausage but any time the children walked past he would look up for a treat and had to be told to go back to eating again. Once a week or so one of the children would toss a food treat at him whilst he was eating, just to keep the good memory alive.

We changed Bobby's expectation of the outcome of "children arriving whilst eating" from a negative worry about a possible loss of food, to a positive anticipation of better food arriving. If they'd recognised his communication and dealt with it like that as a puppy, no one would have been bitten.

Failing to recognise what a dog is trying to tell them is the single biggest cause of children being bitten and is caused by a conflict in the communication between two species. Children are programmed to hug; close facial contact is encouraged; kissing is a term of endearment.

One of the best feelings a parent can bestow on their child is to give them a hug, a kiss and a cuddle. The child is totally helpless in the arms of their protector and at the same time so very safe. From very early days children know that being hugged, kissed and cuddled is a nice thing, and they want to give that nice feeling to other children and their toys. There is no cuter sight than a toddler cuddling his baby sister, and every time we see him hugging and kissing his teddy-bear we go, "*Awwwww*".

Don't think that adults are any less programmed for close face to face contact either. Our most intimate moments, where we express our love for each other, are just that. Why would we not express our love for our dogs in the same way?

Dogs, on the other hand, don't do kissing; they don't do hugging; they don't do cuddling. Humans have a dense collection of sight receptor cells at the front of our eyes, the fovea, that helps us to focus on objects that are very close to us. Most mammals, including dogs, lack that ability, so things close to their face are consequently very blurred. It is probably very difficult for a dog to discern intention from the expression on a person's face at that distance. It is no wonder then that very close facial contact can be worrying for many dogs. It can appear very threatening if you can't see what the intention is.

Although licking is used as a communication device in dogs, it is used by dogs that are trying to signal they are no threat. It is emphatically not a kiss to say "*I love you*". Developed from the puppy licking at the mouth of the adult to stimulate regurgitation, licking at faces means "*I'm like a puppy to you, please don't hurt me*". When dogs use it to other dogs, it usually has the effect of inhibiting aggression and allows the licker to indulge in silly puppy play behaviour, which is tolerated by the lickee. The appropriate canine communication reply to being licked is, "*Fine, I appreciate you mean no harm and I will not do anything (else) to worry you.*"

Admittedly dogs will snuggle in and up to you, but only on their terms. This usually means that they are free to leave at any time. Whilst dogs will occasionally throw a leg over the body of another dog whilst curled up snoozing in a basket, or on the couch together, the intention is never to actively cuddle. No dog would ever consider saying to another "*Come here while I give you a great big hug!*"

Dogs do not like to be confined. Generally speaking dogs do not like to lose control of their own body to another. They do not like to be picked up, grabbed, cuddled or hugged. They will try to avoid any interaction they cannot walk away from when they choose. One of the most aversive and threatening things a dog can do to another she meets in the park is to throw a leg over his back. It is very threatening because the other dog understands that she is limiting his ability to control himself; his ability to move away. As we will see later, moving away is one of the things dogs can do to reduce their fear of an interaction.

Of course, dogs can learn to like being picked up, hugged and cuddled. My first police dog used to leap into my arms at the end of a round of agility from sheer joy. Teaching them it is a pleasant experience is one of the most important things you can do to avoid them biting through a misinterpretation of human communication. But it is not a default setting for them like it is for us, it has to be learned. Because it has to be learned, the circumstances in which it is learned are also important. Being cuddled by your Mum isn't the same as being hugged by a random toddler.

Whilst writing this, out of curiosity I Googled for images of "dogs cuddling humans". On the first page there were twenty pictures that could be described as a dog and human cuddling: six were of people and dogs asleep together, snuggled in, but not cuddling; in one the head of the dog can't be seen, so we can't tell what she feels about it; in ten the dog is tolerating or mildly cheesed off in a, "*Good grief, here we go again*" kind of way; and in three the dog is positively trying to tell them to stop, and stop now. Not one of the dogs is actively enjoying being cuddled. This is not the worrying part, because most seem to be tolerating it or asleep. The worrying part is that there are so many people who think that their dog is enjoying it when they really aren't!

When I searched for images of "dogs kissing people" it got worse. All the dogs that were licking looked seriously unhappy about the situation.

Why does this matter? Because the mismatch in expectations can force the dog to use aggression when communication breaks down.

I was referred the case of a solid black Cocker Spaniel, Lucy. She'd been bought as a companion for the nine-year-old daughter of the family and for the first few months of Lucy's life she was dressed-up, put in a pram, combed, brushed and otherwise treated like a dolly. At ten months she first grumbled and walked away when the daughter hugged her on the sofa. This happened a few times more and soon Lucy started to grumble whenever the daughter came into the room, then would go and hide under the table.

When the daughter was not around Lucy was her usual sociable self. She would sit on Mum's knee, snuggle up on the sofa and happily played fetch with the fourteen-year-old daughter.

The night before I got the call the nine-year-old had come in and plonked herself down on the sofa next to where Lucy was snuggled in to Mum. She picked up Lucy and hugged her onto her knee, arms wrapped around her as she snuggled her own face into Lucy's neck. Lucy licked at her face and, as the nine-year-old moved to a face-to-face hug, bit her on the cheek, enrolling her in category of children under ten requiring oral/facial surgery for that year.

Admittedly there was some background to this case, as Lucy had built up an aversion to being poked, prodded and generally hurt when she was treated as a dolly, but the crucial miss was a failure to understand that Lucy was threatened by confinement. Being confined obviously had worrying connotations for Lucy as it was often the prelude to being jammed into a frock or tugged with a comb, so it wasn't just a natural reluctance to tolerate it, but a learned one as well.

Lucy found herself confined and in what she considered to be a danger of being hurt. There was little she could do, but she did try to use licking as a means of reducing the threat. When that didn't work there was nothing left in her armoury but proactive aggression. In this case Lucy went straight from attempting to defer, to get the threat to go away by communicating her unease, to biting, because the threat was imminent and there were no other options available.

This is a good illustration of canine communication intended to reduce threat. It doesn't *have* to follow a linear progress by first starting with little worried eye-flicks, through stiffening and head-turning and all the way to the degrees of contact such as snaps, nips, front-tooth bites and full bites. It can skip bits altogether. The dog will use what she thinks is the most appropriate response at the time. If she feels that the danger is too close or she has learned that the smaller signals don't work in this situation, she can escalate straight to the top level from nowhere. However, when a dog does that, there have usually been earlier warning signs that have gone unheeded.

Lucy's was a similar situation to the dog that has run away and hidden under the table, but is pursued because the toddler, "*Just wants to cuddle him*". Trapped, with no other way out, the dog bites. It doesn't matter what communication the dog is giving off, looking sideways and down, dropped ears, tail tucked, grinning, rolling over on his back, he can't avoid the oncoming threat. Maybe he doesn't have time to use all the lower levels of communication because the toddler is in his face now. So he bites, usually on the face because the face is nearest.

Any canine communication *can't* work because the toddler doesn't understand it and the adults aren't paying attention. But who gets the one-way trip to the vet?

Canine social aggression is communication. Often people only consider aggressive behaviour in a dog to be a problem when it reaches the extremes of biting and fighting, but it can include lesser degrees, such as glares, lip-flicking, grumbling, growling, snarling, teeth-baring and snapping at the air without making contact. Bites too can vary from light touches with the teeth right through to punctures, rips and tears that inflict serious injury.

Even before these behaviours, dogs can exhibit their discomfort through less obvious communication: head turning away and down, tail under, dropped or pricked ears, corners of the mouth turned down, eyes averted, lowered body posture, stiff body, tail straight out, eye-flicks, staring, leaning or walking towards (or away). The scale of aggressive behaviour begins when the dog decides to manage the situation through the use or display of force, often well before what we normally think of as aggression because we only stick the label on the extreme forms.

From Bobby the Labrador's point of view he was using threat communication to defend his food. There was always an aggressive intent, but the family wasn't aware of it for two years. Only when the level of aggression he was using proved ineffective did Bobby increase it to biting.

From Lucy the Spaniel's point of view she usually deferred when threatened; walked away and hid. It was only when she couldn't walk away and her other communication, licking and lots of head turning and ear and eye positions, had failed, that she resorted to biting.

Both dogs had been communicating like mad, but nobody was listening.

Rather than being something that switches on and off suddenly, aggression is part of a range of behaviours that dogs have available to them to deal with life's everyday challenges. Many of these behaviours are passive and it is only when the dog changes from trying to avoid a situation, through things like moving away or showing that they are not happy, to confrontationally trying to manage the situation, should we term it "aggression".

The circumstances in which dogs bite and fight often seem to come as a surprise to owners, especially the first time a dog resorts to aggression to solve a problem, but they are remarkably predictable when seen from the dog's point of view. Learning to understand canine communication can help head-off aggressive behaviour before it happens, but it can also help to know why a dog feels the need to bite or fight.

There are individual differences in the tendency to use aggression that we will examine in Chapter 4, but the underlying emotions driving biting and fighting remain fairly constant across all types, and it is to these common denominators that we turn our attention next.

# Chapter 3

# Emotions – Deeds, not Breeds

We have already seen that aggression is not a single response, but a series of behaviours that the dog performs when he feels particular emotions. Biting and fighting are the outward expressions of these emotions. The simple question *"Why does my dog bite or fight?"* has a simple answer, *"Because he feels the need to"*. The next question, *"Why does he feel the need to?"* gets to the very crux of the issue and needs a more in-depth explanation.

The main driving emotions for biting and fighting are fear and frustration, with a third possibility of a positive emotion related to the *relief* of fear or frustration and a fourth, less common, positive enjoyment of the behaviour in play or predation. The final possibility is any combination of the primary emotions. This emotion or combination of emotions provides the motivation for the behaviour and that motivation is the reason he feels the need to bite and fight.

Don't worry, this is less complicated than it sounds and we can usually pin down the cause of an individual episode of biting or fighting by examining it in terms of the motivation. By looking at how the dog perceives the interaction, through interpreting their canine communication, we can assign a motivation to the biting or fighting. Once we have the motivation, we have a range of options we can employ to deal with it. As we have already seen with Bobby, and we will see again later, changing the underlying emotion changes the behaviour.

## Fear

When a fearful dog uses aggression it is almost invariably because he thinks he is under some form of threat, but of course the terms of the threat will differ for each dog. For example, it could be to his personal safety or to take away something, or someone, he values highly. The threat makes the dog fearful that an aversive event is taking place or is about to take place. As always when dealing with dogs that bite and fight, we have to look at the incident from the dog's perception, because it is the dog's perception of what is happening that makes him fearful and the fear that motivates the aggressive behaviour. A threat is a threat only if the dog thinks it is.

Dogs have three genetically prepared ways of dealing with fears. "Genetically prepared" has the specific meaning that they are able to learn them more easily. It is possible for a dog to learn any behaviour to remove a cause of a fear, but genetically prepared ones are easier to learn. It is almost like the wiring is already there for them, it just needs to be joined up.

For example a dog could learn that sneezing makes the postman go away, if it was taught properly, but the genetically prepared strategy of "barking like a maniac" is much easier to learn, without being specifically taught. There is no genetically prepared wiring for dealing with a threat by sneezing and we would need to fix it in the brain through repeated teaching before it could be used. Conversely the connections available to be made for barking at an intruder are so well fixed in some breeds that they find it impossible not to do. This is important to remember when we come to discussing breed differences in behaviour.

Unless taught differently, dogs deal with threats through hiding, moving away, friendly social communication, or using aggression.

The main difference between social threats and threats posed by predators is that with a social threat there is the opportunity to use intra-species communication (dog to dog, which of course includes dog to human as well), whereas with predators, if running away hasn't worked, there will be escalation to all-out defensive aggression without further communication. There is no point in trying to use social communication when your life is in danger from another species that doesn't recognise what you are saying anyway. It is futile trying to surrender to a hungry leopard.

However, as dogs don't consider other dogs and people to be predators, we can confine our discussion to social threats. If you want to stop your dog biting and fighting leopards, perhaps you need a more specialist book.

Hiding and moving away are good ways of resolving social threats as long as the threat does not follow. They are at the more benign end of the scale of dealing with fears. If they do not work, and the threat does follow, or is so close that it cannot be dealt with by moving or hiding, the postural communication we discussed in Chapter 2 comes into play. When this fails biting and fighting can be the result.

Although dogs can learn to be afraid of almost anything, common fears in which aggression is used are:
* approach of home range by strangers ("territorial")
* something which has previously hurt (hair pulled when grooming)
* a type or class of person (toddlers, men with sticks, veterinary surgeons)
* unusual objects (umbrellas, fireworks)
* close social contact (other dogs or humans)
* loss of resources that contribute to emotional balance (food, toys or proximity to a person who is important to them)

This list is by no means exclusive, and you come across new ones all the time. In the park this morning I met a man who told me his dog was afraid of having her photograph taken. She curls up in a ball to hide her face if a camera is pointed at her.

Her owner places an anthropomorphic interpretation on her behaviour, but in reality it is classic fearful hiding. I haven't done a complete investigation and don't have the full facts, but I think the most

41

likely reason for her behaviour is that she was probably startled by a camera flash and has come to associate cameras with flashes, which she fears and tries to avoid. Avoiding cameras also results in avoiding flashes and rewards the hiding behaviour with a feeling of relief, regardless of whether a flash subsequently happens or not. Thus she believes that to avoid the flash it is necessary to hide every time. This could develop from one single camera flash – large oak trees from little acorns grow.

Fears can be simple in that they are sometimes very concrete and easy for us to comprehend, but they can also be more ephemeral, such as the fear of losing control over access to a person. Fears can also be a combination of factors, such as fear of getting out of the car because it sometimes predicts that she will be left at home on her own.

Dogs are very good at chaining events together, as anyone who has ever picked up a lead or opened a tin of dog food will know, so we need to be aware that something frightening can also be associated with anything that predicts it.

I saw a dog that was zapped with an electric collar in an attempt train him to come back when told, that had started to attack people. The reason he was not coming back when told was that he was running up to greet people, but he quickly made the association that whenever he now did that, he felt pain from the collar. He changed from happily, if somewhat annoyingly, running up to greet people, to attacking them because of his fear of the pain they apparently caused him. The fear of people that made him bite originated in the pain of the collar used to train him to come away from them. An original fear can sometimes be disguised by a stimulus that predicts it – like this and my hypothesis for the camera-shy dog.

It is also as well to remember that when dogs are in a state of fear they are much more likely to use aggression generally, perhaps resulting in it being redirected towards someone or something else.

This is one of the reasons why it is not always helpful to place labels on "types" of aggression.

**Frustration**

The other major source of the initial use of aggressive behaviour is frustration, preventing the dog from doing something she really wants to do, which causes anger. Again, it has to be seen from the dog's point of view, with the individual dog's values taken into account. Whilst we might not think it reasonable that a dog bites her owner's leg because he is preventing her from chasing a car, we can at least understand that chasing the car must have had a very high value for her to resort to such a frustrated angry response. Dogs' values are not our values and they do not want the same things as us. We look at canine values in more depth later, but to understand aggression we must also understand the power of frustration.

Frustration causes anger. If your dog really, really, really wants that ball, or to go with you in the car, or to play with the other dog, and she is prevented from getting the result she wants, she will become frustrated. Maybe not just slightly annoyed, but massively frustrated and angry.

That anger drives the dog to attempt to control the situation, and can become so extreme that she directs the aggression towards whatever is nearby, whether that is the dog she previously wanted to play with, the obstinate owner, or even inanimate objects such as a gate that bars the way. She just lashes out to vent her feelings.

There appear to be genetic predispositions in dogs that lack impulse-control, which of course makes them more prone to frustration. We all know a dog that lacks self-control, the ability to control their own impulsive behaviour. This kind of dog can be a real handful because they grab at life, doing what they want when they want. They are usually very reactive, can't resist the urge to be involved and push others out of the way. They appear selfish and very often don't take no for an answer.

Some studies suggest that the heritable aspect of this behaviour is due to a lack of availability of the neurochemical serotonin in the brain, but more work needs to be done on the mechanisms responsible. We don't as yet know how or why they lack serotonin. In lay terms serotonin relaxes you, chills you out. It is easy to see how dogs that lack sufficient of it could become frustrated, without the ability to calm themselves down.

It is thought that Cocker Rage Syndrome, where Cocker Spaniels in certain breeding lines inherit a tendency to explode into uncontrollable aggression, my well be due to a lack of serotonin in the brain. Cocker Rage is now recognised to exist in other breeds and individuals too, and is more accurately termed "impulsive aggression".

Mind, don't go sticking a label on your dog for no reason. Your Cocker Spaniel is far more likely to suffer normal frustrations and fears than she is to have a syndrome. Remember Lucy, the solid black Cocker that bit the face of the over-hugging daughter? She was referred to me as Cocker Rage, but she didn't have a syndrome, just a lack of understanding.

Regardless of inherited predispositions, all dogs have the ability to become frustrated in many different situations, but common frustrations where aggression is used usually centre round their inability to control resources or opportunities that are important to them. For example if a dog is so attached to a person that they find it difficult to cope in their absence, they may try to prevent that person from leaving by biting them.

You see it in rescue dogs that are confined to kennels for much of the day. When they are taken out the interaction with people is sooooo nice they don't want it to end. When it comes time to go back in the pen they become frustrated at the loss of the opportunity and their lack of ability to prolong the interaction that they grab onto the trousers or sleeves of the person as they leave. If that doesn't work, they can escalate to biting arms and legs.

Some dogs become very frustrated over their inability to engage other dogs in the kind of play they want and try to nip them into action. I'm sure you've seen a puppy play-bowing, yipping and jumping backwards and forwards, grabbing at the tail, legs and even the neck of an older dog that just can't be bothered to play. Puppies that aren't provided with sufficient guidance, either from their owner or the older dog, can continue as a frustrated adult, only more forcefully. This is usually not regarded as polite by other dogs and can lead to altercations.

A dog dedicated to chasing that is held back from a predatory opportunity may turn her frustration onto the person gripping the lead. A lurcher or greyhound type with a high chase-drive can be so aroused by the sight of a running cat or other small furry that she'll fight the lead to get at it. When she fails because her owner is hanging on for grim death, she can vent her spleen by biting him. There's no great hatred of the owner, it's just that she is so angry she has to bite *something* and he is the only thing in reach.

Back when football violence was at its height, Ava, a police dog I had the honour to work with, would get so aroused by the chanting hostile crowds as we patrolled the streets around the ground that she would bite my thigh. She really wanted to bite the bands of thugs who were spouting their bile at each other, but I had to hold her tight in to me to prevent any passing innocent supporters suffering her wrath.

Hugely angry and unable to take it out on anyone else, she bit the closest thing to her, my left thigh. Once a fortnight home league games allowed me just enough healing time, but cup runs were a bit sore. There was no animosity in it, she loved me to bits really, honestly, she just couldn't help herself biting *something*, and I was the only thing in reach.

## Combined fear and frustration

Fear and frustration can combine in many cases, especially fear of the threatened outcome of an event and frustration at being unable to prevent or deal with that outcome. This double-whammy increases the likelihood of an aggressive response and both emotions have to be dealt with to change the behaviour. This complex interaction is unlikely to be the initial motivator for the development of an aggressive response in a dog, but frustration fuelling a fearful reaction can make it more intense, resulting in a more extreme degree of biting or fighting.

For example, if a dog is slightly afraid of an approaching dog, and he needs to go closer to puff himself up as his way of dealing with that fear, but he is prevented from doing so by his owner holding him back on a lead, he may become frustrated at not being able to use his coping strategy to deal with the fear. That may result in him becoming angrier than normal, causing him to snarl and spit from afar.

If a dog is afraid and attempts to control that fear through his actions, but is not able to, the fear combines with frustration. Often this type of aggression is directed towards the person causing the frustration rather than the feared stimulus, for example when owners try to make a dog come out from under the bed where he is hiding from firework noise, or where he is picked up to be introduced to a feared type of person.

## Relief

Whilst fear and frustration are both negative emotions they are often followed by relief when the problem goes away. Relief is a positive emotion and can be a huge reinforcer for the behaviour that came before it. This positive effect at the end of biting or fighting can support a great deal of aggressive behaviour. Defeating the problem can be a powerful reward. Don't forget that we have to view "defeating the problem" from the dog's perspective. Being dragged away on a lead backwards, still screaming and snarling his anger at the other dog, can be seen as defeating the problem.

The emotion of relief isn't the initiator of biting and fighting, no dog initially develops fears or frustrations just to feel relieved of them, but it can perpetuate the behaviour long after the initial fear and frustration subside. Never underestimate the power of relief.

## Fear, frustration & relief = fun

The very first time a dog is frightened by a postman rattling the letterbox she is in full fear mode, barking aggressively to make the threat go away. When she succeeds, because the postman *does* go away, she is rewarded with that very powerful emotion of relief. Over the next several times the dog starts to realise that if she barks, the threat does actually go away. And it works every time.

The dog now has a successful strategy for reducing the fear and starts to feel less afraid when the postman arrives because she knows how to deal with the threat. The feeling of relief starts to happen earlier and earlier in the encounter until the dog is able to wait by the door anticipating the arrival of the postman exactly because she has the opportunity to mount a challenge that she knows is going to be successful.

The dog relishes the opportunity to be involved in a conflict that she is going to win, giving her a massive ego boost with accompanying feelings of self-congratulation. "*Well done me! I have vanquished another attempt to invade our property. What a hero I am! Bring on tomorrow so I can do it again!*"

It looks like the dog is enjoying the aggression because she *is* enjoying it. She has lost the fear and enjoys the competition. In the event of the post-delivery this might seem of little consequence, but it

47

can take place in any context. It just happens that the post delivery is a good example because it is a very predictable situation.

If we change the circumstances to a dog that has a social fear of other dogs, maybe though lack of social experience, or from previous aversive experiences, but let's say he fears contact with other dogs up close, and through repeated experiences he has learned that being aggressive makes the problem go away. Maybe he is dragged away by the lead or he is actually a good fighter and chases the other dogs away most times. The display of aggression reduces the threat through repeatedly applying a successful strategy.

The dog now looks for opportunities in the same way that dogs wait for postmen, and the appearance of the dog is of one that is enjoying it because he is enjoying the challenge he knows he can win. This dog now looks for fighting opportunities for the positive emotions they cause. He has no fear because he goes into the encounter believing that he will only experience exhilaration and success.

Of course there are degrees of expressing pleasurable aggression the same as there are for fear and frustration; not every dog that uses it will be on the constant lookout for opportunities, although some will.

The two most common sources of developing pleasurable aggression are towards people invading the home territory and towards other dogs away from home. Breed traits play a part in both of these, with the guarding breeds more inclined towards enjoying defending their patch and the fighting breeds enjoying the competition of combat, but any dog of any breed can develop either.

**Increasing aggression**

So we now have the slightly more complex situation where a dog looks forward to an aggressive encounter which he can normally control. If he subsequently realises that he is losing control, the original fear will kick in, compounded by frustration, driving the aggression to new heights.

Fear long since forgotten, anticipation of a positive outcome is now initially in the driving seat for each incident, but failure to achieve the expected outcome re-installs the original fear and the inability of the chosen (aggressive) strategy to control the fear pushes the aggression to greater intensity through frustration. If the new level of aggression is successful, the greater relief rewards that more extreme behaviour, leading to the anticipation of a greater escalation next time. This is particularly apparent in some dog fighters.

*"Ah, a black dog.*

*They used to be scary because a big Labrador sat on me when I was a puppy.*

*Now I bark at them and their owner drags them away by the lead.*

*I look forward to barking at black Labradors because they are dragged away from me. It makes me feel good.*

*But this Labrador isn't on a lead.*

*It doesn't matter though, because if I bark at it, it will go away. It has always worked before.*

**Bark, bark, bark.**

*It isn't leaving, it is coming at me. Arghh! Scary!*

*Why isn't the barking working?!*

*Bark harder and louder. MAKE it go away.*

**BARK. BARK, BARK!**

*Still not working. Getting closer. Need to escalate! Intensify! Increase!*

**BITE! BITE! BITE!**

*Phew. It's gone. Blimey, barking doesn't work anymore.*

*Have to bite them next time.*

*I look forward to biting black Labradors because they run away from me. It makes me feel good.*

*Let me at 'em!"*

The level of fighting behaviour increases until the dog bowls in every time at the highest intensity, completely missing out all the social communication and lower levels of aggression as they perceive that they do not work.

**Predation & play - more fun**

The final expressions of biting and fighting are also positive emotions, those of predation and play. Although these may not technically be categorised as aggressive behaviour, because they are driven by an underlying positive feel, to the subject it doesn't really matter what the dog is feeling when she has your throat in her jaws.

Predation is part of the feeding process of animals. Animals that eat other animals have to actively take them into their possession before they can consume them. There are many parts to predatory behaviours, not all of which are inherited by each breed of dog. That means that some dogs are more dangerously predatory than others. However, all dogs have the ability to chase and bite another animal or human.

The difference between true aggression and predatory behaviour is that the dog actually enjoys predation. That enjoyment of it is the underlying emotion, not fear or frustration. As it is positively enjoyable, it can be difficult to break off. So the first thing to look for in predatory "aggression" is that the dog looks like they are enjoying the whole thing. They won't be worried and they won't be trying to change the situation through social communication.

They might precede the chasing and biting with stalking, head down, body flattened out, silently creeping towards the target. Silence is an important indicator of predatory behaviour, if the dog is growling or barking it isn't predation. The exception to that is if the dog is being held back and the noise is prompted by frustration, but pure predation is usually silent.

Quite often the behaviour of the target can stimulate predatory behaviour by making prey-like noises or movements. It is thought that some attacks by dogs on babies are stimulated by the mewling noises and jerky movements bringing out previously hidden predatory tendencies. This is supported by the fact that the dog has to seek out an immobile baby to bite them, rather than being threatened by one advancing towards them.

Dogs bred to work are particularly at risk of predatory behaviour becoming a problem if they cannot direct it properly. If you have such a dog that is not under control take a look at my book *"Stop!" How to control predatory chasing in dogs* (available from all good retailers, other dog training books are available; the value of your investment may fall as well as rise; not suitable for home freezing; do not exceed recommended dose.)

Animal targets are usually more at risk from predatory dogs than are humans, although that can also include other dogs, particularly in the case of big dogs chasing smaller ones. Some sight-hounds regard all hare-sized animals as fair game, including small dogs.

Sometimes dogs can switch from play or agonistic (fighting) behaviours into predation. Called by some authors "predatory drift", it is the change in behaviour from relatively benign playing or "handbags at ten paces" fighting into deadly serious predation. It is literally deadly serious because predation can result in the death of the other animal if the predator doesn't break off.

This too is thought to be stimulated by prey-type behaviours such as squealing or trying to escape in a manner that might suggest injury. A little dog screaming and limping away from a fight might trigger a predatory response in the victor, causing her to chase him down and apply a killing bite and shake to the back of his neck. It seems to be fairly unpredictable, but once it has happened it must be guarded against happening again.

Predation can result in horrific injuries as the dog attempts to kill her prey, often by tearing him limb from limb or disembowelling him.

It also seems that the tendency can be picked up from another dog acting in that way, where a group of dogs gangs up and kills a single dog "prey". There are also some cases where running or cycling children have been chased down and attacked by a number of dogs acting together.

Although relatively rare when compared to forms of true aggression, predatory behaviour is extremely serious because the intention of the dog is to kill the prey. In most aggression the intention of the dog is to deter the threat, remove frustration or make the other dog or human leave. In predation the death of the prey is the sought-after result.

Whilst predation can come out of play behaviour, it is much more common for dogs to cause injuries accidentally when playing. In this case there is no intention on the part of the dog, but nevertheless they can hurt.

Most dogs are very good at inhibiting their bites when playing, either with other dogs or with humans, but occasionally one will become too boisterous and overstep the acceptable boundary. This is most apparent in dogs that haven't learned to inhibit the strength of their play-bites as pups.

Many dogs play in a breed-specific way. It's not that they can't play in appropriate ways, they can, but they find breed specific behaviour so enjoyable it slips over into their play. There is a debate to be had as to whether or not this is low-level predatory drift, drifting into little bits of the predatory sequence, but in any case it does happen.

When we play football, if our Collie, Fox, can't get at the ball she will nip our ankles as she drops into Collie-type behaviour. It isn't a problem because once we realised what she was doing we gave her a ball of her own and she plays a game alongside us, but Collie nips can be sore.

If you encourage some dogs into their breed specific behaviour they can forget it is just a game and get carried away. Again, not a problem if you realise what is happening and take care of it, but it can be a bit disconcerting if you have a Staffie that has gripped your sleeve and won't let go. Wrestling with some of the mastiff types and their crosses can cause them to become a bit too competitive and before you know it you are pinned to the ground.

An adult (usually the bloke of the house) can teach a dog that it is okay to play roughly with people by indulging in too much wrestling, which can lead the dog to fail to inhibit his behaviour when playing with the children. Add in some breed specific competitive behaviour and it might become a problem. A dog that plays too hard can be as much an issue as an outright aggressive one.

The key to preventing the escalation of inappropriate play behaviour is to recognise it for what it is and nip it in the bud. Find another way of playing or another way for the dog to enjoy their breed preferences.

On that note, almost as if I'd planned it, it is time we looked at breed and individual differences in dogs that bite and fight. Why are some dogs more aggressive than others?

# Chapter 4
## Differences and Similarities
## Breeds, not Deeds

There is absolutely no doubt that some individual dogs are more aggressive than others. Not all dogs respond to the same circumstances by biting or fighting. Some individuals couldn't be pushed into biting or fighting if their lives depended upon it.

That could lead us to ask the question, particularly if we are looking to buy a puppy or adopt a rescue-dog into our family, *"Are some types generally more aggressive than others?"* However, given the huge range of circumstances in which dogs can be aggressive, is that even a sensible question to ask? Is it really "deed not breed" that we should always be addressing?

Despite the view that breeds should not be punished through all-encompassing breed specific legislation, it is imperative we look at all the possible causes of dogs biting and fighting, and only then make an informed judgement as to the likelihood that our puppy or rescue dog will be too aggressive for us. How much do we need to worry that the tiny bundle of fluffy fun, or the homeless stray bouncing for joy as we approach her kennel, has the potential to maim or kill our children?

I'm not an advocate for banning certain breeds, but I am an advocate for understanding what makes different breeds tick, because that is what determines the circumstances in which they are likely to use aggression, and how dangerous that aggression might be.

All dogs come with the starter-pack of potential aggression identified in the previous chapter, for use in situations where they feel the need, but clearly not all bite and fight every time they are worried by a big dog, or when you walk close to their food bowl or give them a hug.

In order to figure out why some seem to bite and fight inappropriately, we need to look at how aggression develops in individuals. We will do that in the next chapter, but first we need to see if there are any predisposing factors. These are things that, when a dog is faced with a choice to bite or not, push some dogs to make a biting decision and others into deciding not to.

Also, as we have seen that aggression is not an all or nothing thing, but a scale of behaviours that can range from quite mild posturing to deadly attack, we have to look at whether some types of dog inflict more damage than others would do in similar circumstances.

Before we start to examine types of dogs and the ways they bite and fight, I need to state two things emphatically. The first is that it is never, "*Always the fault of the owner*" and the second is that you can take the pup with the worst possible predispositions and make her in to an acceptable pet and one with the best possible predispositions and make her into a biter and fighter. "Environment" always trumps "breed".

Disappointingly, I still keep hearing the old mantra, "*There are no bad dogs, only bad owners*". This is nonsense. The correct mantra is, "*Some dogs are considerably harder to manage than others and not everyone has the skills to manage these types of dogs*", but that isn't catchy enough, so I guess the old one persists in its place.

Adding the non-catchy mantra to "*environment always trumps breed*" means that although I believe that any dog can be managed with enough time and effort, by a person with the skills to do it, there are some really difficult dogs that are going to be beyond the skills of an average pet owner. Conversely, a pup with really nice predispositions can be made into a biter and fighter, through ignorance or neglect.

The more astute of you will have now noticed that whilst this chapter is about tendencies and predispositions that cause a dog to bite and fight, I firmly believe that any and all of those tendencies and predispositions can be overcome through a sensitive and skilful upbringing.

However, I would also add the caveat that some dogs reach a stage in their lives where it is not possible for anyone other than a skilled professional to safely change their already aggressive behaviour. Unfortunately there are more of those dogs than there are skilled professionals to take them on.

This isn't a case of a magician turning up and waving a wand to make the dog better, then handling him back to his previous owner. It would mean the skilled professional adopting each dog and living with and controlling him for the rest of his life. Although the dog's life may be better in those circumstances, the degree of control and commitment required could make the professional's life a misery.

My dream is that one day every dog owner will have the skills to prevent their puppy turning into a biter or fighter, so dogs never get to the stage where they cannot be safely handled. They never reach that level where their behaviour has become so dangerous that they have to be destroyed, or locked up in solitary confinement for the safety of the public. One day... in the meantime, which is more likely to bite you, a dog or a bitch?

**Boys and girls**

If we are looking at how dangerously aggressive our potential pet might be, let's start with an easy choice. Every study that has looked at canine aggression shows that entire males, that is ones that have not been castrated, (or to use the technical term, "had their bits lopped off") show more aggression than either females (spayed or entire) or neutered (castrated) males.

So, the popular advice if you are aiming to avoid having a dog that bites and fights, is to get yourself a bitch for starters. As bitches can also be more aggressive over resources when they are in or coming in to season, you should also have her spayed. If you really don't want a bitch, get a neutered dog, or have your pup castrated when he's old enough.

However, it isn't just as easy as that – you never thought it would be did you? There is some evidence to show that if a bitch is already showing aggression, neutering may make her worse. Also if a male dog is already showing aggression, neutering may have no effect on him, or make him worse.

The eye-opener comes when we examine why dogs of different sexes and neuter states are aggressive. Testosterone is one of the male hormones (although females have some too) and the major source of it, the testes, is removed during castration. Testosterone provides confidence and drives competition. Competitive athletes, both male and female, show higher levels of testosterone than the rest of us, as do risk-taking city traders. Studies on several species of mammals show that winners, for example in fights for territory, have raised levels of testosterone in their body. Testosterone drives that competitiveness.

If we look at that in terms of dogs that bite and fight, if an intact dog meets another in the park and each is unsure of the other, they both put on a *"don't mess with me"* display of raised hair on their neck/back and upright stance. Once testosterone takes over, neither one can back down, as more and more posing takes place, although each dog is really frightened underneath. They work through, *"Don't look at me like that"* to, *"Did you knock into my shoulder?"* each one out-snarling and growling the other until one eventually and literally snaps. Then all hell breaks loose and they continue battling for ages because each one's testosterone won't let him back down. (There are parallels here with *"Did you spill my pint?"* and *"Are you lookin' at my bird?"* to the sound of a hysterical female in the background shrieking, *"Leave it Jeff – 'e's not werf it!"*)

57

If a neutered dog meets another in the park, depending upon what they have already learned (double emphasise that bit!) there is less tendency to see it as a competition and more incentive to get out of the situation without raising the stakes. There is less chance that a fight will break out and if it does it will be less intense without testosterone in the driving seat. We have to double emphasise "depending upon what they have already learned" because as we shall see later, if the dog has already learned to fight like a demon, they will continue to do so. Those are the dogs for which castration will not improve already aggressive behaviour.

Male dogs that are already showing aggression through fear often lack confidence. Castrating these dogs removes a source of confidence (testosterone), which can actually increase the fear and consequently the aggression. The double-edged sword swipes when we realise that testosterone drives both confidence and competition.

Castrating removes some of both. If removing the competitive element reduces the tendency towards aggression, the behaviour will be seen to have improved and castration will have "cured" the fighting. If removing some confidence increases fear, castration can make the aggressive behaviour worse. How do we know which one will win out? Actually we don't. If we know the dog well, or are a good judge of dog behaviour, we can make a best guess that if the dog appears to have enough confidence then taking the competitive edge away may help and that if the dog appears generally fearful that it won't, but it remains a guess-timate, not a sure thing.

When looking at adopting rescue-dogs, consider that some are relinquished because they don't fit their owners' expectations in some way. Many of these expectation-deficits involve aggressive behaviour of some sort, although owners who give their dogs up to rescue are notoriously conservative with the truth, and many forget to mention that little Fluffles is a vicious so-and-so in some circumstances. Consider also that dogs are routinely neutered by almost every rescue, without the benefit of a behavioural history or assessment as to its suitability for them as an individual. You could be looking at a dog that had mild fear-based aggression and has just lost the source of what little confidence he had, giving him the potential to become even more fear-aggressive.

Female dogs do have testosterone, but are more driven by female hormones, progesterone and prolactin. The waxing and waning of hormone levels can have effects on bitches that make them more or less inclined to bite and fight as they come in and out of season.

Some bitches value resources (food, toys, nesting places) more when they are in season or pregnant, including false pregnancy, and can also be generally less tolerant. This can lead them into conflict with people and other dogs, which can cause them to bite and fight. Taking away the hormonal cycle by neutering removes the fluctuations and stabilises their behavioural response. Again, if the response is strongly learned, that is she has been showing aggression before neutering, it may have less effect because the bitch has already learned that biting and fighting are necessary.

Competitive aggression is greater between dogs in the same household that value the same things. It should be obvious that two male dogs will want the same things more than a male and female would, that two male dogs of the same breed will value the same things more than those of different breeds and two closely related male dogs of the same breed will value similar things more than unrelated dogs would. The more alike they are the more conflict over resources there is likely to be.

The same goes for bitches too, but there seems to be an added dimension when it comes to females. Some females, especially but not exclusively intact bitches, seem to resent other females living in the same household to the extent that they declare all-out war on them. Bitch Wars can be so severe that the initiating bitch only seems satisfied when the other bitch is permanently removed, and if this is because she has killed her rival, so be it.

The reasons for this aren't exactly known, but it is thought by some behaviourists to be a genetically inherited breeding strategy. In packs of wild canids, such as grey wolves, it appears to be a way to split up a pack by forcing the younger bitches to move away and set up their own family, propagating the parental genes. However, trapped in a human family, the less assertive domestic bitch has nowhere to go. The two bitches become trapped in a cycle of one trying to force the other to leave and the other being unable to get away. The fights become more and more bloody and bitches have been known to kill their mother, daughter or sister in this way.

So, if you want to keep dogs' biting and fighting to a minimum through your choice of sex and neuter status:

* Get a bitch rather than a dog, and have her neutered, but not if she is already showing aggression (your vet will advise you when to have it done, but halfway between the first and second season is the current favourite) until you can work out why.

* If you really want a dog, have him neutered, but not if he is already showing aggression (again, your vet will advise when to have it done), until you can work out why he's biting and fighting.

* To avoid competition between dogs in the same household, adopt two dissimilar dogs and definitely not litter sisters, mother and daughter, or litter brothers.

* If your dog or bitch is already showing aggression, see a qualified behaviourist who will be able to determine what the cause is and then advise you if neutering will help or make it worse.

## What's in a breed?

## Breeds

Much is made of the demonising of some dog breeds, and critics of the dangerous dog legislation, me included, think it is wrong to punish someone for owning a specific breed, rather than for the dog's actions. However, it is undeniable that some dogs are more of a risk to society than others and it would be unhelpful, to say the least, not to recognise that.

But are some breeds really more aggressive than others? To answer that, we first need to know that a dog breed is basically a group of dogs that has identifiable and inheritable characteristics. It occurs when you mate two similar dogs and get a similar litter: they breed true.

This rules out the mongrels, cross-breeds and designer dogs (posh name for very expensive mongrels), such as Labradoodles, Jack-a-poos, Puggles, Cavachons, Bull-Shih-Ts (French Bulldog x Shih Tzu and probably *the* best name for a designer dog) and any others that do not breed true, because they are a mix of different breeds. They could be regarded as "types" in the same way that the Pit Bull Terrier in the UK is a type, but not a breed. We'll look at types later, but for now we need to can see if we can identify tendencies to bite and fight within breeds.

From time to time the popular press calls for the banning or other punitive discrimination against different breeds of dogs. This is usually after a dog of that breed has inflicted serious injury on a person. Way back it was German Shepherd Dogs (Alsatians), followed by Dobermans and Rottweilers. Since the 1991 Dangerous Dogs Act, the Pit Bull Terrier (or more accurately the PBT "Type") has been demonised and prohibited from legal ownership in the UK, along with the Fila Brazileiro, Dogo Argentino and Japanese Tosa. The last three have all but died out in the UK, but the Pit Bull persists. Huge amounts of public money are spent prosecuting owners and either destroying their dogs or going through a special registration process for them.

Why? Are Pit Bull Terriers bad dogs? Do they bite more often than other breeds? Are you more at risk of being subjected to an attack by a Pit Bull Terrier than a Dachshund? No. You are far more likely to be attacked by a Dachshund but, unfortunately, more likely to severely injured in an attack by a Pit Bull Terrier.

Dog bite figures are really difficult to interpret. For a start nobody properly collects figures for the number of dog bites inflicted by whatever kind of dog. How could they? Nobody reports them all to any particular body. There's no central place where we register the fact that we have been bitten. Consequently the figures we have tend to be those that are collected retrospectively by academic studies asking people questions, and with the best intentions in the world they cannot include the whole population. We should expect some bias, however slight, from people who do not want to be included or who portray their dogs in a better light than they deserve. Do you know of any breed standards that state, "*Can be a nasty blighter if not properly socialised*"?

As seen in the introduction, the other sources of figures are hospital records, but breeds and reasons for being bitten are not logged.

"*Breed differences in canine aggression*" was a thorough-as-it-can-be American study in 2008 by Deborah Duffy, Yuying Hsu and James Serpell published in the journal Applied Animal Behaviour Science. This is the study that says you are more likely to be bitten by a Dachshund, Chihuahua or Jack Russell Terrier than a Pit Bull Terrier. In fact, they found there are nineteen breeds that are more likely to bite a stranger than is a Pit Bull Terrier, and twenty seven breeds that are more likely to bite their owner.

To be fair to the Pit Bull Terrier demonisers, PBTs score very highly for aggression directed towards strange dogs, but Dachshunds were still worse.

We must keep in mind that there is also huge variability within each breed. I'm sure you will not be surprised to find that there is a big overlap where some individuals within a "more-aggressive" breed are less so than some individuals within a "less-aggressive" breed.

However, and it is quite a big "however" given the hospital figures, the study made no distinction in the severity of injury, and it is difficult to see the bite of a Dachshund in the same category as a bite from a Pit Bull.

In the United States almost half the human fatalities resulting from dog attacks for every one of the past ten years have been by Pit Bull Terrier (type) dogs. Rottweilers regularly come second, accounting for about an eighth of fatal attacks, with the rest being a variety of breeds. Only one Dachshund is recorded as being involved in a fatal attack in the past ten years. That dog was present with a Labrador when they attacked an elderly and very infirm lady. With no witnesses, it is not clear how much, or even if, the small dog contributed.

So it appears that breed can make a difference, but it is difficult to say what that difference might be, other than bigger dogs inflict bigger bites. Bigger dog obviously means bigger jaws with larger teeth and stronger muscles to close them.

Does this mean that bigger dogs *always* inflict greater injury? Certainly the potential bite force is bigger in the dogs with larger heads. The Mastiff is computed as having a crushing jaw pressure of 552lbs, compared to humans at a puny 120lbs and a lion at 600lbs.

Unfortunately, it isn't as easy as just computing poundage. Motivation is at least as important as equipment. Depending on the motivation for the bite, a large dog with huge jaws might just go for a front-tooth nip to make the problem back off, causing far less injury

63

than a much smaller dog that is motivated to all-out attack. We also have to consider that modern breeding has developed all manner of strangely shaped jaws, some of which are more useful for biting than others. We therefore have to look at a combination of factors to assess the potential for serious injury: dog size, jaw shape and size, and possible motivations for biting.

How then might we be able to determine if "breed" is going to help us? By looking at what that breed was developed for.

Let's start from the basic premise that…

* Any dog can show aggression.
* Any dog can be an exceptional representative of its breed.
* All dogs require to be well socialised in order to interact with people and other dogs normally.
* Inherited characteristics such as "nervousness" exist in strains within breeds and have a bearing on the tendency to exhibit aggression.

…and never forget those points as we investigate breed specific aggressive behaviour.

At the risk of sounding obvious, the whole point of a breed is that it *is* a breed, and we can determine how likely dogs within that breed are to use aggression in their daily lives by looking at the reason the breed exists, and that is the function it was previously bred to fulfil.

All dog breeds have an original purpose, even if that purpose was simply that of "companion". Bloodhounds were bred to track, Border Collies to herd sheep and the Nova Scotia Duck Tolling Retriever to lure ducks into range of the hunter's gun by gambolling about, then retrieve them from the water when they were shot.

Many of these original functions involved a form of hunting or herding that made use of the inherent parts of the dog's behaviour, the instinct that is bred into them that ensures they are fit for purpose. But there are other uses for dogs, in guarding and in fighting. "Fighting" could be with other animals, or each other. The dogs of war used by the Greeks and Romans to fight their enemies, and let slip by Mark Antony in Shakespeare's *Julius Cesar,* have thankfully died out, although the breeders of most of the European mastiff types claim their dogs are descended from them, and many of those are represented in the guarding breeds.

Since mankind first dabbled in the artificial selection of dogs, those used for guarding or fighting have been bred with the inherited predispositions that make them better at doing it than other kinds of dog.

You will find guarding breeds that are supposed to have a "*mistrust of strangers*" or descriptions of fighting breeds that say "*some aggression towards other dogs is to be expected*". These are dog breeds that have been developed, shaped and moulded to bite and fight in certain circumstances. If they were still being used for their original purpose (some of the "guards" are and, regrettably and illegally, so are some of the "fighters") then they will be *expected* to show that behaviour.

So what predispositions would we expect to find in a guarding breed beyond the "*mistrust of strangers*"? How about the tendency to use proactive aggression to manage stressful situations?

Guarding dogs: German Shepherd, Rottweiler, Doberman, Dogue de Bordeaux, Mastiff, Neapolitan Mastiff, Cane Corso, Boerboel, Akita and so on… have a tendency to use aggression in the defence of their territory. An unfamiliar person approaching their property is stressful for them. They manage that distress through driving away the intruder by biting, or at least warning that they are seriously considering biting.

And in fighting dogs? How about pugnacity, persistence, tenacity *and* the tendency to use proactive aggression to manage stressful situations? That's all Terriers (26 breeds listed by the UK Kennel Club and 44 by the USA United Kennel Club), Bull dogs, Bull Terriers, Dachshunds, Japanese Tosas, Presa Canario, Schnauzers, Shar Pei...

In the original working form both guarding and fighting dogs would be expected to use all-out attack, not back down and inflict serious damage. It is the initial purpose for which they were bred and the reason they exist today.

Luckily burglar alarm technology has largely superseded the need to breed scrap-yard dogs for defending property, and dog fighting has been outlawed in the UK since 1835, so dogs fit for this type of "work" are not as prevalent as they once were. However, the old function's instincts are still there, hovering about in the background; perhaps in a diluted form, but still there. Occasionally the random drift of the gene pool throws up an individual with the behaviour of the old style workers. They can be quite a handful.

There are a couple of major considerations that stem from breeding for a purpose that you might like to contemplate. The first is "reactivity" and describes the distance at which breeds react generally and, particularly for our purposes, react to threat.

The guarding German Shepherd was developed from sheep herding dogs that were expected to control a vast flock of sheep by noticing when one was out of line and running over to push them back. They are therefore very vigilant and react to stimuli at a great distance. When they are guarding or policing they also react at a great distance. When they see a miscreant they immediately tell them they are out of line by barking ferociously. This makes for a very effective guard and police dog.

Unfortunately they have the same predispositions when they bite and fight. When they feel threatened they react immediately. Some might say they over-react. The result is that they tend to show their aggression early, expressively and from a distance.

Conversely the guarding Rottweiler was developed from droving dogs, used to take cattle to market. Their herding style is to use their physical presence to intimidate the stock into moving, with any forcefulness saved for animals that confront them face to face. This does not require great reactivity at a distance as the dog is working in close proximity to the beasts. This has produced a dog that does not react to threat until it stares them in the face.

Back in the 1980s the British German Shepherd dog was a shadow of the breed it should have been and police forces could not source suitable animals for training as police dogs. This was before we wised-up and bought in proper working continental stock. When we cast around for suitable alternatives to the sub-standard British GSD, the Rottweiler was one of the choices, and quite a few were trained and sent out to work. One of the problems we encountered was that handlers couldn't recognise when they were about to bite.

The handler would stand with his dog on the street at pub kicking out time (before CCTV and proper door-staff, when drunken street-brawls were the norm). Some drunks would shout abuse and try to approach the policeman to pat or kick his dog. The GSD wouldn't let them get within ten yards before throwing himself to the end of the lead, snarling and spitting his intentions, and the idiot would (usually) back-off and go on his way. But the Rottweiler doesn't react at that distance.

The handler would look down and see his Rotty just sitting quietly by his side and watching as the drunken fool got closer and closer… until the chump was three or four feet away, at which point the Rott would launch at his throat. The drunk wasn't expecting it. The handler wasn't expecting it. So the dog often made contact. What should have been a warning from the dog to back off turned into judge, jury and sentence, then hospital.

All down to failing to understand the difference in reactivity between breeds.

And it isn't just GSDs and Rotties. Anyone thinking of buying a pup and looking to avoid the consequences of biting and fighting, or looking to correct a biter and fighter, should consider reactivity as a contributing factor.

Reactivity ties in with another major contributing factor, that of breed tendencies in communication. Taking the GSD and Rotty as our examples again, it could be said that the GSD will communicate their feelings excessively and at a distance. They do not hide their unease, whereas the Rotty does not express itself at a distance; they hide their unease until the last moment. This is an inherited tendency.

We can find these breed communication tendencies in other breeds too; think of the Akita's famous stoicism or the yappiness of the Pekinese. These are demonstrations of tendencies to display or not display different styles of communication. They exist in all breeds to a greater or lesser extent, but the most worrying tendencies are in the dogs that were originally used for fighting other dogs.

In dog-fighting, communicating fear, deference or any non-proactive threat-reducing behaviour would be a serious hindrance. The dog they were fighting would immediately know that they had an advantage. It would be like a prize-fighter crying when he was punched by his opponent. Therefore fighting dogs were bred not to display anything but outright attack. No bluff, no bluster, just pile straight in and grapple for a biting hold that would disable or kill.

Likewise, backing off when an opponent showed threat-reducing behaviour is also a tendency that would lose a fight. Consequently the best dog-fighters were bred not to show or take notice of deferential threat-reducing communication. Because this behaviour is inherited, although dog fighting is no longer legal, in breeds that were originally dog-fighters the behaviour (or lack of it) can still re-surface. It produces dogs that bite other dogs as first option when threatened and/or don't back down when their opponent is obviously beaten and trying to give in.

On the plus side, this lack of inhibition should be shown only to other dogs, as any aggression shown towards people by fighting dogs would result in their removal from the gene pool with extreme prejudice.

Fighting dogs are expected to be friendly towards people, and this trait is highlighted in the Kennel Club breed standard for the Staffordshire Bull Terrier and the American Dog Breeders Association's standard for the American Pit Bull Terrier.

Unfortunately, even these types of dogs can go wrong; can develop fears and frustrations; can play excessively. When they do that the aggression they show is expressed in a breed specific way, just like the GSDs and the Rottweilers do. And that means not showing signs of fear and not backing off when their opponent is beaten.

Whilst many of the non-fighting and non-guarding breeds still fulfil their original purpose, although sometimes with modification of the circumstances, some breeds have also been captured by the pet market.

Historically the pet market has taken failed workers, the dogs that were no good for their purpose, but the last hundred years or so has seen the "pet-ication" of breeds. Domestication is a process that dogs went through about twenty thousand years ago, after which humans bred them into the diverse purposes that gave us the three hundred or so breeds we now have. Pet-ication is the term I use for when a breed (not the individual) is removed from its original purpose and made fit for the pet market.

German Shepherd Dogs were captured from the pool of workers and pet-icated by breeding quieter, less reactive, more amenable ones suited to pet ownership. In the UK now the gene pool of pet-icated GSDs is considerably different in inherited behaviour from the old-style workers. The same can be said for Dobermans and Rottweilers, most of which are considerably nicer to own now that the breeds have been pet-icated.

Why has this happened? Because they were not nice to own in their working form. In a two-up, two-down with children running about the place they were downright dangerous, so breeders diluted their predispositions to make them more pet-friendly, and more saleable. Gradually the less appreciated aspects of their working behaviour have been diluted. Hence most of these dogs are now very nice pets and, also hence, every now and then a throw-back appears with the original characteristics and causes mayhem for the breed.

So, some breeds have become pet-icated and are the better for it, but others haven't. Spaniels are a good case in point. They retain their original working drive to stick their nose to the floor and run about as if flushing game. There is no need to pet-icate them as their working characteristics are not dangerous. Place a Spaniel in a pet home and it might not have the best life it can, but "running about with nose on the floor" will not endanger anyone in the way that guarding or fighting behaviour might.

Other working groups straddle the working/pet divide. Working Terriers (Jack Russell, Irish, Patterdale) exhibit all the fighting behaviour that one would expect of a dog designed to kill wild animals in a confined space, and it can cause them problems in a pet environment when that tenacity is directed into aggression towards people or other dogs. Luckily they are not very big and bites tend to be tolerated more easily. It smarts, but it doesn't usually result in hospitalisation for two days, or death.

Finally we have the recently pet-icated breeds. These are the breeds that do not have a very long history of breeding for the pet market. They are they breeds that have recently been captured from the working population. They are often quite fashionable; new things often are. They are also quite often of the guarding or fighting type. Examples would be the Dogue de Bordeaux, the Presa Canario, the Boerboel, the Kuchi (Koochee/ Coochie, so recently introduced from Afghanistan the spelling hasn't been standardised). All of these breeds retain high levels of their original working behaviour in their gene pool, and many of these involve biting and fighting.

We know that breeds inherit tendencies that were required for their original working purpose and that, as the breed pet-icates, those tendencies, particularly the problematic ones, become watered down.

As I said, this was particularly apparent during the 1980s when British police forces found it increasingly difficult to source German Shepherd Dogs of the right temperament to train as police dogs. We eventually bought-in continental-bred working dogs because the British GSD was just too nice a pet. Great for the breed, but now we are seeing two different strains of GSD in the UK, the pet type and the working type. If you want a pet, don't get the working type.

If you want to minimise the chances of your potential pet dog biting and fighting, or at least minimise the injury they might cause whilst doing so, consider what the origins of the breed are, how far from those origins the breed is currently, and what their inherited predispositions may be.

How does this fit with the reported fact that the three breeds most likely to bite and fight are Dachshunds, Jack Russell Terriers and Chihuahuas?

Okay, starting with the obvious fact that all three are small dogs and when small dogs bite and fight they do not inflict as much damage so aggressive behaviour is more likely to be tolerated, then taking each breed in turn:

*   The Dachshund is a dog that was bred to hunt like a Terrier, which gives us independence (doesn't take direction from you)

71

and the typical stubbornness, tenacity, refusal to back down and to use aggression in competition against a cornered badger. The dachshund knows what he wants, won't back down and is prepared to use aggression to back himself up.

* The Jack Russell Terrier is still a working dog, bred to go to earth and kill or drive out small mammals (including foxes fighting for their lives), hardly if at all pet-icated and with all the potential to bite and fight that entails. Pet dogs are still being captured from the working population.

* As Chihuahuas are a companion dog, you would think that should make them ideal pets, but they are famously one-person dogs. A companion dog that is strongly bonded to one person is not sociable towards other people and defends her attachment-figure from all-comers. Fear or threat of loss of attention from, or proximity to, her attachment figure is an extremely efficient way of developing aggressive behaviour.

And, hey, it's kind of cute when the little guy barks like that, isn't it? Oh, and they are all handbag dogs as well, picked up, cuddled and people's faces thrust into theirs – all potential trouble hotspots.

So, given a reasonable amount of information on the breed we can work out if our potential pet might have aggressive tendencies, but there's one more thing about breeds that might have a bearing on a dog's tendency to bite and fight, their degree of inherited breed specific behaviour. We will look into this in greater detail later, but for now we need to know that breed specific behaviour, the behaviour that the dog inherits to do its intended job, is necessary to help balance their emotional state.

Although it varies in individuals, not being able to perform their job-behaviour can cause some dogs to become distressed and unable to cope. Being distressed and unable to balance their emotions can cause dogs to be more prone to biting and fighting. These are the working Collies and Spaniels that become stress-heads when kept in small flats and walked on a lead for ten minutes a day. Chronic stress causes over-reaction to small annoyances. Over-stressed dogs can bite and fight. Dogs with a high degree of active working behaviour easily become stressed in pet homes because they are not fulfilling their behavioural needs.

Beware the advert that says, "*Puppies for sale – good for work or pet*". Firstly because a dog that's good for work shouldn't make a good pet (and vice versa) because they are different functions, and secondly because the breeder doesn't seem to know that, or doesn't care.

## "Types" and mongrels

Moving away from pure breeds though, remember we mentioned "types" earlier? What about "types" that aren't breeds, like the Pit Bull Terrier? I'm going to use the PBT as an example, because the "type" is a good example of cross breeding, but you can apply the principles to any mongrel dog.

In the United Kingdom, owning, breeding and selling Pit Bull Terriers has been banned since 1991, so at the time of writing in 2013 a pure-bred UK Pit Bull would have to be twenty-two years old. In short, there aren't any (except for a very few that are being illegally imported from Eastern Europe and through Ireland – and you won't be reading this if you have one of those). However, the law, no matter how much you may or may not like or agree with it, states that the Pit Bull is a type, not a breed. The type is defined as a dog that has "*characteristics that substantially conform to the standard set for the breed by the American Dog Breeders Association for the American Pit Bull Terrier*", even though it does not meet that standard in every respect.

73

This type of dog can be bred from two other dogs, usually a mastiff type and a legal Bull Terrier type, such as a Staffordshire or English Bull Terrier or crosses of them (or crosses of crosses), although I have known other breeds such as Boxers, American Bulldogs and Ridgebacks to be used.

But of course types don't breed true. You don't get relatively fixed heritable behavioural and physical characteristics when you breed two of a type together, you get much greater variability. This is our first take-away lesson for the difference between breeds and types.

Selecting a dog of a known breed gives you a rough idea of his heritable characteristics. For example, if you were to breed a St Bernard and a Chihuahua together you would be (apart from an idiot) unlikely to get puppies the size of either parent, but neither would you get puppies exactly halfway in-between sized. The offspring would be various sizes and shapes.

In the same way that they would not have the physical characteristics of either parent, nor would they have the behavioural characteristics of either parent, but some variation not exactly halfway in between.

If we take a typical dog that has the physical "*characteristics that substantially conform to the standard set for the breed by the American Dog Breeders Association for the American Pit Bull Terrier*" it will most likely be the product of a mastiff type and maybe a Staffy. The mastiff breeds often include guarding dogs such as the Boerboel, which are typically described as "*extremely protective of their family and territory*". This is what guards are for and a good example for us to use.

Staffordshire Bull Terriers were originally pit fighting dogs and can still develop aggressive tendencies towards other dogs, but are renowned for their friendliness towards people. As pit fighting dogs they needed a high degree of competitiveness; they don't back down when in a competition. Our Boerboel X Staffy (Boerffy? Staffboel?) may well look enough like a Pit Bull Terrier to be classified as such, but what about his behaviour?

Whereas a breed inherits similar characteristics from both parents, the parents of a mongrel (cross-breed/type) do not always have the same characteristics, so the offspring have a wider range of possible inherited behaviours.

Let's look at the possibilities for inheriting only one tendency from each dog when crossing a Boerboel with a Staffy: the dislike of strangers of the Boerboel and the persistence of the Staffy. Now bear in mind that these tendencies can be inherited on a scale from almost none to a huge amount. Our cross-breed may inherit very little "*dislike of strangers*" from the Boerboel or a massive amount. He may inherit very little "*persistence*" from the Staffy, or a huge amount. Or any amount of either, anywhere in between.

For a dog that's expected to be a pet, that gives us a best case and a worst case scenario, plus all the intermediates, from the raw materials, as this figure shows:

| Qualities | **Staffy** <br> Low persistence | **Staffy** <br> High persistence |
|---|---|---|
| **Boerboel** <br> Low distrust <br> of strangers | A dog that likes people and isn't the slightest bit pushy. Not threatened and not frustrated easily. Low potential for biting and fighting. | A friendly dog that refuses to stop licking and jumping up. Medium potential for biting and fighting, mostly due to frustration. |
| **Boerboel** <br> High distrust <br> of strangers | A dog that hates people but doesn't show it until they are in his face. Medium potential for biting and fighting, but explosive performance when close. | A dog that hates everybody unfamiliar and doesn't back down. High potential for biting and fighting through threat and frustration. |

And that's only from two inherited tendencies. We would need to factor in all the others too, such as "tendency not to display threat-reducing signals", "attachment to owner", "boldness/shyness" "reactivity" and many more. Because we have so many variables which often play off each other or cancel each other out, it is almost impossible to predict which ones will come to the fore, other than to say those found in both parents are more likely than those that differ. That is why there is such variability in cross-bred dogs. What crossing two breeds can't ever do is provide standard behaviour for the "type", whether it is a Labradoodle, a Cockerpoo or a Pit Bull Terrier.

What you will get is a combination of the parents' *possible* behaviours, so don't expect anything you don't find in the parents. Any behaviour that is represented strongly in both parents is more likely to be passed on, so you are likely to get guarding offspring if the tendency to guard is present in both Mum and Dad. Most guarders and most fighters both pass on a tendency to resort to aggression easily in some circumstances, and the tendency not to back down. These are therefore tendencies you should expect to be represented quite strongly in the offspring of a guarding breed crossed with a fighting breed.

Working breeds are exactly that because they are selected to have standardised behaviours – like begets like. Only when breeding from dogs that have the same tendencies can you have a reasonable expectation that the offspring will inherit them. Breeding two dogs that do not have the same tendencies simply provides greater variability in the litter. I guess you could call it "like-parts beget like-parts" because although the two parents' behaviour isn't totally alike, the parts that are tend to come through. The bits that aren't alike can be inherited from either Mum or Dad.

From the dogs that I have assessed as having the physical conformation of a Pit Bull Terrier I have seen the sweetest natured to the abominable; far greater variability than within exists within most breeds.

If someone were to breed our Boerboel/Staffy cross to another of the same cross, with the same tendencies, you would expect a greater standardisation from some of their offspring. Selecting the "standard" of those for further breeding would promote that standardisation in the next generation, and so on until they became another breed. That's how all breeds started. The Labradoodle will become a breed when people stop crossing Labradors and Poodles together and start a process of standardising the cross-breeds.

Pet owners usually only have limited experience of a few individual dogs from any breed. The variability of the Pit Bull type is the reason that people are so polarised about them. Some see only a few nice ones and some see only a few nightmares. The truth is that their behaviour cannot be accurately predicted because they do not breed true.

And first crosses are the easiest to determine. If you then breed the half-breed to another unrelated half-breed, the behaviour takes on an even greater level of complexity, and so on *ad infinitum*. You may still be able to identify breed traits in an individual once she grows up, but you won't be able to predict which ones they will be before she is born.

Fancy buying a pup or adopting a young dog that will have the eventual physical ability to inflict serious injury, without knowing his inherited behavioural tendencies? Maybe he has easy predispositions and will bring himself up to be a sweetheart, or maybe he will be a nightmare that will take careful handling all his life and can't ever be trusted near children or other dogs. Do you have the skill for such a demon? If you do, you'll probably know you don't want to take one on. Who needs the grief?

**Generalisations and exceptions**

There will always be exceptions in any sex, breed or type of dog. That's why we love them so much, because they are all individuals. But, as you can see, there are generalisations we can make that will usually reduce our chances of starting out with a dog that has predispositions to turn into a biter and fighter.

Consider the sex, remembering that statistically in order of least aggressive tendencies it goes: neutered bitch; entire bitch; neutered male; entire male; with the stated provisos!

Look at the breed. Those with a guarding or fighting temperament may resort to aggression quicker than those without. Those not bred for the pet market that are close to the original working stock will retain their working behaviour, which may include aggressive tendencies. Avoid the unpet-icated guarders and fighters. For those that used to be bred as guarders and fighters, make sure they have been pet-icated for long enough to make a difference (measured in several decades). Workers that do not include aggression in their breed tendencies can be frustrated if they are deprived of the opportunity to work. Don't discount them, but take it into account.

Cross-bred dogs don't breed true, so you can't predict their probable adult temperament with certainty, but you can take a guesstimate if you know their type.

Cross-breeds with guarding and fighting dogs as their forebears may inherit potentially problematic behaviours. Those close to the working stock or only recently pet-icated more so. Equally, they may not, but why take the risk? Usually the size and physical capabilities of these types of dogs means that if they do bite they will cause serious injury. The risks of injury when a Pit Bull type goes wrong are greater than those if a Cockerpoo type goes wrong.

But, as I've emphasised throughout, you can start with a dog with difficult temperamental predispositions and if you bring him up well he can make an acceptable pet. We now need to look at what to do to avoid turning your pet into a nightmare biter and fighter. How to bring him up well.

# Chapter 5
# Environment – the Whole Thing

Having seen how breed and type dispositions affect the potential of a dog to be a biter or fighter, we can now look at the factors that are common to all sexes, breeds and types. It starts earlier than you think.

## Genetics

There is a vast amount of scientific evidence that some of the temperaments involved in biting and fighting behaviour are inherited by individuals within breeds.

Nervousness, or low confidence, is certainly heritable. It is possible within a few generations to breed nervous pups from nicely confident forebears. Think of the damage a nervous sire could do to a breed if he had a particularly good conformation, or a nicely shaped tail that breeders wanted for the show ring. Within a few generations of this prize-winner spreading his genes for prettiness and nervousness they could be in half the breed.

Another well-investigated example of heritability is in dogs that lack impulse-control. These dogs often rush around acting impulsively without inhibiting their behaviour; in lay terms they snatch and take what they want when they want, like a badly behaved child. Often these dogs have a reduced amount of a brain chemical called serotonin when compared to more relaxed dogs. We know that serotonin is required to aid relaxation in all mammals and a lack of it contributes to the inability to cope with frustration.

One of the theories of aggressive behaviour mentioned in the last chapter is that an inherited lack of serotonin availability, contributing to a corresponding lack of impulse control, is behind the so-called Rage Syndrome that has been identified in some strains within some breeds. My own view is that it is not helpful to call it a "syndrome" or label it "rage" but there are undoubtedly dogs that find it difficult to cope with what should be normal levels of frustration, and consequently react with undue aggression.

Both lack of impulse control and low confidence (nervousness) contribute to a dog that is easily distressed, and dogs that are easily distressed can be prone to biting and fighting. If both of these traits are inherited it produces a dog that is nervous and can't cope with frustration. Such a dog would need very careful handling to prevent her turning into a biter and fighter.

As in many matters of inheritance these are not all-or-nothing traits, but exist in all dogs to a greater or lesser extent. Dogs at the "nervous" and "impulsive" end of the scale will be difficult to deal with and those at the "confident" and "relaxed" end will be easier, but there will be a whole series of combinations of more-or-less of each in between - for example, very confident and impulsive is also a challenging permutation. These dogs will be more or less easy to live with depending upon the guidance they receive and the environment in which they are brought up.

As a prospective pet owner, looking to avoid your puppy turning out to be a biter and fighter, if you see a Mum or Dad that is exhibiting nervous or impulsive behaviour you have to ask yourself if you have the skills to take on a puppy that may also have these traits. Can you supply the guidance and environment needed to contain the inherited behavioural traits?

## Mum

The first true environment to consider is a pup's Mum. She's the place they spend the first nine weeks or so of their existence. There are lots of studies that show an easily distressed Mum produces offspring that are more susceptible to becoming distressed. This is not just genetic, but also because of Mum's hormonal soup to which they are subjected in the womb. This circulates the hormones of distress through the placenta from Mum to pups, and results in lasting changes to their brain and hormonal configuration even before they are born. This is one of the reasons that puppy farms are one of the worst disservices we've ever done for dogs.

There is some fascinating work being done in the relatively new subject of epigenetics (Greek: epi - above/on top of/over), that is finding connections between the environment in which the pup is grown and the expression of particular genes. It seems that genetics isn't the fixed thing we thought it was and that some genes are switched on or off in response to certain environmental conditions.

Studies in rats show that pups that get a lot of licking from their mother - the equivalent of human cuddles - are subject to permanent changes in their genes that grow parts of the brain that can help them deal with stress more easily when they grow up. We always knew that a good mother is worth her weight in gold, but maybe the theory that good parenting makes for happy offspring has a solid genetic basis.

In terms of development, slight stress is good for you because it prepares your body to deal with it, but too much distress creates an individual that becomes easily distressed in the future.

In practice this means that Mum needs to be in the bosom of a loving family, not subject to undue distress, as she is carrying her pups. It should go without saying that a Mum who is easily distressed may not cope with pregnancy and may not be a good mother. Breeding from bitches that are easily distressed produces pups that grow up to be easily distressed and breeding from them perpetuates the problem.

The first environmental factor that affects if a dog is going to grow up to be or not to be a biter and fighter is whether his Mum was a nice confident pet in a happy home. Dad has a contribution to make too, but more in terms of the genetic basis of his confidence and impulse control. If he is a stress-head he will pass on his stress-head-genes (note for geneticists – I know that it is more accurate to say that he will pass on his genes that support the behaviours involved in being a stress-head, but "stress-head-genes" is catchier because it sounds like the latest denim fad).

Anyway, meeting and evaluating Mum and Dad should be the first step to investing in your puppy. Do not even consider buying a puppy without at least seeing Mum. A puppy on his own could be from anywhere, maybe a puppy farm or a batch of illegally imported pups from Eastern Europe. At the time of writing unscrupulous people are illegally importing batches of underage pups for sale in the U.K. It could just be a matter of time before one brings in rabies.

People find it difficult to walk away from puppies when they go to view or buy them. This is weird. You don't buy the first house or car you see, and I know lots of people who will reject several dresses or pairs of shoes after trying them on. Why do we treat our purchase of a living being with whom we are going to spend the next ten to twenty years of our lives so superficially?

Even worse are those who buy the little puppy, "*To save it from…*" usually the conditions in which it is living. You do realise that if you buy this one it gives the dealer and/or breeder the incentive to produce another lot exactly the same? That you are responsible for perpetuating the misery? "*I felt sorry for her*" is not a good reason to buy a pup. You then become part of the vicious circle of wretchedness. You spend fifteen years of unhappiness with a dog that is nothing but a burden and very little joy. The dealer pockets your cash and does nothing to improve the standard of their pups. And do you think your dog is happy being stressed, anxious not to be left alone, fearful of other dogs and people?

See the Mum and, if possible, the Dad. If either shows the slightest aggression, lack of confidence or nervousness, walk away. The bitch "*being protective of her pups*" is not a good reason for her to be aggressive. She may also be "*protective of her...*" bed? food? toys? home? owner? And there's every chance her pups will be too, because that's the lesson she is teaching them every time a new person appears, "*It's OK to be aggressive to people*". What a great start in life for a biter and fighter! Mum should come out to greet you wagging her tail with pups following behind.

## Socialisation

But come out from where? A shed in the garden? "Socialisation" has become a bit of a buzzword and a lack of it is blamed for all kinds of behaviour problems. It is true that what people call socialisation is immensely important, but many still don't understand what it is.

Let me explain it in a different way because the frequently trotted out, "*show your dog lots of stuff and people and it will be alright*" is far from true. For a start the word "socialisation" doesn't do it justice. I prefer the term "social and environmental referencing" but that's a bit of a mouthful, so I'll stick with the convention for now for no other reason than to save my two-fingered typing.

Pups in the womb are subject to Mum's hormonal soup that affects their future behaviour through the ways that hormones act on genes, kind of promoting or restricting their action, and when pup pops out Mum has set them up for life. Keeping Mum in a noisy boisterous family home, assuming that is where she is used to being kept, is best for her pups. This should be normal for her if it is to become normal for them. If it isn't normal for Mum to live in a boisterous family home, we are already looking at adopting a pup from a less than optimum source.

Whilst puppies are not exactly a blank canvas when they are born, it is the time that we can start to seriously have an effect on them as individuals. Pups' brain connections don't get fully wired up for this kind of input until about three weeks old, when their senses start to develop, but there is some evidence that they are able to discriminate

84

scent/taste right from the first day, so early input could be very beneficial.

Pups should be picked up and gently handled several times a day, from birth. Senses don't just suddenly switch on, but fade in gradually. If pups are used to being touched, accompanied by the sound, smell and sight of people right from the start, there is no sudden shock for them. The familiarity fades in with their ability to experience it. Their brains develop with the expectation that people are part of life.

The same goes for other sights, sounds, smells, tastes and touches. Gently fading in a wide range of them as normal is a great start for pups. Living in an environment where they are normal is the best way to do it. Do I need to tell you that a shed in the garden doesn't provide that? Neither does a barn on a puppy farm.

When I helped to raise police dog pups they were in a police dog kennels because that is where they would spend time in the future, not your average household pet's kitchen. To compensate for the lack of activity (ha-ha! "lack of activity" – dogs barking, handlers stomping about, buckets clanking, radio playing, kennel-man singing out of tune…) we had gaggles of school-children visiting them every day, played sounds CDs, fed them on a big plastic sheet (associating slippery floors with a nice experience) and every handler's family that called in to visit their own pup picked up and cuddled all the others too.

If your pup is going to be a pet he should experience everything that you expect him to have to deal with in the future as early in his life as possible. At the early stage, don't worry about making him a nervous wreck, because before he is five weeks old his brain is in a state of parasympathetic dominance, meaning that it is not yet set up for what is known as the flight or fight response.

After five weeks you need to take a bit more care because he can be frightened, so you need to make sure his introductions to new things are not done in a scary way.

But rather than think of it as introductions to individual things, try to view it as the building of a collection, or general set, of experiences that are OK. Each time pup encounters something he will do a split-second sub-conscious brain search to help him to decide how to react to it. Anything that compares favourably to things in his established set will be approached in the same way. If the outcome is positive, or at least not negative, this too will be added to the established set. In this way he can build up a set of stimuli which will be regarded as safe, or at least benign.

When we get it wrong, or we are taken by surprise, the stimulus might scare him. In this case the event goes into another set, that of frightening or "unsafe" things. When another similar stimulus is encountered, that too will default to the unsafe set. Thus our pup has three ways of viewing any new stimulus: "safe", "unsafe" and "not yet allocated". Every time he encounters a new stimulus it is transferred from the "not yet allocated" set based on similarities to stimuli already allocated to "safe" or to "unsafe" sets, and how it works out.

Obviously the more stimuli that are in the "safe" set and the fewer that are in the "unsafe" set, the more chance a new stimulus has of being viewed as benign. That is why dogs that are scared of one stimulus that we would consider to be safe are also scared of similar ones, for example dogs scared of hair-driers are often also scared of other things that whir or blow air, such as vacuum cleaners and fans.

Building up a solid set of positive experiences for your pup is the best favour you can do for them. Unallocated stimuli or those close to or designated as unsafe are the biggest source of fear for pups. Fear is the biggest source of threat for a dog and threat the biggest source of aggression. Reduce the fear in the pup and you reduce the chances of biting and fighting in the adult.

But there is an important time-line here. Three to five weeks old is a crucial time for these experiences and we don't usually have our

86

pups by then. The breeder has responsibility for this period of their lives. How then can we have any influence over what happens? By only buying a pup that has had the upbringing that we know is the optimum for their future mental development. Walk away if she hasn't.

Don't feel sorry for her because she is hiding under the table, or buy her to get her away from Cruella De Vil. If we continue to buy pups from Cruella she will continue to produce them in a cruel way. If we leave her, this puppy may suffer, but that's inevitable anyway. Think of all the future pups that won't suffer when breeding practices improve. Consumers can improve breeding practices by only buying well brought up pups. If you buy a badly brought up pup you are perpetuating the problem. You are part of the problem, not the solution. Of course it's tough to walk away, but dogs as a species deserve better from us.

And there's a better than average chance that she will turn out to be a biter and fighter. Would you buy a house suspecting that in a few years it is likely to collapse on your family? Would you buy a car that you know has a good chance of developing a steering and brakes fault on the school run? Why buy a pup that might develop a propensity to bite your children, or cause you to acquire a criminal record for being the owner of a dangerous dog?

The 2012 PDSA Animal Wellbeing report showed that 79% of people with an aggressive dog thought that a lack of positive experiences as a puppy leads to aggressive behaviour, but only 21% of them had trained their dogs at all in the first six months of the dog's life. It seems that people know how important socialisation is, but they neglect to do it anyway. Or perhaps in hindsight they realised their mistake and are paying for it for the rest of the dog's life.

Make sure pup's Mum and the Dad are pleased to see you, and make sure the pups have been brought up in a busy home environment. Good puppy breeders will go further than that and include additional sensitive socialisation up until the time you can take her home with you. If you can find one of them, you can be safe in the knowledge that your pup has had the best start in life.

It almost goes without saying that you should continue that process. Not just for a few days or weeks, but forever. Yes, that's not an exaggeration; you have to keep it up forever. It doesn't end at fourteen weeks or the "onset of a fear response" as some authors would have you believe, it doesn't end at all. Although the initial sensitive period fades away as the pup grows older, dogs are susceptible to developing fears of novel stimuli at any time during their lives, so they need to be introduced to them sensitively at any age.

There is also strong evidence for a second sensitive period for learning about social behaviour around the onset of puberty. This is the time when a pup changes from puppy behaviours to adult ones, determined by a change in hormones, much as it is in humans. It is difficult to give an exact age because big dogs tend to mature more slowly than smaller ones, but look for it around nine months onwards.

Of course if the number of experiences in their safe set far outweighs the ones in their unsafe set there will be far fewer challenges for them at any age. That is why starting out well is important, but continuing is also necessary. The second sensitive period makes dogs doubly susceptible to acquiring social fears at a crucial time in their development.

**The world**
Strangely to us, a dog's world is quite small. Our personal worlds are big. We travel to exotic lands, watch the wonders of nature and fantasy movies on TV, read thought-proving books, surf the wonderful world wide web, have virtual, real and Facebook friends with whom we argue philosophically, and are generally encouraged to think outside the box. Dogs have only their direct experiences of things that act upon them.

In most cases this involves the people and other animals they live with, a few regular visitors, their home, regular walks, the back of the car (which I always think must be like going to the cinema for a dog – scenes passing before their eyes, but none of it experienced as reality) and not much else. Sure, some dogs have a wider existence that involves visiting Grandma and some go on holidays with us, but the experiences within those experiences are much the same, a home, familiar people and dogs, and a walk.

It is when something new is introduced to this world that problems can occur. A dog with a broad set of safe experiences will cope with novelty better because, even though it is new, it is likely to be similar to something the dog has already experienced. For example if a dog is introduced to a train travel for the first time, he will accept it more easily if he is already comfortable in a car.

I once met a two year old dog who had lived only in a bungalow and then in kennels. She was scared stiff by a staircase when she was rehomed. It was a novelty that did not exist in her world. Because the staircase scared her she tried to bite the man who was making her walk up it. Because he handled the situation badly, by forcing her up the stairs, the experience didn't go from her "not yet allocated" set into her safe one, but into the set of experiences she considered to be unsafe.

If, rather than trying to drag and push her up them, he had been a little more considerate, perhaps by placing a treat on every other step or throwing a ball for her to chase up them, she would have accepted steps as normal and safe, rather than being worried every time she approached them. Although we managed to get her to walk up and down them eventually, she never really got over her worry. And because staircases in general were in the not-safe set every individual staircase had to prove it was safe, every new staircase was a mountain to climb.

The big benefit of building a full set of positive experiences as a puppy is that as they get older dogs lose the ability to generalise. For a puppy, if one staircase is okay, they all are; if one man with a beard is okay, they all are. For adults, generalisation is more difficult. If the puppy hasn't seen a staircase or a man with a beard then, as an adult, each staircase and each beardy-man are recognised and treated as individuals. *Some* generalisation can and does take place, but not to the same extent as in puppyhood. This is why it is important to introduce your pup to as many safe experiences as possible whilst they are young, to take advantage of the generalisation effect.

Unfortunately, it is easier for dogs to generalise bad experiences than good ones. Good experiences are taken one at a time. Bad experiences generalise easily. It doesn't seem fair, does it? But it makes good evolutionary sense.

If I open a box and find a cake inside I would receive a minor boost to my genetic survival and would like boxes as a result, but I would not expect there to be a cake in every one. If I open a box and find a venomous snake inside I may receive a potentially devastating blow to my genetic survival potential and, if I escaped, it would make good sense to avoid boxes altogether. One cake gives me a positive feel about boxes, but not to the same extent that one snake gives me a negative feel about them.

## Practicalities & babies

What to do if your impressionable pup is caught by surprise and spooks at something we would consider safe, such as a bin-bag flapping in the hedge at dusk? Don't push him at it but laugh heartily in a jolly uncle kind of way and approach it confidently yourself. Encourage him to come with you to investigate in his own good time and keep up the, "*It isn't a problem*" impression. Don't use, "*There, there, the nasty bin bag won't hurt you*" in a sympathetic Mumsy voice, but go with, "*Ha-ha-ha, it's only a silly old bin bag – look, if I can stand on it whilst laughing so can you!"* loud and confidently.

Admittedly, it can be difficult to cover absolutely everything in the first few weeks of your pup's life, but keeping social and environmental referencing jogging along as an everyday occurrence makes your dog less likely to develop specific fears at any time.

Your personal environment may comprise of stimuli that are specific to you, for example particular types of machinery, or other animals, which you should obviously include in your loose programme of introduction for your pup.

If you have cats or horses they will need to be benignly factored in to your pup's experiences as soon as you can; if you are an avid walker who delights in roaming through flocks of sheep, you should introduce him to the woolly-backs as soon and as often as you can - with a "come away" request. The earlier dogs are introduced to any animals, the less likely they are to later regard them as prey. It is much easier to show your pup that a species is not prey from very early on than it is to change his mind later.

There will be some specific stimuli that are difficult to produce at the right time, for example babies. We need to specifically consider babies because of the disproportionate number of dog-bites that happen to children. Socialising to babies is a good start to preventing your dog and your child adding to the figures.

I'm told it is not always possible to produce a baby just for the purposes of socialising your pup. You might be able to borrow one for short exposures by visiting a new parent, but you may not know of any. In view of that, despite your best efforts it may be that your dog grows up without the benefit of knowing and understanding what a baby is.

Most new parents don't actually consider that they may have missed part of their pup's socialisation until their dog first growls at their baby, but with a little forethought you can do some social-add-ons to

91

prevent that. We look at what to do about him growling at baby in part two, but savvy parents don't wait for the problem to develop before addressing it, they introduce their dog to their baby-regime even before they bring their new-born home.

There is much that can be done as Mum nears the end of her pregnancy, such as training the dog to go to his bed with a long-lasting treat as Mum practices changing a doll on the floor. On-the-floor has been almost exclusively doggy territory up to now and soon there will be a new occupant in his environmental niche. Show him that not everything that happens down there is of importance to him.

Training in going for a walk whilst you are pushing a pram or buggy is also useful, so your dog gets used to this different way of walking on the lead.  Bring the buggy, carrycot, bedding, changing mat, potty, nappy-bundle and all the other baby gear into the living room for him to investigate in advance, so it doesn't all arrive as a shock on the first day baby turns up. Drip-feeding new stimuli is easier for him to cope with than a heap arriving at once.

You might also think about digging out that Sounds CD you played when he was a puppy and playing the baby-crying noises again as a warm-up for the real thing. Keep it low-volume and at times when he is having a good experience, eating or playing games. Progressively turn it up and take the player round the house so he gets used to full baby-lung volume (which in my experience is extremely loud) from upstairs too. Maybe *not* go the full hog and get up to play it at 1am. And 2am. And 3am. And... He, and you, will have to cope with that when the real baby comes along.

Once baby arrives at home most dogs will show slight interest but no more. Don't make a massive deal encouraging him to approach at every opportunity, but structure it so you are in complete control of the circumstances when you invite him to come and see.

Under no circumstances should any dog be left alone in a room with a baby, toddler or child until you are absolutely sure there is no risk. Depending upon the individual dog and child, this could be anywhere between the child being six and twelve. That's years, not days, weeks or months. It doesn't matter how friendly your dog is or how asleep your baby is, just don't do it. We look at risk assessment later, but in this case even if the likelihood of the dog biting is tiny, the potential injury itself is just too severe to take any risk. Take the risk away completely by never allowing your dog unsupervised access to your baby.

It is possible that the night-time feeds and disruption may make you a bit grumpy, despite this bundle of joy being the best thing that ever happened to you both. Your dog may well be feeling a little emotionally delicate too, so a little one-to-one quality time for him with both partners at different times gives you an occasional break. A little extra walk, game or fun-training will help you all.

Expect your dog to show interest in baby-food and dirty nappies, but don't get into conflict with him over these resources. Let him see what is going on, but when he becomes too bothersome for you, ask him to go settle on his bed (see part two for more details), with any necessary rewards.

To introduce your dog to your baby, and reduce the chances of him considering her to be prey, from the earliest days when baby comes home sit her on your knee and call your dog over for a stroke. It doesn't have to be extensive, you're just building up a nice association between dog and baby. You are also in a very good position to take control if he gets too stressed and send him to bed to calm down, but if done sensitively it shouldn't come to that.

Post-socialisation socialisation is possible, and even easy if your pup has had a good early foundation, because he expects new things to be non-threatening. If his set of safe stimuli is large and his unsafe set is miniscule, he will expect this new arrival to be safe too. Approaching a baby not expecting to be worried is the best introduction he can have.

Ultimately, it is your job to make sure every new experience goes into your dog's safe-stimuli set. Socialisation is a matter of keeping your dog well balanced. Forming and keeping a mental collection of positive experiences is the key.

## Coping with the world

It is worth recapping on what we have so far with regard to the environment, as we are going to build on it. We have a dog that lives in a relatively limited world by our standards and is only able to understand things that she directly experiences. Since she was a puppy she has been building a model of that world in her head. She has experienced things that are safe and things that are not, but hopefully the set of safe experiences is much wider than the one of unsafe experiences.

As she grows up she begins to rely on the safe set of her experiences in her model. This is her world, predictable and stable around her, and modelled as such in her mind. She relies on it staying that way. When her world view is challenged by something that isn't usually in it, for example by a thunderstorm, she relies on her proximity to safe things to maintain her emotional equilibrium. She has a set of safe stimuli that she uses to maintain her emotional balance and protect herself from undue distress.

Her safe-set view of the world or "maintenance set" of familiar stimuli supports her when she becomes distressed by unexpected or unpleasant events. The thunder may crash but she can rely on her home, bed, fireside and owner to be there for her. Maybe the thunder isn't so bad after all. The things that she does when she becomes distressed grow into her coping strategies and these are inevitably aspects of her maintenance set of positive experiences; the world modelled in her head that she can rely on from past experience.

Coping strategies from the maintenance set can be split into those that are environmental and those that are social. Being at home when thunder rolls feels safer than being away from home; being with her owner when thunder rumbles feels safer than being on her own.

"Being at home" and "proximity to owner" are coping strategies from her maintenance set of positive experiences that are useful for reducing her distress when a thunderstorm worries her.

By using coping strategies gleaned from their maintenance set of positive experiences most dogs can cope with life's challenges most of the time.

## Stress, eustress and distress

Stress can be defined as the response of the body when a biological or psychological demand is placed upon it. We are all, dogs included, subject to stress many times throughout the day. Stress can be negative (not enjoyable), which is the way that we normally mean it, *"Oh, he's stressed-out."* But it can also be positive (enjoyable), for example the kind of stress felt when you are trying to score a goal, driving in a race, or even writing a book. Dogs indulging in breed specific behaviour are in a state of positive or eu-stress. However, please remember that both positive and negative are stressed states.

Stress in itself is not necessarily a problem. Eustress can be exhilarating and sought after. Even negative stress is acceptable to the body up to a point, providing we have a way of coping with it.

Distress describes the state of the dog when he is not able to cope with a stress that is placed upon him. Chronic distress happens when the dog is in distress for a long period of time. It is characterised by the panting, pacing and whining that is seen in some kennel-distressed dogs. If left to suffer for too long chronic stress can have serious long-term consequences for the health of the dog.

Acute distress describes a sudden or extreme onset of stress with which the dog is unable to cope. During acute distress and acute eustress impulse-control and social inhibition processes are bypassed and consequently the threshold for aggressive behaviour is lowered.

Also consider is that stress is cumulative, whether it is distress or eustress. Both demand an increase in arousal and both can build upon what has gone before. Single stressors can build up inside a dog towards a tipping point where the dog has to deal with the latest addition. This should not be a surprise to us as we acknowledge it in ourselves. When we are having a bad day we snap at the point at which the final straw breaks the camel's back.

I saw Jim, a Beagle dog that had bitten a child who had taken him by the collar to pull him off the sofa. The bite apparently came out of the blue because he was used to being guided by his collar and was used to being turfed off the sofa when there was no room for the many children in the house to sit there.

The difference was that on this particular day he'd been beaten up by another dog on his afternoon walk, his owner was late home from work, he hadn't been fed, and a teenager was taking advantage of his Mum's absence to play rock music at full volume. Jim just wanted to curl up on the sofa (a good environmental coping strategy) and couldn't deal with that option being removed.

All the little stressors added up to a lot of distress which boiled into acute distress when the hand grabbed him to turf him off the sofa. He was having a bad day and the hand was the straw that broke the camel's back.

Dogs in eustress, playing hard at rough and tumble, are so fired up that they can flip into acute distress. This frequently happens when dogs in a play-fight realise that they are losing control of the situation. I have seen it when assessing Pit Bull Terriers. By starting a rough and tumble game with a push and shoulder barge they respond in the spirit of the game by jumping and barging back. However, if I continue to take the game to higher levels through rougher contact there is quite often a point at which they feel they are losing control and need to re-exert it. They flip from extreme enjoyment to a burst of serious aggression.

You only need to look at professional football players to know this happens to people too. They over-react to a situation from which they could normally walk away because impulse control and social inhibition goes out the window and the lower threshold for aggression is easy to step over.

Many dogs, and especially the competitive and fighting breeds, escalate play beyond the level with which they are able to cope, and flip into a burst of aggression. The only answer is not to let them get to the stage when eustress turns into acute distress.

A dog is subject to lots of stressors throughout the day, positive and negative ones. The positive eustress is exciting and fun so long as it remains within boundaries. The negative distress is okay so long as the dog has coping strategies in place from her maintenance set of positive experiences. Now you can see why it is important that every dog is sensitively socialised.

Stressors come and either stay or go, as they are, or are not, coped with. Multiple stressors push the dog towards the tipping point at which she needs to react and the next one, which might normally be innocuous, could be enough to force her into responding.

When stresses are too much she moves into distress. If it happens slowly over time with no trigger that pushes her over the tipping point, she will remain in a miserable state of chronic distress, with resulting health consequences. If the trigger arrives suddenly she can flip into acute distress. If she can't cope with the build-up or sudden arrival of the stressor, she has to get out of the situation immediately.

The usual coping strategies must have failed, otherwise she wouldn't be in distress, and she must cast around for alternatives. Because impulse-control is reduced she can act in ways that may be normally uncharacteristic for her. Because social inhibition processes are bypassed she no longer has the good manners that you have come to expect from her. Because the threshold for aggressive behaviour is lowered she drops into fight mode.

From an evolutionary perspective the breakdown of normal inhibitions in times of acute distress is very effective. The normal processes haven't worked, so more extreme alternatives are sought. In dogs this translates into instinctive strategies of hiding, running away, and more extreme social communication (aggression). In this case the term aggression has its specific meaning of "actions to attempt to proactively control a situation through the use or display of force".

Good social and environmental referencing prevents a dog becoming distressed by providing a wide range of safe experiences with which to compare new ones and a broad set of maintenance stimuli to help them cope with challenges to their emotions. Such a dog will very rarely feel the need to use aggression, unlike the dog that is regularly distressed and has no means of coping.

But even the most well-balanced dog may face a challenge to which the best answer is to bite or fight. What happens if they learn that this is actually a very effective strategy? Learning from specific events is very important in the development the behaviour of all dogs, but particularly in those that bite and fight.

# Chapter 6

# Learning - How Aggression Develops

## Development

We should acknowledge the importance of what we have so far before we take the next step, because nipping the development of biting and fighting in the bud at any stage is easier and more effective than dealing with it afterwards.

We know that biting and fighting are normal parts of dog behaviour that only cause us a problem when we think that the dog's judgement is unsound, when they do it in what we would consider to be inappropriate circumstances. It is okay to bite a burglar, but not a neighbour who has popped in to borrow a cup of sugar.

When a miniature dachshund snaps at the man trying to grab her owner's purse the newspaper headline describes her as *"bravely defending her Mum"*, but when the same dog snaps at a boy-scout taking her owner's arm to guide her across the street she is described by the prosecutor as, *"an uncontrolled fear-biting dangerous dog"*. Context is everything.

Although there are dog breeds that are more or less predisposed towards the use of aggression because of the purposes for which they were bred in the past, and there are sex and neuter differences in the tendency to bite and fight, these predispositions can be overcome through sensitive upbringing and guidance. Good nurturing can always improve natural tendencies.

It is also undeniable that some breeds cause more damage than others when they bite and fight. The conformation of the jaws and musculature of different breeds and types can cause more or less damage, but the motivation behind the attack is at least, if not more, important. A large dog with huge jaws that gives a single front tooth bite to make the problem go away may cause less injury than a smaller dog that wants to engage in a prolonged ferocious battle.

Within individuals there are temperament traits that make dogs more prone to developing inappropriate aggressive responses, such as nervousness or lack of impulse control. By selectively breeding emotionally well-balanced pets we can reduce the incidences of biting and fighting. Until that happens we must be careful in selecting our pets from only the most stable of parents.

Having recognised and bought into the production of the best raw material for a pet we have to take responsibility for how our pups are brought up. Having the best genetic material is directly linked to keeping the environment at the optimum for the development of our pups because it starts with Mum's physical and emotional state when they are in her womb. Afterwards, the initial period of infancy is vital in the development of a well-balanced pet because this contributes to the maintenance of the ever-expanding positive experience-set necessary for emotional wellbeing.

A wide maintenance set of positive experiences supported by a solid set of coping strategies is a buffer against distress, a negative emotional state in which dogs are prone to over-react because impulse-control and social inhibition processes are bypassed and the threshold for aggressive behaviour is lowered. Keeping distress down in this way reduces the potential for aggressive behaviour throughout the dog's life.

And if we can arrange all that will we have a dog that never has the need to bite or fight? Unfortunately, life's not like that. We can, and should, attempt to arrange all those things, but sometimes we make mistakes, and sometimes life just throws unexpected stuff at us. This is where the value of understanding the aspects of learning that affect the development of biting and fighting comes in.

## Growing up

Although the learning processes for puppies and adult dogs are the same, the deferential behaviour given off by puppies usually diverts social threats. Most dogs recognise that another dog rolling on his back and urinating in the air is not going to be a threat and back off accordingly.

Whilst this gets the puppy away from the situation, he is still learning that certain other dogs are to be feared; they are still going into his unsafe set of stimuli.

When puppies mature they go through a change of behaviour from that of a puppy to that of an adult dog. They lose puppy behaviour from their repertoire and start to use behaviour more appropriate for adult interactions. They stop being so extremely deferential and start to be more proactive; more interested in being in control of the situation and less likely to roll on their back and urinate in the air.

This change from puppy to adult behaviour is responsible for a vast number of what owners see as unpredictable bites and fights that occur when the dog is about twelve months old. For the past year he has been afraid every time he has met (a spotted dog, a bearded man, a toddler... fill in the blank as appropriate) and he has dealt with it in a deferential puppy fashion (by running away, hiding, rolling over and urinating... fill in the blank as appropriate). But he's all grown up now. He doesn't do puppy behaviour any more. He does adult behaviour.

This isn't a conscious decision on the dog's part, but a variation in his available motor patterns, driven by the hormonal changes as he matures. Whereas once he responded to a particular emotion with a puppy motor pattern, the change in hormones stimulates an adult motor pattern in its place.

An adult is less likely to back down from a challenge and more likely to engage in conflict than a puppy. So when the puppy that has been half scared to death grows up, he has different ways of dealing with the fear, the threat and the distress. One adult way of dealing with social threats, those from other people or dogs, is to meet the challenge head on. To *make* them go away.

This is often the first time an owner will have seen the more proactive threat-reduction behaviours in their dog, starting with stiffening and glaring, standing up to the protagonist, not backing down, holding their ground and challenging back again. Many aren't expecting the change and simply don't understand what's going on. Quite often they don't recognise the stiffening/staring for the aggression it is and it is only when their little darling bursts into a screaming fight they exclaim *"Well, he's never done that before!"* Their baby has grown up.

It would help if owners were to pay attention because this is another very sensitive time for the development of social behaviours. Teaching a dog good adult manners is as important as teaching a puppy. Think of him as a stroppy teenager with few social skills. He needs to be guided as to the right course of action or he could turn into a proper thug. It doesn't take a great deal of effort, but it does require guidance and consistency in the process of learning how to become an adult.

## Learning

Notwithstanding their need for guidance, dogs are far from stupid. They are very good at associative learning, both classical and operant conditioning. This means that when they experience or do something that has a consequence they are likely to remember what their actions and the consequences were, so that they can do or avoid the same thing again. They know that what works, works. Important consequences, such as the removal of acute distress, are learned particularly easily, as they are particularly important.

We have already seen that the communication used by dogs to reduce threat runs on a scale from little movements away, through other body language that can easily be missed, such as lip-licking, yawning and head turning, right up to full blown in-your-face biting. So why do some dogs continue to operate this communication at a level that we think is appropriate throughout their lives, with never a need for escalating to biting and fighting, but others somehow lose their way and end up as biters and fighters?

The behaviours lower down the scale of threat reduction are sometimes called "appeasing" "submissive" or even "pacifying", but what's in a name? I prefer "threat-reducing" because it describes the effect they have on other dogs, rather than attempting to place intentions upon them, which would indicate a level of a theory of mind that no one has yet conclusively proved a dog to have.

When used towards another dog that understands them, and despite my caveats about the strange shapes we have bred dogs into, against all odds many dogs *do* understand them, the behaviours have the effect of reducing the threat to the dog exhibiting them because the other dog usually backs off.

Remembering our definition of attempting to proactively control a situation through the use or display of force, we wouldn't label these behaviours aggressive because the force element is absent, but the desire that the dog is communicating is the same; to get the other dog or person to back off and reduce the perceived threat.

Nobody teaches dogs these behaviours in the same way that nobody actually needs to teach a dog how to growl or bite, although they can be taught when to do it. They are among each dog's inherited batch of motor patterns, discrete chunks of behaviour like the parts of the breed-specific-behaviour we discussed earlier. Initially they display and understand them automatically without any learning being necessary.

Many are converted puppy behaviours, such as licking at the face, which is pinched from the puppy behaviour of licking at the dam's mouth to stimulate regurgitation, and which could be interpreted as "*I am acting like a puppy and therefore am no threat to you*".

It should be noted that because these behaviours are inherited, individual dogs within breeds can inherit a lot or a little of the tendency to display them.

As we saw earlier when discussing breed tendencies, it is thought that dog-fighting breeds, those that have been selected to be good at dog fighting behaviours, have a reduced tendency to display threat-reducing behaviours and also to react to them by backing off in social interactions with another dog. This makes good breeding sense as any dog that either rolled-over when threatened, or backed off when another dog showed signs of being worried, wouldn't last long in a dog-fighting pit.

At a basic level a dog displays behaviour based on the emotion that she feels, therefore if she feels a little intimidated she might display what we would consider a low-level behaviour and conversely if she is hugely threatened may exhibit behaviour at what we would consider to be the top end of the scale.

But behaviour doesn't operate in a vacuum. Each time she uses a threat-reduction motor pattern there is a feedback loop. Is it working to get what she wants? If it is, keep doing it and use it again in the same circumstances; if it isn't, change it now and next time for something else. This feedback is going on constantly. Throughout an interaction the dog is throwing out behaviour and receiving feedback in terms of the response of the other person or dog, and then keeping or changing it to fit the next move.

When dogs first meet there is inevitably at least a small degree of threat because they don't know how the other is going to receive them. Normal canine greeting involves at least some threat reduction. The communication is like a dance. Where the dog is very familiar with the other dog or person (or cat or any other animal) the dance flows like the best ballroom waltz, with each knowing where the other is going to place their feet next. You can whirl through the greeting almost without thinking about it.

On the other hand a stranger is a completely new partner and you have no idea what dance they are going to do, let alone if they are any good at it. It is no wonder that dogs sometimes metaphorically step on the toes of others in first encounters. This is where skilled trainers quite literally take the lead to show the dog exactly what is expected, guiding them and providing feedback in all the right places.

Bear this in mind when thinking about adolescent dogs learning adult behaviour. They can't use the dance they learned as a puppy because it's too childish for a grown-up. They have to learn a whole new one. One where they are not allowed just to stomp clumsily on people and other dogs who get in their way. They have to learn sensitivity at a time when they are still a bit giddy and ungainly. But just think of the huge learning opportunities this whole behaviour feedback process provides.

We need to think of a single simple interaction as experienced by a puppy to use as an example. Let's say she's been born of genetically well balanced parents and she and her Mum have been living in a steady and happy home. She is no more likely to develop tendencies to bite and fight than the next dog, in fact, probably less so.

At ten weeks old she goes to a puppy class with her new owner. She is a bit concerned because of all the new smells, sights and sounds, but is expecting a positive experience because that is what she is used to. Things go quite well to start with; people give her treats and she is quite happy to go up to the Boxer puppy opposite and touch noses. The Boxer is quite a nice chap but as Boxer's do he bats her nose with his paw in play. It hurts, so she backs away. The Boxer follows so she hides under the chair her owner is sitting on; she grins;

she tucks her tail under; she hides her head; she rolls over on her back; she urinates in the air. Still the Boxer stuffs his face into hers. She is terrified. So she launches at him, snarling, snapping and biting his nose... and he backs off. All this took place inside three seconds.

What has she learned? Anyone who said she has learned, "*biting works*" can go to the bottom of the class.

Anyone who said she had learned, "*This Boxer is unsafe; dogs are unpredictable; be wary of unfamiliar dogs; puppy class is a dangerous place; hiding doesn't work; deferential social threat-reduction behaviours don't always work; my owner doesn't protect me; my owner doesn't guide me; biting works.*" can go to the top of the class.

We also need to be able to understand how the emotions surrounding this experience will project into the future. Repeating the full Boxer-in-puppy-class experience would bring on the most distress, but little parts of it can also cause little bits of distress because they also have part of the value that predicts the whole. For example if you'd travelled to the puppy class in the car, then getting in the car might trigger memories of the puppy class, which triggers memories of the altercation, which causes distress because she does not want it to happen again. Picking up her lead, putting on your coat, walking from the house to the car, all might be predictors of feelings of distress because of what happened at puppy class.

What happened in terms of learning is that our pup was subject to a relatively small threat, a tap on the nose, a challenge to her emotional balance that she tried to deal with through firstly moving away, then through hiding. Had either of these worked to reduce the threat and return her to emotional balance she would have learned that these were appropriate strategies, which they were.

However, they did not work and the threat increased. Her distress levels increased exponentially as she worked through all the deferential threat-reducing behaviour in her repertoire, as each failed to remove the Boxer. Then she tipped into acute distress where her impulse-control and social inhibition vanished, and she bit the Boxer in the face.

At the point at which her level of distress was most acute she used another normal instinctive behaviour for dealing with threat. She bit the nose in front of her. And it worked.

When the feeling of distress is extremely high, the feeling of relief when it passes is correspondingly very warmly felt. This feeling of relief is a huge emotional and physical reward, and a reinforcer for the previous behaviour. This means that biting as a strategy is learned very strongly. The next time pup is confronted with a predicament from which she must extract herself, biting will come high on the list of possible solutions. After all, it worked really well last time.

The next time she is nose to nose with a Boxer, if the Boxer leans forwards as she leans backwards, she might miss out all the deferential communication and simply go straight for the hugely distress-relieving face-bite.

That was an example of one big learning experience that is all too common in the development of a biter and fighter. But it didn't have to happen. All along the route were possible exits to better behaviour; behaviour that doesn't result in her being taken out at midnight because she hates all dogs on sight.

After the paw hit her nose the Boxer's owner could have recognised his dog was too invasive and called him away. Then, moving away would have been the solution for our pup. Small problem, small solution; slight increase in distress followed by a slightly rewarding feeling of relief. Everything on a small scale.

After she went back to her owner he could have protected her by gently blocking the Boxer's approach and she would have seen that coming back to him worked. If he'd then given her a treat or lots of praise, or both, the added reward would also serve to reinforce the behaviour of "coming away to Dad when worried".

She'd have had a slight increase in distress but used a good coping strategy to get over it, reinforced by her owner so that it would be used again in similar circumstances. She'd have learned that this Boxer, and therefore some dogs, can hurt a little bit, but she can quickly get over it. It's not a problem.

Boxer communication is a little bouncier than most and he was just indulging in the same play that he had practiced with his litter-mates. He lacked a bit of guidance too. But had the Boxer been more in tune with her communication and backed off at any time before she bit, she could have learned that any of the strategies in use at the time would work for her; then and in the future.

Any of these would have been preferable to learning to use a biting strategy this early in her life.

Those who want to take the exercise a little further might now consider what the Boxer learned, too. It takes two to tango.

Of course the fact that it happened this early in her life is important too, because she now has the opportunity to practice it more often as she grows up. Puppy classes, Boxers and unfamiliar dogs are moved from the not-yet-allocated to the unsafe set of experiences. They in turn will influence other similar experiences.

This simple example of learning how to bite and fight can and does happen in exactly that kind of way, but more often pups and even adult dogs learn in stages, as opposed to a single big event. Many learning experiences where moving away doesn't reduce distress can cause a feeling of a lack of control over the situation. Little repeated events where the dog growls and gets away reinforce a general move from deference towards managing the situation proactively.

One reason that predicting dogs' biting and fighting is sometimes difficult is that each dog goes through a slightly different path of learning to get there. Even though big learning events do happen, no dog goes from benign friendliness one day to being a public danger the next without a series of stages in between. It is these stages that differ ever so slightly in each dog, and each time a stage is passed other options become available.

Depending upon the learning experience, the dog can quickly leap to a biting and fighting outcome, or can learn other ways of dealing with the challenge. It is this individuality that can make it seem unpredictable, but it isn't if you take notice of what your dog is trying to tell you.

## Fighting other dogs – fear & relief

Although one big event can have huge potential for changing future behaviour, because repetition is such an important part of strengthening learning, the fear-response often builds through a series of events, and a dog can learn that there is no point in sending out deferential low-level threat-reducing signals that never or rarely work.

This particularly applies to dogs whose shape or hairiness causes other dogs difficulty in interpreting their communication. They can give off small signals that are not noticed because of the way they look. If other dogs ignore or do not notice their low-level leave-me-alone signals they quickly learn to use the bigger ones, barking and snarling at a distance.

Humans contribute to the development of this kind of behaviour by thinking they are controlling it when they are actually rewarding it. If their dog barks and snarls at another dog the owner, quite naturally, pulls her away on the lead and walks in the other direction. Embarrassment is high on our list of things to avoid.

If we follow this from a learning theory point of view the dog experiences a rise in distress when he sees another dog. Due to previous learning experiences he knows that smaller "*leave me alone*" signals don't work so he fires off big ones early. The barking and snarling are so obvious to all, even his owner and the owner of the other dog, that they drag their dogs away before they've ever got into combat distance. For the owner, the problem is solved for this time because no fight took place. For the dog, the rise in distress was dealt with by way of combative intent. Distress went up, anger came out, the other dog didn't get close and the relief flooded through him. The relief he felt at not being in contact with the other dog rewarded the aggressive behaviour. Problem solved for the dog, too.

Next time the rise in distress, which is itself distressing, can be dealt with sooner because now he has a solution. Bark and snarl and the dog goes away. In fact from our dog's point of view there is now no need to experience any distress at all. The moment another dog trots into view, use the fighting strategy and he feels relief as it goes away.

Many dogs operate this strategy with their owners; they are the midnight walkers who can't allow their dogs to see another without him kicking off. Most have their critical distance, beyond which they don't react but within which they do. It might be ten metres or a hundred metres. In some dogs I have met it is any line of sight at which they can identify that it is another dog. In others they can cope if they remain outside actual touching distance. Both of these have their challenges, the former because they are so sensitive and the latter mostly because they inhibit their signals right up until the last minute, when they explode as the other dog comes in for a sniff.

However, these are the easy ones to deal with, straight fear with a coping strategy that works at a distance, and we'll look at how to change that later. The trickier ones are those who start to look for the relief as a source of positive emotions.

Quite often these dogs lack stimulation, or come from the breeds that have traditionally been bred to enjoy combat. Sometimes they like the experience because their environment is restricted and any form of excitement is better than none at all, for example because they live in a situation not compatible with their breed dispositions (Collie in a bedsit springs to mind). In this case it is their boredom that leads to delinquency. They still feel the fear, but the need for excitement overrides it. They are literally thrill-seekers.

The other kind of dog that looks forward to fighting is to be found in the combative breeds for whom it is part of their original breed specific behaviour. Not all of the individuals in these breeds inevitably have to be fighters, because good breeding for confidence and impulse control, coupled with sensitive upbringing, can always trump any breed dispositions. But it doesn't take much poor upbringing to develop it.

The issue we have to acknowledge is that some dog breeds have been manipulated by us to enjoy biting and fighting, otherwise they wouldn't do it. Dogs that have been bred to guard find seeing-off an intruder enjoyable. Dogs that have been bred to destroy vermin find killing small furry animals enjoyable. Dogs bred to fight other dogs enjoy the combat. This enjoyable aspect of fighting is fuelled by the brain chemicals of reward. The dog gets an exciting, gratifying buzz from doing it.

Like all breed specific behaviour it can be inherited on a range from low to high but, no matter how strong the tendency to perform it is inherited, it can be kept to a minimum, and in some cases none, by not providing outlets to practice it. Practice, of course, makes perfect.

Every time the dog does it he gets a thrill and every time the thrill happens it strengthens the neurological connections that support the behaviour. In lay terms the more he does it, the more he enjoys it and the more he wants to do it.

These dogs may initially feel the fear, but it is eventually replaced by the pure enjoyment of the fight. The fear/enjoyment balance differs in different dogs, and this could be seen as the continuation of a scale from the pure fear-based to the pure enjoyment based fighters.

The big difference when trying to deal with it, and that is the reason we need to understand the underlying motivations, is that the fear-based dogs are trying to maintain distance and the enjoyment-based dogs will actively seek out opportunities. Those in-between will be flipping between the two, wanting to get close but dreading it.

The emotions supporting the behaviour differ, in that fear is a negative emotion (distress) from which the dog is trying to escape, and breed specific combat is a positive emotion (eustress) in which the dog is trying to indulge. Knowing whether we are dealing with distress, eustress or a more complicated mixture of the two is vital for resolving problematic behaviour.

## Fighting other dogs - frustration and anger

Although fear is by far the most common motive for dogs fighting with other dogs, there are two more reasons we need to consider. The first is what appears to be anger in response to what they perceive as an insult and the second is pure frustration that stems from their inability to make contact.

"Perceived insult anger" is often the flip side of the fear-aggressive encounter that we looked at earlier, and one of the ways that many Staffies get themselves into trouble. If one dog barks and snarls, it is bound to have an effect on how the other dog feels. After all, barking and snarling is not appropriate greeting behaviour. It is threatening.

If our normal, well-behaved, average dog wanders towards another in the park, just to say, "*Hello*", and this other dog suddenly kicks off into a snarling monster at the end of her lead, because she is afraid and trying to keep him away, how would our dog respond to that? Well, lots of dogs will perceive such aggressive behaviour as threatening and we know that dogs have ways of dealing with threat. In this situation he can move away or engage in social threat-reducing behaviours.

Moving away is an option that many dogs can and do take. However a significant minority, most often to be found in the combative breeds, deal with this threat by engaging in the fight. Remember that some breeds have been especially developed not to back down from a challenge? Remember that some breeds actually get a buzz from fighting? These are the ones that respond to the threat with what appears to be anger and a good excuse for a rumble. However, this is just the underlying fear being disguised by the breed specific combative behaviour.

Inevitably when this is recounted in court the snarling monster that initiated the fight has been picked up and, from a human point of view, cannot be a threat to the dog taking up the challenge. But dogs don't think like that. They perceive a threat as being issued but don't think through whether or not it can actually be carried out. So long as the snarling monster continues to spit threats, they will attempt to deal with it by responding with their own. Unfortunately they are not attempting to place distance between themselves and the monster, but to defeat her in combat. That is what these types of dogs have been bred to do, not back down.

You can see how, when this has happened a few times to a nice placid dog of one of the combative breeds, he might decide to get his retaliation in first, and it won't take a full-blown snarling monster to set him off, but maybe only being looked at in the wrong way.

This leads us nicely into frustration as a cause of fighting, because we have to look at what might happen if both dogs are on a lead.

Frustration is caused by an inability to do something that you want or need to do. It is difficult to separate wants from needs and often the difference is only in the eye of the beholder. My need might be perceived by you as only being a want. Rather than get into an argument over semantics I think it best to point out that they can both result in frustration. We should also note again that frustration is most apparent in dogs that lack impulse control. They find it difficult to deal with frustration of any kind.

Barriers cause frustration because they hold you back. Most dog-on-dog frustration stems from being held on a lead and not able to approach the other dog. The motivation for wanting to approach the other dog can vary. It can be because he has a strategy for coping with his fear that involves being close to them, or it could be because he wants to engage in play, but in each case the outcome is frustration at their inability, which turns to anger.

Let's take the first scenario. Many dogs have a mild fear of other dogs that they can overcome by using strategies such as going close and having a sniff, or standing sideways on for a few moments until the fear subsides. These are fine and relatively unproblematic strategies, except when the dog can't utilise them. Then he becomes frustrated at his inability to deal with the distress building up inside, which causes more distress, which, as we know, can lead to an increase in aggressive behaviour.

A variation of that is when a dog of a combative breed is challenged, and their method of dealing with the perceived (not necessarily real) threat is to engage and defeat the challenger. If they are being held back on a lead they can't do that and again frustration builds to more anger.

The second scenario is often seen in dogs on the cusp of maturity. Puppies often want to run up to other dogs in a sociable puppy way for the enjoyment of playing with them. This puppy behaviour frequently persists as they begin to mature and they still want to run up to other dogs to play when they are full-sized, but not yet adults.

Because we owners know that this kind of behaviour is sometimes not tolerated in a full-sized dog we tend to hold them back on the lead. Depending upon the value our dog places on playing with the other dog they can become very frustrated if they are unable to do so. The higher the value of the play, the higher the frustration. Think of bored dogs with little stimulation available in their environment again.

What starts out as a desire (want, need?) to go play with another dog turns into anger through frustration at being prevented. Again we have distress at the inability to fulfil a need fuelling an increase in aggressive behaviour. Unfortunately because our dog is focussing on the other dog his frustration and aggression is also focussed on her.

The reality is that although he is angry at his own inability he projects that anger towards her because she is in front of him. The result is that the original intention to play is replaced with anger at her because he can't. To a lesser extent this can also happen when a playful dog runs free up to another that doesn't want to play. The lack of the expected play causes frustration and a fight can break out as a result.

Finally, the inability to control their own actions because they are held back on a lead can also contribute to frustration. As we will see later, not holding them back on a lead, and instead providing them with a safe way to explore options other than fighting, can be an effective solution for some fighters.

## Fighting known dogs

We will look in more depth at dogs that fight within the family home later, when we examine how to deal with it. These are the distressing occasions where dogs that appear to have happily lived in the family home now can't get on together. In some cases they can't even be in the same room together without a fight breaking out.

The origins of this fighting and the ways in which it develops from a breakdown in communication are the same as with dogs that don't know each other. The fears and frustrations are slightly more tilted towards resources and fear of loss, which drives competition between dogs, and the proximity of the two dogs means that neither can avoid the other.

When you consider the combination of competition for restricted resources, including a finite amount of owner attention, and living virtually on top of each other, it isn't so much a wonder that some dogs in the same family fight, but more a miracle that so many don't. This has to be testimony to the ability of dogs to learn how to live in harmony.

Having looked at some of the different ways that fighting behaviour can develop in a dog, there is a common factor that stares us in the face. The build-up for all these fighters stems from experience and practice. The more of the wrong kinds of experience they have and the more they get to practice the wrong ways of dealing with them, the more likely they are to turn to fighting. The same applies to dogs biting people.

## Biting people

If your dog is biting strangers, or attempting to bite them, or even giving them the impression that she might bite them, you can get into a lot of trouble. Section 3 of the Dangerous Dogs Act 1991 covers it – go read up on it. At the time of writing the penalties for being the owner or person in charge of a dangerous dog that bites someone is a maximum of two years imprisonment and/or an unlimited fine, disqualification from owning a dog for as long as the court sees fit and the dog destroyed. Where the dog does not actually injure anyone the maximum penalties are six months imprisonment or a fine of 175% of weekly income, disqualification from owning a dog for as long as the court sees fit and possible dog destruction.

If your dog is biting family members you are much less likely to report yourself to the police, so only risk maiming your nearest and dearest.

Nobody wants their dog to bite anyone, except the idiots who use dogs as a weapon, so why do we let them? Make no mistake, the fault lies with us, not the dog. Every dog has the potential to bite someone, but only some do. Those are the ones over which we do not have sufficient control. We fail to control the dog by failing to provide guidance for her at some point in her development.

It is not the fault of the person who left the gate open, not the fault of the deliveryman for putting his hand through the letterbox, not the fault of the person who tried to pat her, not the fault of the child who tried to cuddle her, or approach her when she was eating, or take her toy from her. It is the fault of the person who should be looking after her. So where are we going wrong?

## Strangers

As I said in the introduction, nobody records details of all dog bites, but in my experience it is extremely rare for a dog to randomly bite a stranger in the street without extenuating circumstances. Extenuating circumstances would be such as being involved in a drugs dispute where one of the protagonists is using a dog as a weapon, or maybe someone intervening in a fight between two dogs. You can decide in which one you are more likely to be involved.

As a normal average person you are extremely unlikely to be approached in a public place by a dog intent upon biting you. However, this risk increases massively if you go to someone's home, for example if you are delivering a letter or parcel.

The different layouts of average United States and United Kingdom properties makes comparison difficult, but UK postal workers are a hundred times more likely to be bitten by a dog than their US counterparts.

The UK tradition is a home with front garden set behind a wall, hedge or fence, with a garden gate being the portal and edge of the dog's territory; the US home usually has a mailbox set at the end of the property, by the road.

The US system discourages conflict between a delivery person and the dog because the mailman does not set foot on the property, but the UK front garden provides the dog with a territory-marking barrier that is regularly breached by postmen, and so we should expect (but not condone) more conflict in this set-up.

The UK Royal Mail records a "dog event" where a postal worker is bitten or otherwise seriously intimidated by a dog in the course of their duties. 3,251 such events were recorded in 2011, an average of ten every day, costing £400,000 in lost working time. Despite the more favourable set-up, but because the country is so much bigger, the United States Postal Service (USPS) recorded 5,577 dog bites on postal workers, almost eighteen bites every day, costing $1.2 million, in the same year.

The USPS delivers to 150 million different addresses and the Royal Mail delivers to 28 million, so we shouldn't tar all dog owners as irresponsible and all dogs as dangerous, but that's eighteen American and ten UK postal workers every day too many. The monetary cost may be high, but the cost in trauma to the postal workers, who have to go back day after day to the same premises, must be horrific.

The reason for it lies in the territorial behaviour of dogs and lack of understanding or training by their owners. Nearly all dog breeds are territorial to some extent and the 2012 Langley Report into dog attacks on postal workers was not able to identify any particular breed that was more responsible, but we still have to consider that some breeds (the guarders) will be more likely to engage in this kind of behaviour than others.

The development of territorial behaviour is extremely simple to understand and we've looked at it before but, as a check, we can work more closely through what motivates it.

The start point is fear. The dog is surprised by the sudden knock at the door or arrival of letters and reacts defensively with a "*woof*" of alarm. Then the postman leaves. On the dog's emotional level it is a simple rise in distress, use of an aggressive strategy, followed by a feeling of relief. The relief rewards the aggressive behaviour and makes it more likely next time.

You can add in frustration because the dog inside the hallway can't actually get at the person on the other side (which causes some dogs to rip up the mail as it comes through the door) and you can add in the confidence at being on the dog's own patch, which makes the dog more likely to use a proactive social response to the threat of incursion.

Finally, the reward from the feeling of relief repeated every day, time and again, makes him more likely to develop a positive association with the arrival of the post as he anticipates the pleasant feeling of winning this challenge again.

Every day, all over the world, dogs sit waiting for the challenge of the post-delivery so they can defeat the intruder and gain the reward of that winning feeling.

Which is great, for dogs that never meet a delivery worker. But what happens on the day the door is accidentally left off the latch, or the day that Postie is early and coincides with the time that little Fluffles is down the side of the house doing his business?

Well, we can work that out too. Bear in mind that we are dealing with a dog that is used to seeing-off this intruder every day. He has a good strategy for dealing with the distress of what he sees as an incursion onto his property. He may even look forward to it.

Remember that a dog in stress (either distress or eustress) has an increased tendency to use aggression. Our dog is already using an aggressive strategy. Do you think that when he comes face to face with his opponent he will decrease his level of aggression, or increase it? Do you think that when he is actually faced by the intruder who is on his property he will back down? Does he have another strategy to deal with the distress?

No, he doesn't. So what can he do? Ramp up the aggression. This is where some variation in the level is possible. Some of the less confident dogs, or those from the less combative breeds, will bark louder and harder, and back off. The barking will become more ferocious but he won't actually launch into a full attack. Others, more confident or more combative, will bite.

The first time this meeting happens can be extremely difficult for an owner to tell which way it will go. A professional with all the information and history at their disposal will be able to make a good assessment and maybe get it right 99% of the time. But there's still that 1%. And owners are considerably worse at this judgement. After all, their little Fluffles has never bitten anyone before; they have no idea that this first time was just waiting to happen. That's why they think it came out of the blue. Court statements are littered with phrases like, "*He's never done that before*", "*I had no idea she was going to bite him*" "*I thought he'd be fine*"...

But once you project it backwards for them they realise that it was inevitable. What owners need to do is to be able to gather the information and project it forwards before a bite happens. With the knowledge you've gathered so far, you should be able to do that, or at the very least identify the risk factors that make it more or less likely.

## Family

The biggest problem with dogs biting familiar people is that it is even less predictable for owners, although equally predictable for us. There is generally no obvious build-up of previous barking and lunging. The behaviour leading up to the bite is usually much more subtle than that.

It could be said that there is a greater culpability when a dog that has always barked at the post-delivery bites the Postie, that the owner should have known that if the dog barks behind the door they will bite when the door is opened. After all, the barking should be a clue that the dog is at least not completely reliable.

But usually the signals given off by dogs that subsequently bite family members are missed by owners. They don't comprise of barking like a rabid baboon every time they meet the family, but of subtle glances and avoidance.

Regardless of how subtle they are, they are still there to be read by anyone who takes the time and effort, and why would you not?

If we think about it we also have the answer to why dogs develop behaviour that ends in them biting a family member. It may not be as obvious and noisy as the development of the bite to Postie, but the same principles apply. The difficulty owners have is that they don't understand what their dog is telling them.

You know how aggression towards family members develops because we have covered the basics already. All we have to do is apply them to the circumstances that lead up to the biting. Again, every owner should be projecting forwards to prevent bites, rather than waiting until a bite happens then projecting backwards to understand why.

The development of aggression towards family members is usually rooted in a lack of proper social interactions when the dog is young enough to understand what is normal. If the puppy is made to be bomb-proof it doesn't matter what happens later, within reason of course. But good raw material subjected to a good upbringing goes a long way towards prevention.

Why does it? Because poor raw materials and a poor upbringing increase the chances of distress in a dog, and a dog in distress is much more likely to resort to aggression.

Why would a dog feel distress? The list is too long to be specific, but there are many reasons why a dog could be in conflict over social contact. Firstly, as we already know, there is the dog/child conflict of expectations:

* Children like to hug; dogs don't like to be confined by hugging.
* Children like to kiss; dogs don't like face to face contact.
* Children like to poke and prod; dogs can have very sensitive ears/eyes/nose/tummy/tail.
* Children like to treat dogs as toys; dogs aren't toys.

Then there is the over-attachment to owner conflict. Dogs that have not learned to be independent over-rely on proximity to their owner, which then becomes so valuable that the opposite, anything that predicts they will lose the possibility of owner-attention, becomes aversive, distressing and to be dealt with. This can result in aggression towards a third party who tries to come between them, or through frustration at not being able to control them, towards the owner.

And then there is the straight frustration effect of not being able to keep the toy, stay in the warm place, eat the food; failure to secure anything the dog finds valuable either to alleviate distress or to perpetuate eustress.

Although obvious, we also have to include straight fear. If the dog has had her ears pulled for the third time and can't get away she may launch a pre-emptive strike the next time the ear-puller comes towards her.

Biting in play can either be due to the dog failing to learn appropriate bite inhibition, simple over-enthusiasm, or an escalation of breed-specific behaviour.

Predation, when something triggers a predatory response, although relatively rare, still deserves a mention, most especially because it can have such deadly consequences for the "prey".

So, like everything else it boils down to fear, frustration and fun (play & predation) or some combination of them. In every case, except possibly predation, the dog will have communicated a lower level of the same behaviour previously. The glances, the moving out of the way, the stiffening, the staring, head turning and tail tucking, the lip licking, the eye flicking, the nipping and lunging, the stalking, chasing and grabbing.

In some dogs it may build up over days, weeks or months, in others it may be within the first interaction, but it will have happened. And if it happened and the dog still felt the need to bite, we let them down because we missed the communication and failed to give them the guidance they needed.

You'll have noticed that guidance, or rather the lack of it, looms large in the list of how we fail dogs that bite and fight, but many owners seem to be in constant conflict with their pets. Before we leave learning theory, perhaps we need a closer look at what might be happening.

## Relationships

The values that dogs place on resources are different to ours, and they view competitive outcomes differently to people as well. Our apparent inconsistency is very hard for them to handle. For example she may be stopped from grabbing a piece of toast from the floor when it falls butter side up, because I want it back, but encouraged to eat it if it falls butter side down, because I don't want it and she might as well have it. A hairy piece of toast may have little value for us, but huge value for her.

If your dog sees you defer your option to take the hairy toast on one occasion, she may form the expectation that you will do so on the next occasion too. She expects that you will concede this valuable resource to her. If she expects you to defer to her in this situation, what does she presume in other situations where there is a you-or-her choice? Unsurprisingly she uses the same expectation she has formed from previous experience.

Other apparently innocuous interactions may also form her opinions in ways that we don't anticipate. For example if she jumps on your knee any and every time that she wants, because you never really mind, who is then regulating access your knee? From her point of view, who owns this valuable, comfortable resource?

Add in the thousand other, to her, hugely important little interactions, which she takes when she wants because they aren't that important to us: a look, a stroke, a tug toy, the comfiest bit of the sofa, and her *Resource Holding Potential* builds up.

Resource Holding Potential (RHP), proposed by Parker in 1974 (Parker, GA. (1974) *Assessment strategy and the evolution of animal conflicts.* Journal of Theoretical Biology 47, 223-243), is a measure of how and why an animal engages in social conflict, and is now a widely recognised and accepted biological model.

A resource is simply something the dog wants. It could be a comfortable resting place, a look or pat from Mum, to chase a ball, sniff a tree or eat a treat. Of course different dogs place different values on different resources. For example a Labrador may place high emphasis on food and a Collie may think that chasing a ball is extremely important but, be assured, every single dog is different.

Dogs are not dissimilar to us in that all the time they are thinking, *"What do I want now, and how do I get it, now?"* This causes us and them to engage with others to fulfil our needs.

Dogs *do* differ from us in that they depend on us for what they need, and how your dog goes about acquiring the resources she values depends upon her relationship with you. You are access to many of the good things in life such as food, games and your attention. Your dog wants them. You have them. There is the potential for competition and possibly conflict if the expectation of supply does not match demand.

However, and I can't emphasis this enough, if there is no conflict, then there must be no mismatch in expectation and therefore no problem. Having high RHP is not a problem in itself, it only becomes problematic when conflict arises between the two parties. Nevertheless, as we are dealing with dogs that bite and fight despite their owners' wishes, they are definitely not living in perfect harmony.

As we discussed back in Chapter 1, there are costs to engaging in competition. No animal wants to take part if she has little or no chance, therefore each animal has to judge her own potential for gaining what she wants. One of the ways she does this is by looking back to see how successful she has been before. Starting from scratch, if she has been successful once, she is likely to be successful again. She will lose some, but win others.

If she continually gains what she wants in particular circumstances or against a particular individual, she will always fancy her chances against them next time. Thus a dog develops expectations of her chances of securing particular resources from another individual. She judges her *Potential* for *Holding* (keeping or gaining) a *Resource*.

The value of the resource is also important in judging RHP. Dogs that really, really want the resource will put more effort into securing it. If a dog perceives that the other competitor does not value the resource very highly, she may put more into the competition in the expectation that the other will back down first. This is why dogs that place different values on resources are more likely to live in harmony than dogs that value the same ones – remember bitch wars?

But it's not so much about fighting and competing as it is about deferring. If I constantly defer to her, perhaps because I do not value the resource as much as she does, she would be entitled to form the idea that her RHP in relation to that resource was very high indeed, because she always gains it with little effort. Perhaps I'm the fussy clumsy kind who never eats toast that has dropped on the floor, always leaving it for her. Which in itself is fine, but if the deferring happens with many different resources in many circumstances, she would probably form the impression that she could take anything from me, anytime.

However, resources change in value over time. If I have just eaten, food is less valuable than it was; if she has chased a ball for half an hour, ball-chasing is less valuable than it was.

Similarly, when I reach the stage of resource deprivation, when I am starved of the resource, my value of it increases. Perhaps it is the last piece of toast and I am hungry enough to want to scrape the hairs from it before scoffing it. If I reach down to take it from between her paws as she is about to pounce, it would not go down well with a dog that has a history of gaining whatever she wants from me in lots of circumstances. She would regard it as hers by right, and may well insist on exercising that right. As we both become more and more insistent, frustration and anger can break out as conflict develops. She growls, I bridle and grab the toast, she bites my hand.

From her point of view I'm not doing as I'm told, which I have done so most, if not all, of the time up to now. She is used to me deferring to her in lots of small interactions. In effect I've inadvertently raised her expectations of her ability to control toast by allowing her to control many circumstances when it wasn't important to me.

In terms of toast this may not be very important, but in terms of my attention it might start to have wider implications.

Human attention is a highly valuable resource for dogs because we have bred them to be like that. We saw earlier how interaction with people who are important to them can help a dog balance her emotions when she is subject to challenges. These interactions can form part of her maintenance set of coping mechanisms that serve to minimise and reduce distress.

Attention is at least as, and probably more, important than toast to most dogs. The ways that a dog interacts with her people determines her RHP in relation to their attention. If her person defers their attention to her every time she wants, asks or demands it, she may form the idea that she can take it any time she wants. If she can take attention from you any time she wants, why should she pay you attention when *you* want her to? Perhaps when you ask her not to fight the other dog, or bite your nephew?

Behaviourists quickly establish a relationship with a dog that they are visiting. They have to. They have never met the dog before and they have to establish the cause of the problem behaviour before teaching the owner how to change it. This often entails training the dog to do things that the owner has not been able to do, for example paying them attention, in the very short time they have available in the consultation; less than a couple of hours.

As soon as they walk through the door they start to interact with the dog by establishing their own RHP. They give nothing away for free, including a glance or a word. Every aspect of their attention is designed to reward the behaviour that is wanted in the dog. Initially this is usually just staying calm, but the skilled behaviourist soon starts to work on other aspects, such as building confidence, or leaving one thing for the reward of another. Food treats will be used sometimes, as will toys, but it is attention that is most effective.

127

By the time the consultation is halfway through the behaviourist will have established a relationship in which the dog knows that behaving in a certain way gains approval but, more importantly, when she behaves in a way that the behaviourist considers inappropriate, that approval is withdrawn. The dog actively starts to want to please the behaviourist.

Owners often attribute this to some sort of magic or special powers, and are astounded at the well-behaved pet they now see in front of them, but it is down to RHP. The behaviourist has taken the lead in their short relationship with this dog, and the dog knows that the behaviourist's RHP so far exceeds their own that she defers to every request. This guy has loads of good things going on and all she has to do to get them is whatever he wants.

Attention is any kind of interaction. To her it can be a meaning look, a pat or stroke, or a word. It doesn't even have to be a kind word, as attention-deprived dogs (as defined by the dog) will do things that they know will result in punishment in order to gain some form of attention from their owner. Even negative attention is better than none at all. That's why shouting at dogs rarely succeeds in stifling attention-seeking behaviours - it may not be the best reward in the world, but it is still attention, and any attention is rewarding to a deprived dog.

Dogs are driven to find ways of fulfilling their needs, as are we all. Their needs, the resources they value, are mostly supplied by us. If they take them from us whenever they want, they can form the impression that they can take whatever they want when they want. They perceive their personal RHP to be higher than ours. If we give our dogs the impression that we are always a push-over they may not bother to pay us any heed when we want them to. Why should they?

A mismatch in expectation can cause us problems when we have given the dog the impression that she is entitled to something that we believe she is not. I guess you could say that we sometimes inadvertently over-promote dogs. If a dog believes that she is entitled to our attention because every time she asks for it she gets it, on the odd occasion when she doesn't get it she can become frustrated. And if she gets frustrated enough… we know where that can lead.

If a dog has the impression that she can take our attention whenever she wants, because we always jump to her every desire, on the odd occasion when we don't jump she can be very insistent. She is used to us asking, "*How high?*" when she shouts, "*Jump!*" If we don't jump at all, she could get annoyed.

Think of the dog that sits on her owner's knee. She gets on and off whenever she wants. Of course her owner is kindness itself and acquiesces every time. We want our dog to be happy sitting on our knee. Then the phone rings and her owner has to get up to answer it.

*Hey! Wait a minute! That's my knee you're taking away! I wasn't finished with that! Come back!!* The dog is quite annoyed, but doesn't follow it up this time.

Next time the phone rings the dog knows it signals the knee's disappearance and becomes more agitated. She growls quietly, but her owner still ever-so-gently slides her off.

The next time the phone rings she is really cheesed off. She wants this knee to stay put, and she's prepared to enforce it. She looks straight into her owner's eyes and snarls. Her owner is in a very vulnerable position, with the dog sitting on his knee threatening to bite him. The phone's probably just another cold-caller. Maybe he should stay put this time.

Now who owns his knee? And what happens when he *really* needs to turf her off?

This slightly simplified example shows how important little interactions can be in terms of overall perceptions if we don't consider them from the canine viewpoint. We will look at the solutions to this problem later, when we revisit the vital subject of relationships to explore how we can facilitate what our dog wants through taking a perspective she understands.

Not all dogs will develop biting and fighting or any other problem behaviours because of high perceived RHP, but the imbalance it causes in relationships can contribute greatly to owners' inability to deal with dogs that do bite and fight.

## Causation

We must be careful to distinguish between the ways in which breeding, development and learning can influence a dog's tendency to bite and fight from the actual cause.

Although I have given numerous examples of ways in which it is possible to result in a dog that bites or fights, it is also possible that the same dog may not develop any inappropriate aggression at all.

It does not follow that each dog bred with low confidence or poor impulse control will later bite and fight. Nor do poor social referencing, breed tendencies, attack(s) by another dog, an out-of-kilter relationship, or any of the other learning possibilities mean it is absolutely inevitable.

True, the single possibilities if taken cumulatively may add up to more and more probability, but it is conceivable that each disposing factor alone may not. Each is not an all-or-nothing prospect. There are so many interdependent factors it is impossible to know why one dog edges towards biting and fighting whilst another with what appears to be the same predispositions, even in the same circumstances, doesn't. On the other hand we know that dogs do develop inappropriate aggressive behaviour as a direct result of one or more these influences.

Consequently what we can and should do, through an understanding what the factors are, is take each opportunity to carefully manage every stage of our dogs' paths through life so that we can direct them away from showing inappropriate aggression, which will result in a pet less likely to indulge in problematic biting and fighting. Every learning opportunity for our pet is an opportunity for us to get it right.

Unfortunately, if you haven't been able to do that, or have inherited a dog that already bites or fights through whatever combination of factors, you now have to accept that it has happened and deal with it.

The issue of course is that now it *has* happened, what can we do about it? Was it a one-off or will it happen again? How can we tell? *Can* we tell? We usually can, and before we look at how to change dogs that fight and bite, first we need to know how possible, how realistically achievable, and how safe it will be.

# Chapter 7

## Assessment

## Can We Stop Biting and Fighting?

When a dog starts to bite or fight our main concern is how to prevent it happening in the future. Some people insist that all dogs that have bitten a person must be destroyed; others think they all deserve a second chance. The truth, as usual, lies somewhere in between. What's past may be past, but we can learn from it.

The first step in looking into the future, without a crystal ball, is to look to the past. We have to try to assess the danger this dog represents in order to decide if we can save him. This is bread and butter to experts examining the behaviour of dogs whose owners are brought to court, where the more information we can gather the more informed judgement we are be able to make.

The same assessment process can be used by owners, or those helping owners, to deal with their own dog biting or fighting. Dogs can be dangerous. There is a limit to the amount of risk to human safety that is acceptable and no person should be placed at risk of serious injury by a dog. I'm not an advocate for destroying dogs at the drop of a hat, but I am a realist. As I've already said, I am a firm believer that any dog can be handled by someone with the skills to do it, but people with the skills to manage a seriously aggressive dog are few and far between.

From what we have already learned we know that a dog with serious aggression issues (as defined shortly) isn't going to be cured. There is no cure because it isn't a disease. Such a dog has to be managed. Yes, some are managed more easily than others, and that's what we have to look at. Can this dog be safely managed by this person, with as much support as is available? If he can't the options are

132

limited. Could you hand over a dog that you know is likely to bite to someone else?

People do, you know. People who have a dog that has bitten someone or gets into serious fights with other dogs have been known to give their dog to a re-homing organisation. Of course they don't tell the organisation, otherwise the re-homers wouldn't accept him. And of course he bites again. Is that fair? I think not.

Our aim is to establish if this dog, the biter and fighter we are dealing with, can be handled with safety and managed to the point that he will not cause serious injury in the future, in the environment in which he must stay.

In Health & Safety speak this is a "hazard", and to determine the risk we must look for risk factors to establish the severity and likelihood of it happening again.

Risk factors for a dog biting in the future include:

* The severity of injury caused previously
* The length of time the behaviour has been expressed
* The frequency of the aggressive episodes
* The number of different circumstances in which aggression occurs
* The warning he gives before actually biting/fighting

## Severity of injury

This is the first consideration, because it is the biggest significance in the risk this dog poses, but what to measure isn't always as simple as it might seem. The obvious answer is overt aggression, bites inflicted or snaps aimed, but teeth baring, growling and snarling should not be ignored either. What then of lip-licking or grinning? Do they count or not?

What should count is the intention of the dog and how he perceives the problem to be resolved. Aggression becomes a problem to us when the dog proactively uses it to resolve the situation. Whether

133

the communication is used *towards* you, not *away* from you. It is the difference between a dog that growls and walks away and a dog that growls and walks towards you; a dog that bares his teeth and hides and a dog that bares his teeth and puts his front feet on your leg. The former are actively avoiding conflict and the latter are proactively engaging in it. *They* are telling *you* what to do.

Attempts to avoid conflict start with subtle communications that dogs use all the time: turning the head away or down, eyes closing or long blinks, lowering the ears, yawning, lip-licking, lowering of the body posture, lowering and tucking of the tail, turning and walking away. These are all ways that the dog can communicate that he isn't happy with the situation he is in, but that he would rather not engage in an argument about it. Growling and teeth-baring are ways of emphasising the communication for the hard of understanding.

The distinction between avoiding conflict and proactively controlling it is important because of what comes next. In active avoidance, even if that includes growling and teeth-baring, the dog is trying to remove himself from the situation. If he is allowed, he will disengage from the conflict, although if not allowed he can quickly switch into proactive control. In proactive control the dog is taking steps to take charge in the conflict. He will not disengage until he gets the result he wants. He will escalate the level of aggression to achieve that.

When assessing the severity we should include the lesser manifestations of aggression where the dog is proactively managing the situation as well as those where bites or attempts to bite have occurred. On a rising scale for aggression directed towards both humans and other dogs these will include:

- Staring whilst growling, snarling or teeth-baring, standing over or on, moving towards, lunging, snapping at the air, snapping attempts to bite.

- Bites to the clothing or hair only, gentle placing on of teeth, nips, front tooth bites, superficial bites to the skin leaving no mark or slight reddening, bites causing grazing or bruising only, bites causing slight puncture marks.
- Single full mouth bite and release, single full mouth bite and hold then release, bites causing deeper puncture wounds and crush injuries, bites causing skin tearing.
- Full mouth bite hold and shake, multiple bites, frenzied multiple bites, bites causing muscle tearing and breaking small bones (eg finger or tail).
- Bites directed at vulnerable parts of the body, facial bites, throat bites, groin bites, ringing joints, bites breaking major bones (eg arm), failure to stop biting even though the goal has been achieved.
- Bites causing death.

There is no way to precisely categorise dog bites in order of severity that makes total sense. I am aware that even in my attempt above, a single mouth full bite and release may inflict more severe injury than multiple smaller bites. What it can do is to give a perspective by which biting events can be assessed against each other, to give you an idea of just how bad the one we are dealing with might be. Was it a nip to the trousers of the delivery girl or was it a frenzied attack that ripped the small dog apart?

I do not use a severity scale as a measure of what should happen to the dog, but as a way of assessing how difficult he will be to deal with in the future.

I could have suggested a kind of a 1 to 10 of how severe, but I don't want to be too prescriptive. When we come to totting up the total later, does a three in this scale mean more or less than a two in the "length of time it has been happening" scale? I think it is better to bring everything together then look at the whole package, perhaps trading some parts off against others to get a general idea of this dog and the environment in which he lives.

But I would recommend writing it down so you can cross-reference it all. Make a note the severity of this dog's biting or fighting for each occurrence you are recording. Look for patterns. If there has been more than one occurrence an increase in severity over time is to be expected, so listing and comparing the incidents gives you an idea of the scale of the escalation, and what's likely to be next.

## Length of time

For what length of time has the dog been using this method to deal with problems? If he has been using aggression in this particular way for a considerable length of time it is because he considers it to be a very effective strategy for resolving the problem he sees in front of him.

No one, dogs included, is quick to abandon an effective problem-solving strategy, so it is likely that the behaviour will be resistant to change. The more time the dog has been practising the strategy, the less likely it is that he will change to another when offered the opportunity.

It is generally true that a dog that has been biting for the whole of his eight year life is going to be more difficult to change than an eight year old dog that bit last week for the first time.

Documenting the first time and the last time any of the aggressive episodes defined in "severity" took place gives us an indication of the length of time this strategy has been in use. Measuring it in terms of the dog's lifetime gives an indication of how fixed the strategy is likely to be. For what percentage of this dog's life has he been pursuing a proactive aggressive strategy?

## The frequency

Allied to "length of time" is the *frequency* of times that the dog has used the aggression defined in "severity". If the dog is practicing the strategy

136

daily, he is more likely to be entrenched in the behaviour than if it happens only once a year. Practice makes perfect. Combining "length of time" and "frequency" will give the total number of aggressive episodes for this dog, for example "once a week for three years" will be more fixed than "twice in five years". Measuring the frequency gives another indication of how fixed the strategy has become.

An increase in frequency obviously indicates a worsening of the problem, both from the dog's point of view and from the point of view of dealing with it.

## Number of different circumstances

Text books are full of categories of aggression, such as "territorial", "possessive", "maternal", "dog to dog", "food-guarding" "defensive" and the ephemeral "dominant". These labels can be too prescriptive when describing the actions of an individual dog. If a dog growls and lunges at people who approach her when she is in her bed with toys, is it territorial, possessive, pseudo-maternal, defensive or "dominant" aggression?

Labels can be a useful shorthand, but fall short of describing what is often a multifaceted behaviour with complex motivations. It is not surprising that in a list of categories for aggression there is usually one called "idiopathic aggression." "Idiopathic" means we don't know what causes it.

Far better to describe the behaviour as observed, such as "growls and lunges at people who approach when she is in her bed with toys". If we collect all the circumstances we will start to be able to identify patterns. Rather than a bland "aggressive towards dogs", it would be far more help in understanding causation if we see the behaviour as "stands over and growls at unfamiliar dogs when off-lead on walks".

List all the different circumstances in which the dog uses the aggression defined in "severity". Expect these to be diverse, from "growling and staring if approached whilst eating", to "biting the face of an approaching toddler when under the table" or "jumping up and down and barking on the lead when she sees any other dog" to "growling and staring at small white dogs".

The higher the number of different circumstances, the more the dog has learned that the strategy is successful in varying situations and the more likely she will be to use it in novel circumstances. If it works in situation A, B, C, and D, it will very likely work in situation E as well.

## How much warning?

If the dog gives lots of communication towards the lower end of the scale of aggression before he feels the need to bite or fight, we have the opportunity to intervene before the worst happens. If he launches straight from being relaxed to full-on in-your-face, we have little chance to avoid it.

Despite people telling me that their dog's aggression is completely unpredictable I have never yet seen a dog that goes from zero to attack without some kind of warning. Most often the people involved either don't see it, or don't recognise it for what it is. In some cases this is because the signals are disguised by the shape of the dog and in others the dog has learned that the lower signals don't work, so doesn't bother expressing them as a means of coping, or sometimes both. However, even if they don't intentionally give warning signals, their increased distress is reflected in their body language.

Recognising these miniscule signs can be the difference between being bitten and not. It might only be a slight stiffening of the body and cocking the head, but they are there to be read.

If the dog provides recognisable warning signs that he is about to tip into proactive aggression, we can predict when it is going to

138

happen. If we can predict it, we can avoid it. The problem lies in the word "recognisable" warning signs. If the dog is barking like a rabid maniac over the garden gate, you would be foolish to try to enter. The reason you would be foolish is that the signs are recognisable as being a warning that the dog will bite.

On the other hand take the case of a dog that enjoys attention and fuss, but can't cope with the back of his head being stroked. This is a common situation, often initiated by people who grab the back of the dog's collar to tell him off, or to remove him from the room. Scruffing, shaking the dog by the neck as a punishment, used to be popular. I sincerely hope it is dying out.

From this the dog understands that a hand over the back of the head means trouble and wants to prevent anyone taking hold of him. This dog wants to be petted, but fears having his collar felt, so is very happy being petted on top of the head, but quite literally snaps when the hand strays towards the back of his neck. Unless the person is paying particular attention, and many aren't, they won't see the slight tension in his face the split-second before the hand reaches the point of no return, and he bites them.

Now in terms of how much warning we have before he bites, we have a reasonable situation, because we know he only bites when a hand reaches over him. But the owner has to explain that to anyone who comes into contact with him, and deal with the, *"Oh, he won't bite me. I've had dogs all my life – ouch!"* idiots, because very often *they* can't recognise the signs.

How much warning we have determines the predictability of the nest episode of aggression. The more predictable it is, the easier he will be to work with. Although it is difficult to quantify, this too needs to be factored in to the risk assessment. If it is unpredictable for the people at risk, as opposed to a professional who is able to recognise small signs that the owners' can't, they will be in greater danger. Of course, teaching the owners the warning signs will be a vital part of any behaviour modification, but getting it wrong is a hard lesson if they end up hospitalised.

## History

We will now have a complete history of:
* The severity of injuries
* The length of time
* The frequency
* The different circumstances
* The warning given

Why is this important? Because we are looking at the danger that this dog represents and we need to be able to assess that as objectively as possible. It is easy to obscure the facts because aggression in a dog is seen as personal. Is a dog dangerous if it has bitten a toddler in the face causing wounds to their cheek? The answer is that we can't tell from that amount of information. Sure, there is a possibility of a repeat of the incident, but we don't know how likely that is until we have the full history.

If Belle is a twelve year old dog that has never been proactively aggressive (never stared and growled, lip-curled and lunged) at all until the time when she and the child were left alone, and we see a boy with a torn cheek with blood everywhere and find the dog hiding under the table, how dangerous is she to the next child that comes into the house?

If Nell is a four year old dog that has chased a child in the street, knocked him down and bitten his face, when she has a three year history of chasing people as they walk past her garden gate, snapping, snarling and spitting venom several times each day, and also has to be muzzled because she "nips" when groomed, has to be put out of the room because of barking and growling at visitors and fights

140

any other dogs she comes into contact with, how dangerous is she to the next passing child?

If Nell, the second dog, hadn't actually bitten the child, just knocked him to the ground, which dog is more likely to injure the next child she meets?

I hope by now that you are able to see that Nell is far more of a risk because even if the injury was less, the circumstances, percentage of her life spent biting and fighting, and frequency are much greater. Both dogs are now reasonably predictable and we have ample warning of each circumstance, and Belle probably gave lots of warning communication before biting, if only anyone had been there to recognise it. Belle has had one episode and no practice. Unless the same circumstances come up again, she is unlikely to bite again. Nell is an injury waiting to happen. In Health and Safety terms, Nell's hazard is less, but the likelihood of it happening is far greater.

Taking the history is not a precise science, but it helps us understand what the dog is capable of and likely to do in most circumstances. If we know what the dog is likely to do in future, we can take steps to control the environment and train the dog in a different strategy, reducing the likelihood of aggression.

It is possible to modify the biting of both of these dogs, but the programme of intervention required for twelve-year-old Belle is going to be much less involved and protracted than the one for four-year-old Nell.

## Safety

The first measure to take to reduce the chances of future biting in a dog that has already shown aggression is to avoid the circumstances that trigger it. The more triggers there are for this dog, the more difficult they are likely to be to predict and to control.

In the example of Belle, the simple expedient of not allowing the dog into close proximity with a child would probably be enough to prevent further aggression. In the example of Nell, it will be much more complicated; controlling access to the street and to visitors, and changing methods of grooming, which all seem to have been unachievable up to now.

The second measure is to assess the possibility of changing all the aspects of aggressive behaviour that this dog exhibits. With Belle it may be possible to instigate a training programme that changes her attitude towards children, but we need to take into account that she is an older dog and it may be necessary to protect her from children for the rest of her life. If this is possible in her environment then the chances of success are extremely good, she need never show any proactive aggression again.

Yet again, Nell proves more difficult. There is a training programme that will modify Nell's behaviour, but it will be much more complicated, having to address so many different aspects of her use of proactive aggression. Because there are so many different circumstances we may miss some, or it may pop up in one that we hadn't yet considered, making predictability more difficult.

This combination of physical manipulation of the environment to reduce the risk of proactive aggression, whilst training is put in place to change the dog's emotional response to all the different circumstances in which they have previously done so, can be applied in every case. The likelihood of success can be judged by the assessment.

Dogs displaying proactive aggression that you have assessed as very severe, for a very long time, very frequently, very many circumstances and very little warning, are going to be considerably more difficult to change and pose a greater risk than dogs that are assessed as not exhibiting those extremes.

And yes, I am of the opinion that some dogs cannot be helped because they pose too great a risk. There is a point on the scale where the risk is not tolerable. It is a subjective judgement exactly because the factors interact in many complicated ways. Is a Neapolitan Mastiff that has maimed a child on a single occasion more or less tolerable than a Border Collie that has nipped a child three times this week? What if the Collie had nipped three different children over a year?

Yet, it seems to be a relatively easy decision to make in each individual case. Add up the risk factors and ask, *"Am I sure that the measures I can put in place will ensure that this dog will not cause an intolerable fear or injury in the normal everyday circumstances in which she will continue to exist?"* If I cannot answer *"Yes"* then the risk is not worth taking.

"Intolerable fear or injury" is also subjective, and another reason for documenting the reasoning behind the decision. If the dog is a Mastiff, his bite will have more risk attached to it than the bite of a Chihuahua. If you think that is unfair, well, tough. I may be prepared to tolerate the bite of a Chihuahua within a training programme because of the limited damage it can do to a consenting human being. A single bite from a Mastiff can be life threatening and, whilst I may be prepared to risk a scratched hand, I'm not prepared to risk anyone's life.

If that is biased against big dogs, consider that small dogs are much more likely to figure in the bite statistics. Life isn't fair.

There are times when we have to take responsibility for preventing injury in the future. If I cannot walk away from a situation believing that I have sufficient preparation and control measures in place to prevent a dog causing injury to a person or another dog in any circumstances I can reasonably foresee, I believe that taking the ultimate sanction of humanely destroying the dog is the only safe way to proceed. Yes, it is sad. Yes it is our fault. But once an animal becomes so dangerous that we cannot prevent it from causing injury to a person or another dog we do not have the right to allow that to happen.

To close the assessment chapter, let me reiterate my position on the question of dog behaviour problems, including dogs that fight and bite:

* I believe that it is possible to change the behaviour of any dog for the better.
* I believe that there are some dogs that are so extreme in their behaviour that it takes a handler with high levels of skill, patience and determination to make those improvements.
* Many of these Most-Difficult dogs cannot be just improved and handed on, but require sensitive skilled handling for their entire lives.
* Not all people have or can acquire the necessary skills, not because it is a difficult skill to learn, although it isn't easy, but unless you are doing it full time you are not committing the necessary effort to it.
* Those that can do it, let's call them Super-Handlers, know how much time and effort these Most-Difficult dogs require to bring them to the point at which their behaviour is acceptable, and can only work with so many at a time, if indeed they have the desire to do so, as it can be mentally and physically exhausting if done properly.
* There are more Most-Difficult dogs than there are Super-Handlers prepared to take them on.
* Without Super-Handling, the potential for a proportion of the Most-Difficult dogs with aggression problems to cause injury is very high, to the extent that it may be unacceptable to society.
* Therefore some dogs will be un-saveable.

* There is a far larger subset of dogs whose behaviour problems are, although currently difficult, much more amenable to change.

* Owners tend not to initially have the skills to change the behaviour of difficult dogs without increasing their knowledge, but that increase in understanding and skills is within the grasp of an average pet owner.

* It is therefore possible for difficult dogs to be handled by average pet owners, both from the point of view of safety and the relative ease with which their behaviour can be changed, if they increase their understanding and skills.

* The information that follows can provide owners with the necessary understanding and skills to handle the difficult dogs.

The percentage of dogs that are un-saveable is very small in comparison to the overall population of pets, and in Part Two we are going to look at the others, the less-difficult, saveable, dogs. The ones whose lives we can improve, with safety as our top priority. We will look at how to change the behaviour of dogs that bite and fight, and the first step is to prepare them, and us, for that change.

# Part Two
# The Practice of Changing Biting and Fighting

In which we examine how to change the behaviour of dogs that bite and fight.

## Chapter 8
## Groundwork - Preparing to Change

In this section you step up a level from the average pet owner. We are part-way there by now because if you've got this far you've already increased your understanding of why dogs bite and fight. Well done, it took me years! This is a solid grounding for changing their behaviour but, before we start, let me remind you that nobody said it would be easy, especially not me.

We've established that there are basically three motivations for aggressive behaviour, whether it is directed towards people or towards other dogs: Fear, Frustration and Fun. There are breed, sex and other inherited dispositions that make some dogs more susceptible to using aggression than others, and the way that the dog has been brought up will also have a major bearing on their tendency to bite and fight.

Adding all those together with how-and-to-whom aggression is directed will help us to establish the underlying motivation and how it has developed from there (what the boffins call "aetiology" or "etiology" if you are using an American dictionary and prefer not to have your Greek-origin words start with an old Saxon letter æ).

We must remember that the origins of the motivation may be obscured by how the dog is now dealing with the stimulus, and that

146

they may be combined in some cases. Although this sounds complicated, it is far less so than trying to establish causation through looking only at the target, "*my dog is aggressive towards children*", or just through the trigger "*my dog is aggressive around food*".

Therefore what might be labelled "food", "guarding" "protective", "defensive" or "possessive" aggression can probably be traced back to an original fear, even if the dog's body language doesn't reflect that fear now.

Likewise it is less than helpful to distinguish labels such as, "aggression towards household dogs" from "aggression towards strange dogs" as both could either be fear, frustration or fun based. Remember, labels aren't always helpful for understanding what is going inside the dog.

But looking at the aetiology, the trigger and the target can help us determine what the dog feels in the circumstances, which is the single fundamental factor that we must change in order to change the behaviour. Change the emotion underlying the behaviour and the behaviour becomes susceptible to change too.

Saying, "*He is food-aggressive*" doesn't help us change the behaviour, but saying, "*He is worried that someone is going to take his food away and so he defends it by snapping at anyone who goes near,*" gives us an understanding of what is going on in his mind when he behaves the way he does. It's just not as snappy a label.

Saying, "*He is aggressive towards strange dogs*" doesn't really help us, but saying, "*He bounces up and down on the lead when he first sees another dog and if he is allowed to run up to them he leaps all over them and sometimes starts a fight,*" probably gives us an insight into the frustration he feels when other dogs won't play with him how he would like them to.

Saying, "*He is aggressive towards family members*" isn't much help either, but saying, "*He doesn't seem to know when to stop wrestling with Jonny and often eventually ends up drawing blood by biting his hands,"* points us in the direction of fun with a tinge of frustration, and probably some breed tendencies.

You will remember from Chapter 7, that dogs that have been exhibiting biting and fighting for longer are more difficult to change. As a rule of thumb, the longer it has been happening, the more fixed the behaviour is. The reason is that the dog has a successful aggressive strategy he is using to cope with whatever environmental factors are causing the distress.

It should be obvious that if the dog continues to exhibit biting and fighting the problem will only become worse. In fact, every time it happens it fixes the behaviour a little more. Such are the laws of learning theory and reinforcement. Every time it happens makes it more likely to happen again next time.

The very first step that must be taken, therefore, is to prevent the circumstances that stimulate the behaviour. No arguments, it has to stop now. Prevent it, avoid it, do whatever it takes but stop it now. Take a different route on his walk, feed him on his own in the yard, stop Jonny wrestling with him, ban the Mayhem twins (politely of course), and don't touch him *there*. This isn't the long term answer, and the avoidance isn't necessarily forever, but it is the first step to the solution.

Because there are different underlying emotions for biting and fighting, there are different procedures for dealing with them and we will get to them in due course, but we should start with the theme that is common to all dogs that bite and fight: *control* or rather, the lack of it.

## Control

Control has become a bit of a dirty word in some modern dog training circles because it has been used oppressively by some trainers in the past. But what many people don't seem to realise is that all behaviour is about controlling something. Whether it be pulling on an extra layer to control my temperature, flicking the switch to control the light, eating a biscuit to control my hunger, or throwing the last morsel of it to my dog to stop her salivating.

*Control* isn't therefore the problem; the baby to be thrown out with the bathwater. Control will happen anyway, in one way or another. It is *how* you control that is important.

So, when I say we should exert or take control I do not mean making or forcing the dog to do, or stop doing, something using punitive methods. I mean controlling the circumstances so that the dog wants to do what we want her to do.

No dog ever attempts to control anything just for the sake of control; they are not trying to take over the world. If you want to see my take on "dominance" please see this article on my website, an edited version of which was first published in the Veterinary Times Vol 40 No 7 on 22nd February 2010 entitled *Dominance meme: out-lived extreme?* http://www.dog-secrets.co.uk/why-wont-dominance-die/

But dogs do acquire control of things when we allow them to. As we saw when examining RHP, this need not necessarily be a problem; we can delegate management of particular resources to dogs whenever we think it suitable. Conversely, we should take back management of resources and situations that are not helping dogs.

That is what I mean by "control": control of the situation so that the dog wants to make the appropriate decision. I guess I could call it management, but control is a perfectly good word as long as we both understand what we mean by it.

Dogs that bite and fight are making decisions that we would prefer them not to. From a human perspective, biting or fighting is rarely the correct decision for a dog to make in any situation.

If he bites or fights when we don't want him to (and no one in their right mind should want a pet dog to place themselves in that position) they are making a decision to control the circumstances. Remember right back at the start we said that it is difficult to separate out what is aggression and what isn't? And we plumped for a definition of attempting to *"proactively control a situation through the use or display of force"*? Well, this is where "control" comes home to roost.

The dog must be in control in order to make what, from our point of view, is the wrong decision. Because the dog is able to feel in control, he feels able to make the decision. If we change the degree of control the dog feels in the situation in which he bites or fights, he will be more susceptible to following the guidance we give him. But it is almost impossible to take control of our dog in just the circumstances in which he uses aggression. We have to take control of him generally so that he is used to deferring to our decisions and looks to us for guidance.

When we have control of him generally we can provide guidance that changes his aggressive behaviour, provide him with alternatives and then give him back his self-control of the situation. Eventually he will be more confident about how he deals with circumstances in which he previously felt sufficiently vulnerable or annoyed that he needed to bite or fight. We take away his control, teach him the alternative and then, bit by bit, give him back control where he doesn't now need to use aggression.

Gaining control is the underpinning skill necessary to change biting and fighting. Not just control of the biting and fighting, but control of your relationship with your dog, your dog's degree of self-control, and your own self-control to determine to work with a difficult dog.

Dealing with your own self-control first, because that is the easiest to tell you about, the crux is this: you need some. No, I'm wrong, not "some", you need lots and lots!

When first taking control of your relationship with your dog you need to micro-manage him. This takes time, commitment and patience.

For a short while you will need to guide your pet almost constantly. This does not mean being on his back all the time, nagging at him, but being there mentally as well as physically, to provide guidance in every little thing he does.

## Learn to Earn

Taking control means developing a relationship where your dog looks to you for guidance. This is where, as we have seen with the issue of socialisation, many pet owners fail. They allow their pups to slide into habits they actually prefer them not to have, through lack of guidance. They leave their pups to sort themselves out, to get on with things on their own.

If left to their own devices pups will get into all sorts of trouble. However, with the right guidance they only need the occasional nod in the right direction and they can make all the right decisions. Errorless lifelong learning might be unachievable, but as-error-free-as-possible lifelong learning shouldn't be.

We do, however, have to acknowledge that if we have a dog that is biting or fighting we have made some errors that need to be corrected, or at least someone has! These are human errors, not canine ones. We failed to provide the right assistance at the right time. That means we will have to go back and re-do, starting with our relationship together.

What does this mean in terms of hands-on living with your dog? Well, for a start-off it means more interaction and more communication, and more awareness of what your dog is doing and how he is feeling at any time. It means taking the stress out of his life by helping him make the most appropriate decision in everything.

It isn't oppressive and it should all be done with positive reinforcement included, guiding him away from making the wrong decisions and rewarding him for the right ones. And before anyone goes out to buy shares in hot-dog sausages it isn't about constantly throwing treats at him. It is about rewarding him with what he wants in any given situation by allowing access to it dependent upon appropriate behaviour.

Whatever your dog is doing, ask yourself, "*What does he want?*" If you know what he wants, and it is usually perfectly obvious, ask yourself, "*What would be an appropriate way of him getting it?*" Much of the time he will be getting it right anyway, but if you don't monitor those times, you won't be able to gain an understanding of where he is going wrong.

This kind of supplying what your dog wants, conditional upon appropriate behaviour, is often called Learn to Earn by behaviourists, but the term seems to have become corrupted through misapplication and the overbearing withdrawal of attention that ends up less as guidance and more of a punishment.

Mat Ward and I became so concerned that the very useful Learn to Earn paradigm was becoming degraded that we wrote our interpretation of what it should mean for the Association of Pet Behaviour Counsellors. You can find it on their website at www.apbc.org.uk and Mat has kindly allowed me to reproduce it in an appendix at the end of this book.

It doesn't really matter what you call it, because labels are for the benefit of humans, not dogs, but if you understand and follow the principles outlined in our version of Learn to Earn you are following the least confrontational and most effective programme of relationship change for your dog.

That, then, is your first real hands-on task when preparing to change a biter and fighter. Read Learn to Earn and practice it with your dog. It should become a way of life for you both, as you start working with him to take control of your relationship. It isn't just important for an owner with a dog that bites and fights, it is essential. It is the most efficient and kindest way to persuade your dog to look to you for guidance. If your dog won't look to you for guidance, you won't be able to change him. Every protocol for change you will read later depends upon you already having taken control through Learn to Earn.

## Training

However, if you are going to develop an ability to guide your dog into appropriate behaviour, you both have to understand what appropriate behaviour might be. Whilst you may have some inkling, your dog may well need to be taught.

Let's start with the basics. As well as Learn to Earn and playing games (of which more later), you need to teach your dog three things so you have a basis for change. There may be others specific to you and your dog, but the generic three are:

1. To pay attention when asked.
2. To sit when asked.
3. To relax on his bed when asked.

You will use these three behaviours as alternatives to inappropriate behaviour in a variety of situations, but they will ultimately be very challenging situations, so your dog needs to be 100% rock solid in understanding and complying.

If you have a dog that bites or fights and think you have already trained any the above, ask your dog to do them in the circumstances in which he is aggressive. If he doesn't immediately comply, you haven't taught him properly. Start again. Here's how...

In all dog training you must teach any new behaviour in a place without distractions. When the behaviour is perfect, introduce minor distractions and then increase them. For the early stages of training it will be useful to use treats, but phase them out and get the behaviour under stimulus control quickly. Train for short bouts, and lots of them, in a variety of environments. If you don't understand the basic training principles re-read Dog Secrets, where they are laid out in greater detail (available from all good retailers; not packed in a nut-free environment; minimum monthly payment required; can only help with weight loss as part of a calorie controlled diet).

## 1. Paying attention

Fix on a word. You can use your dog's name, but it is often devalued through over or inappropriate use, for example when telling your dog off, or by constantly repeating it. "*Ba-a-a-d Cindy!*" or "*Cindy come, Cindy, Cindy, Cindy…*" If you waste your dog's name like this, use another word, such as "*look*" or "*watch*". Make it upbeat and friendly.

Most police dogs respond more readily to their handler's excited "*Wat-sis?*" ("*What's this?*") than they do to their own name. In fact, why not? It's got all the right tones to encourage a dog to look at you and usually predicts something good on offer. You can say it quietly and keep the excitement in. No wonder it works.

Give it a try if you are retraining your dog to pay you attention. Say it fast and enthusiastically, "*Wat-sis?*"

Start off by simply saying the word and tossing a treat to your dog. Walk about and wait until your dog isn't looking at you then say the word again. After three goes she will look at you and after five she will keep looking at you when you say the word.

You have your dog's attention. Now stretch out the time that your dog looks at you when you say the word. Two seconds then reward. Five seconds, then back to three next time. Mix and match but always keep it within her capability.

Use a variable interval schedule of reinforcement and provide a conditioned reinforcer of praise from you. This simply means reward after she has been looking at you for a random amount of time, and give feedback of quiet praise between when she looks at you and the delivery of the reward. Once you have the behaviour you can also change the reward depending upon your dog's preferences. For example, sitting looking at you can be rewarded with lavish praise, a game, possession of a toy or an activity; a hug, a dance, or jumping into your arms, whatever tugs your dog's rug.

Once your dog is reliable, don't reward un-asked-for continuous attention to ensure stimulus control, and occasionally chuck in big rewards, as unpredictability increases resistance to extinction. Back to Dog Secrets if you're not getting any of these basics.

Pretty soon you will have a dog that looks at you when you say "Wat-sis?" and holds that look in anticipation of a reward. Now get this bit... this paying attention is reinforcing in itself and can be used as a reward for doing the right thing.

Admittedly there are breed variations in how rewarding dogs will find looking at their owner; dogs that have been bred to work with a person will find it more stimulating than the ones that have been bred to work on their own, but all will enjoy it to some extent. Dogs bred to work with people include herding and retrieving breeds. Those bred to work on their own include the terriers and hounds. Terrier and hound owners have to work harder, that's all.

You final port of call in this training, as in any other, is to use it in a complicated environment so your dog gets used to other factors competing for her attention at the same time... and chooses you. But don't jump straight from simple to complex, chuck in some in-between-ies for a gradual progression. You don't leap from learning your two-times-table to your nine-times, you do fives, tens and threes before fours, sixes, sevens, eights and eventually nines (although personally I'm still not 100% with eights).

## 2. Sit

I'm not to bore you by going through it all again for the "sit" but the most common fault is in failing to generalise. The dog will only do it under specific circumstances. So make sure that you train in those complicated environments. Be inventive, dog training should be fun! Have you tried asking your dog to sit with your back to him? How about on a chair? In water? On a see-saw? Or asked from a different room? Use props like mirrors and the view in a glass door to check. Use a clicker if you have the ability and the desire, but don't rely on it because one day when you really need it you will have left it at home. Be inventive: today's task is to train your dog to sit in a way/place/manner he has never done it before. Go for it, it's a game you can both enjoy!

### 3. Sit on bed

Every dog should have a place to go to in the home. Not too far away from people, so he still feels part of the family. It isn't an exclusion punishment, it isn't any kind of punishment, so don't banish his bed to the outhouse or a far room. It isn't necessarily the place he goes at night-time, although it can be if it suits, so I guess you could call it his day-bed if you like. Think of it as a place that is his, like Granddad's chair (don't sit in Granddad's chair – he won't say anything outright, but he will glare at you and mumble about the impudence of the younger generation).

There are only really three requirements for his day-bed. Firstly it is part of the family space, secondly it is comfortable, and thirdly it is identifiable to the dog. After that you can decide if you want it washable, disposable, expensive, luxurious, a posh hand-stitched fluffy quilt, a hard moulded-plastic chew-proof (ha-ha!) oval, an old blanket on the floor or a fleece on the sofa.

Now you need to train him to go there when you ask and wait for a reward. You can enhance the desirability of going there by having a treat-pot full of goodies on a shelf above the bed, so he knows there is always the possibility of a treat on offer. Make sure that you reward on a variable ratio and interval schedule, so he will never know when one or more treats will be forthcoming.

156

Train him to scamper there and wait until he is released every time you ask. This is particularly important for dogs with tendencies to bark at the door so you should put knocking-at-the-door noises into the training programme. Tap on the back of the door, give him the, "*go to bed*" request and treat him for staying there.

For those of you who don't think sit-on-bed training is important and it won't apply to you because your dog only growls at dogs he meets on walks, think again. It allows you to take control of your dog in a myriad situations: to stop him drooling at you when you are having your tea; to give him somewhere safe to go when the Mayhem twins from next door visit and run riot; to keep him calm before the walk whilst you put on your coat and pick up his lead; to give him comfort when fireworks crash; as a place to relax when you leave him alone… All are there to reduce stresses that may be contributing to him fighting with other dogs.

## Training v real life

Training and real life should not be mutually exclusive, but having done the training you will need to factor it in to real life situations to help you build a relationship in which you have control of your dog.

Going back to the observation and communication, if you observe that your dog wants to go out, and you should do because you are now paying attention, how does she behave in order to access that privilege? If you go to the door does she leap about, jump up and bite your elbows in excitement? Does she simply barge past you when the door is opened a tiny crack? Some dogs do. Take control through the imaginative use of an opposable thumb. Ask for your trained behaviour; you can decide if paying you unreserved attention or sitting, or both, is more appropriate and, when it happens because you have so excellently trained it, grant her the very wish she desired. Open the door as a reward that releases her from the behaviour.

Barging doesn't get, neither does leaping nor biting. Only the alternative more relaxed behaviour is enough to grant the wish. You'll start to feel like a fairy godmother; it's quite nice and the tiara and wand are optional.

Now the real, real-life bit. We want the correct behaviour and nothing else. Anything else should be given an understood signal for non-reward (see Dog Secrets) such as "*ah*", "*oops*" or "*wrong*", although I currently quite like the "*Sorr-eee*" as spoken by Miranda Hart in her eponymous TV programme.

Be very firm with this though, wrong is wrong. Not, "*That was close enough*"; not, "*Okay, that'll do*". If she's wrong, she's wrong, and doesn't get the magic reward. The more you let it slide the more she will understand you are inconsistent and learn that it isn't really necessary. What basis is that for a relationship? Do you think she'll defer to your judgment when the chips are really down if she doesn't have to just to go outside or to have her lead put on? Sit quietly instead. Barking at the doorbell, jumping up at visitors, begging at the table? Sit on her bed instead. Use "*Wat-sis?*" first if you need to get her attention.

If you are struggling to get the message across, as you well might with a very impulsive dog, you may benefit from attaching a house line to her. This is just a light line, lead or piece of cheap curtain cord, about three to four feet long, that stays attached to her collar all the time she is in the house. This allows you to guide her, not by grabbing at her collar, but by quietly taking hold of the other end of the line. (The most useful and under-used piece of dog training equipment, the long-line, will be used outdoors later.)

There are only two options for her, do it voluntarily, or do it with guidance from you, backed up by gently manoeuvring her with the line. Either way, let me say it again because it is important, wrong is wrong. And you must make that point consistently, firmly and quietly.

158

Cinderella didn't get to go to the ball by grabbing the fairy godmother's jacket, or bouncing about in the hallway so she tripped her up, or yelling at the newly arrived coachmen. She had her wish granted because she behaved impeccably.

It's not abusive, there's no shouting, there's no losing your cool. Just a simple, quiet, calm, relaxed, request for the appropriate behaviour. She knows what the request means because you've trained it so well. Say it once. If she doesn't comply you have a signal for non-reward of the inappropriate behaviour to tell her she got it wrong ("*Sorr-eee*") and the ability to lead her to the right course, with the line if necessary. Never, ever, just communicate, "*Don't do that*" to her, but always suggest, "*Do this instead*".

Even better still, guide her in the right direction *before* she makes a wrong decision. Pre-empt her choice and steer her to make the right decision. Monitor her to see what she is about to do. If it is the right decision, tell her. If it is the wrong decision, channel her into making a better one and then you can tell her what a good choice she made. If you don't get appropriate behaviour you can guide her into pay-attention/sit/bed, whichever is the most suitable, then reward with what she wanted in the first place.

Of course the upside is that when she does get it right the magic happens and her wish is granted. Poof! Stars appear with a twinkling of fairy dust and Cinders shall go to (play with) the ball! I may have taken the analogy ever so slightly too far now, but you know what I mean.

Although I've used the context of going outside as an example, the principle applies to all her behaviour; everything she wants. Food, toys, games, affection, even the opportunity to get in or out of the car, or to go sniff-and-greet another dog. Everything is conditional on your approval and your approval is conditional on relaxed and appropriate behaviour.

This can be quite labour intensive for a while, especially if your relationship is on an uneven keel to start with, but it gets easier as she understands that you hold the key to her happiness, as you slip into the fairy godmother role. Although you should be aware that if she comes in after midnight wearing three glass slippers you should expect a knock on the door from Prince (a Corgi from the palace) a few days later. And you can take that tiara off now, you look ridiculous.

You get used to monitoring and guiding her. As the relationship develops she starts to understand that you want what she wants and how to make the magic happen. You can now apply the guidance with a lighter touch because she doesn't make so many mistakes.

## Environmental management

We know that distress can build and that small background stressors accumulate to cause a dog to tip into biting and fighting. The main cause does not have to be the trigger stimulus in front of her, but a minor emotional jolt on top of chronic distress can flip her into needing to deal with it immediately.

For that reason when we are changing the behaviour of dogs that bite and fight we need to take the distress out of their lives as much as we can. Remember that some dogs are more prone to suffering from it than others, due to their inherited tendencies and early experiences.

Much distress relief can be bought through an even-keeled relationship with you, but there are other factors that you may wish to consider. Many of these factors are facts of life and can only be removed temporarily, but that might be enough to set her on the road to coping.

Only you can be specific because I don't know what distresses your dog, but I'm thinking of things like being bullied by other dogs in the household, or by people for that matter, noise phobic dogs, dogs

160

without an appropriate outlet for their needs (Collies trapped in a flat without enough exercise), and even illness. Dogs are good at hiding pain, but not good at hiding the grumpy feelings caused by being in pain. Lack of tolerance is a good indicator of a dog in pain and should be checked out by a veterinary surgeon. In fact any unusual behaviour could be caused by illness and should be checked.

Because stress inhibits learning, once you take out the stressors, whatever they are, you will be working with a dog that finds it easier to learn and is much less reliant on the previous strategies because they were for dealing with distress.

If you look at it as emotional balance, would you rather introduce her to a new dog or kid on the block when she is in deficit, feeling miserable and touchy, or when she is feeling that all is fine with the world? Which one has more potential for disaster?

Would you prefer to meet a new work colleague when you have just accidentally shredded the accounts you have to present to your boss in the next hour, have an aching tooth, and spilt coffee over your laptop, or when you've just been given a deserved pay rise, finished your project ahead of schedule and are on a chocolate-break? Arrange for every day to be a chocolate-break type of day for your dog.

## Breed specifics

Having earlier pointed out that breed-specific behaviour can be problematic, I want to highlight how we can use it to our advantage. We can use breed-specific behaviour to communicate, reward and divert our dogs.

This subject bestrides control, training, environmental management and stress-reduction, fitting within and alongside all of them. Most problem dogs' lives can be improved by careful manipulation of their inherited behaviour and it is the aspect that most owners and many trainers fail to address. It goes to the heart of what a dog is, and more particularly, what this dog in front of us is. Sure, all dogs have basic doggy needs and respond to basic treat-training learning theory, but until you have an appreciation of their breed specific behaviour you don't really have an understanding of your dog.

Modern pedigree breeds have all been through a developmental genetic bottleneck in the last one to two hundred years and dogs alive in the western world today are descended from their offspring, even those not recognised as a pedigree.

When I was a nipper my Grandparents had a small-ish wiry-curly-haired, short-legged, stump-tailed, floppy-eared, grizzle-coloured, short-ish-faced, indeterminate mutt. When asked what breed the dog was, Granddad would say,

*"Oh, he's very rare, he's a Bitsa."*

To which the reply would inevitably come, *"Never heard of one of those, what's a Bitsa?"*

*"Well, he's bitsa Collie an' bitsa Terrier an' bitsa Spaniel an' bitsa something we don't quite know what!"*

At which there would be a groan, then, *"What's his name?"* and Granddad would say,

*"Guess."*

The poor questioner, realising he was out of his depth by now would say, *"I don't know, what is it?"* and Granddad would again say,

*"Guess!"*

At which point, depending upon their level of exasperation they would say either, *"Fido? Rex? Spot?"* and so on, or go straight to, *"How can I guess? I have no idea? What is it?"*

Eventually Granddad would put them out of their vexation with,

*"No, you don't understand, his name is 'Guess'."*

Oh, how we laughed. Please don't judge, there were only two TV channels in those days and we had to make our own entertainment.

But getting back to the point, even if your pooch, mutt or cur isn't a breed that is recognised by a kennel club, he will exhibit traits from an ancestor that was. Even a Bitsa is bits-of-something. Bitsa-Collie, bitsa-Terrier, bitsa-Spaniel, and some bitsa-breed-specific-behaviour leaks down with them.

How do you know what he has, what he likes, what he needs? Observation. Watch him, see what his preferences are. Does he like to run ahead and lie down watching you (bitsa-Collie), enjoy playing grab-and-growl with furry toys (bitsa-Terrier) or root about in the hedgerow when let off the lead (bitsa-Spaniel)? You don't have to attach a breed label to it because the behaviour is more important than the brand and there may be combinations such as rooting about in the hedgerow and staring at any hedgehogs he finds, (bitsa-Spaniel _and_ bitsa-Collie), but knowing what makes your dog tick is vital for balancing his emotions.

If you still don't get it, think of the breed or breeds involved and then ask yourself, "*What were they for?*" and, "*What tendencies would they need to fulfil those functions?*" You might get some less-than-pleasant answers, such as, "*Fighting other dogs*" or, "*Ripping up small animals*", but don't worry because now you know, you can temper that behaviour into appropriate games rather than its original purpose.

These games are the final part of the things all dogs should be taught, and you are going to use them to balance your dog's emotions and as an opportunity to reward him when he decides not to bite or fight. For some dogs they will be more valuable than food treats or praise from you, so don't underestimate their significance.

You don't have to indulge all of your dog's inherited breed tendencies; in fact doing so may be counter-productive. Allowing your Collie to herd everything in sight is not the solution to anything, and neither is allowing your Staffordshire Bull Terrier to tug on a rope-toy until he pulls your arms from their sockets, but when we know what their breed tendencies are, we can manipulate them to our own ends.

163

Our own ends also coincide with the ends of a happy dog, content in his skin and environment.

The important part to remember is that any breed-specific behaviour that your dog has inherited is rewarding for him to perform and, up to a point, the more he does it, the more he enjoys doing it. Whilst this can be a pain for owners whose dogs dig for fun, or chase deer, or search for road-kill to eat, when we direct a dog's breed tendencies it can help us to control him.

Breed specific behaviours are quite varied, but once you have established what they might be, you can use whatever your dog has inherited. It also has to be said that some characteristics aren't much use as they are usually exhibited in ways that we can't control - tracking springs immediately to mind. It is difficult to reward a dog with a track, but most dogs that are focussed on tracking are looking for an end to the track and if we practice controlling the end result of the track, the object at the end starts to have high value for the dog.

Don't worry that you don't have a recognised breed. All dogs pick up some form of behaviour from their ancestors that you can use. Whatever your dog has inherited you can find a way of using it, even if it is the opportunity to be stupid in some way.

Chasing him three times round in a circle, then changing roles and letting him chase you when you tig him is a brilliant game that uses some social and predatory motor patterns. Teaching him to jump into your arms for a cuddle is great social attachment behaviour. Teaching him to run and pick up his favourite toy gives him focus and taps into predatory motor patterns. Even something as silly as quickly moving a toy back and forth in front of him, then placing it on the floor whilst he waits for permission to pounce on it provides a boost of predatory endorphins that the right dog will enjoy.

People dismiss these games with, "*He's not a circus dog*" and talk disparagingly about, "*Trick-training*" as though it is somehow demeaning, but dogs benefit from the mental stimulation and find that interacting with their owners in an appropriate way is much less stressful than bouncing off them in ways that neither really appreciates. You just need to work out what it is your dog likes to do most and how to control it.

The simplest one that applies to most dogs is the desire to chase and catch/hold something, but you can project it onto almost any behaviour and scenario with a little thought. There are variations of this such as just the opportunity to hold something gently in his mouth, or to grab hold and rag the toy in his grip, shaking his head to and fro or tugging backwards, or to make the toy squeak, but most dogs will be able to take pleasure from some form of toy-acquisition.

If you build up a focus on a single toy so that it becomes desirable through using it as an outlet for breed specific behaviour (of course using the training principles of starting in a place with no distractions) then you instil the toy with value. If you control the toy, then you too increase in value.

Just a slight word of warning here, keep it proportionate. If you have a dog that tends towards the obsessive, take care not to over-do the focus on the toy. Whilst it will help with your dog's focus on you, especially in times when your dog may otherwise be biting and fighting, you don't want to exchange an aggression problem for a compulsive behaviour that may also develop into a problem. People who have accidentally built up too much of a tendency for their dogs to make a toy squeak know all about this, and about the resulting tinnitus.

Keep the toy proportionate, ensure your dog has lots of other opportunities for emotional balance and above all make sure your dog learns to relax by rewarding lots of calm sitting-on-bed type behaviours. Massage, or even just sitting stroking your dog, is a vastly underrated opportunity to encourage him to relax, and incidentally has also been shown to have beneficial effects in relaxation for the human involved.

So you have one more training task, training him to play the game. If this involves training a retrieve, and most do, it is one of the best games over which you have control. If your dog focuses at all on an object for their game, they need to be able to feel good about giving it back to you. Time spent in training a good retrieve is well-spent. It will stand you in excellent stead in all manner of interactions with your dog, and especially in using a retrieve toy to reward behaviour that isn't biting and fighting, if that's the route you are taking. To teach a retrieve, guess what? Yes, it's all in Dog Secrets and also in "Stop!" (available from all good retailers; may contain sulphites; your knees may be at risk if you fail to keep up payments).

The idea of proportionality is perhaps best explained through the method of using of a ragger to teach a terrier-type to retrieve. Many terriers will not want to let go and will manically tug on the rope, which is not the result we want. Controlling this breed specific behaviour comprises of asking for a short game of tug-the-rope after which the rope goes dead by locking it out against your leg. When she leaves it, she is rewarded by another game, initiated by you inviting her to tug again. This rewards the letting-go with another tug and from the dog's point of view every let-go of the dead rope has the potential to bring it alive again. The control of short games like this prevents the dog from becoming over-excited and escalating the game beyond your ability to control it.

The next stage is to make the rope die and, when our dog lets go, to throw it a few feet to one side (throwing it over her head encourages her to grab up at it, which is not our aim). Still excited and expecting it to come alive again, she will pick it up from the floor, and probably give it a few shakes of the head.

This is where your trained "sit" comes in. She will probably run around you, still quite excited. A quiet "sit" request encourages her to plonk her bum on the ground whilst she still has the rope in her mouth. When she does, immediately reward her by taking hold of the rope for

166

another quick tug game, making the rope dead before she gets over-excited again. This time, take the opportunity to encourage calm behaviour, and ask for the sit before you throw. The throw now reinforces the calm sit. The final refinement is to extend the calm sits before you throw and also after she has picked it up.

You are developing calm behaviour, sitting to have the rope-toy thrown and sitting with it in her mouth for a game, reinforced by an appropriate level of breed specific behaviour. When you offer the rope as a reward, for example for coming away from a potentially aggressive dog ("*Wat-sis?*"), it has a high value, but not only will she come away for a short tug game, she will calmly sit to ask for the reward. You have a dog that runs back to you for the chance to indulge in breed specific behaviour, but waits calmly as a way of asking for it. Leaving the rope is never a problem because when it dies she again sits calmly to ask for a throw of it. Neat, tidy and you both get what you want.

Our Collie, Fox, used to get distressed when she was approached by other dogs. We taught her to walk to heel whilst looking at us to earn a throw of her ball, and then gave her that option when another dog appeared. She is now able to control her own distress when she needs to by coming away from dogs and walking to heel, rewarded with a throw of the ball when the other dog has passed by.

You are aiming to increase your potential for reward by having another string to your bow. Many biters and fighters expect nothing more from their owners but to be told off. Building a better relationship with them gives your praise more value and enhancing that through the use of a toy or game not only raises their general opinion of you, but also gives you something else to use as a reward. Whereas previously all you had of value to give them for not biting and fighting was a food-treat, you can now use praise and the most attractive part of their instinctive behaviour.

By training an appropriate level of breed specific behaviour, you've gone from the possibility of one small reward for being good, to three, increasing the value of all three, and your own value, on the way. Now your dog has the possibility of any of three different but big rewards. You can pick and mix which to apply when and where. For coming back to you when there is a dog in the distance you can reward with a, "*Yay, good dog!*" For sitting on her bed when the Mayhem twins visit you can give her a stuffed Kong. For coming to you when the elder (by seven minutes) Mayhem twin tries to grab her, let her leap into your arms and give her a cuddle - then pop her on her bed and have a word with him. For walking away from the snarling challenge of the neighbourhood bully-dog, play rag (or fetch, or squeak, or hold) the toy with you for two minutes. She deserves each one.

Oh, I nearly forgot tracking. I said it might be difficult, but you should find a way of using it somehow. Here's how. If your dog's only breed-specific-behaviour is tracking, you need a way to control it for your own ends. You may have a Beagle or a Basset type.

Take a short piece of rope and a purse-type porous bag of smelly treats. Use a doubled training lead for your dog and on walks loop it around a stout tree or fence post so she is quickly tethered. Walk away, dragging the treat-bag on the ground for fifty yards or so, drop the bag and come back by a circular route. Untie your dog and walk with her as she tracks the treat-bag. When she finds it, take it from her and toss it back to her in the air. Play a short fetch-game, then give her some treats from it and toss it a few feet away for her to pounce on and fetch. She is still attached to a lead and the purse is still attached to a rope, so getting it back from her won't be a problem. Play on from there with tracks and fetch, and your game will develop until one day the treat-bag will be empty and she will be playing fetch games with it for fun. Keep the tracks going though, because they are such a stress-buster, and she loves it!

## When you are ready

It is not always easy to balance your dog's emotions and if you are having any difficulty with this it is worth getting help from a properly qualified behaviourist. At the very least they will be able to point you in the right direction with regard to what your dog might find rewarding. If you are consulting a behaviourist about your dog's biting and fighting, they should factor all of the preparatory emotional balancing into their behaviour modification programme, which should be tailored especially for you and your pet. If they don't, sack them and look for a proper behaviourist.

However, with a bit of savvy and attention to detail, and some serious application to addressing your dog's needs, you should get to a point where you have balanced her emotions, have taught her basic control and response to your requests, and have a variety of ways of rewarding appropriate behaviour in the face of confrontation.

You'll have taken control in all but the most extreme circumstances of biting and fighting, which is great, but not the full monty. We now need to look at how your newly balanced dog responds to the mutual control provided by your new relationship and can be rewarded for not biting and fighting with your newly acquired tools for high value reinforcement.

# Chapter 9
# Forward Planning

Having got all your preparation in place, you might just find that the problem has resolved itself. This isn't unexpected as, if the biting and fighting was caused by undue stress, and the distress is removed, there's no need for the coping strategy any more. Although this isn't a quick-fix, it does mean that our work here is done. Or at least if not done, then at a point at which we have no need for further intervention.

If the biting or fighting was caused by a small stressor that broke the camel's back when it was added to other stressors, when you reduce the cumulative distress, your dog may be able to cope with the one that previously caused her to use an extreme aggressive response.

Of course you'll still have to keep the improvements or she will fall back onto using the previous aggressive coping strategies, but if the overall distress levels remain below the point at which she needs to tip into problem behaviour, she won't need to do it ever again. This relies on you being able to monitor her and keep her below the tipping point but, having got this far, it is eminently achievable for many dogs.

These are the, "*I just increased her exercise from one walk to two a day and she stopped fighting*" dogs, at the easiest end of the spectrum. But many don't resolve, often because they've got themselves into a stimulus-response-relief rut, where they believe that the response is necessary to deal with what they perceive to be the aversive stimulus every time, or those that have had intermittent reinforcement and have come to expect the worst on each occasion.

For example if once a toddler grabbed the dog's ear and hurt her, the next time any toddler approaches she may growl as an expression of the internal emotion and a warning that she is feeling fearful. If the toddler stays away after she's growled, the dog will learn that growling keeps toddlers away. And she won't learn anything else about toddlers. She won't learn not to growl because she feels growling is keeping her safe. It may not be, but her perception is that it is necessary to growl to keep safe from toddlers. The relief rewards the growling and prevents the dog learning it isn't necessary; that all toddlers aren't going to hurt her.

Unfortunately there are many circumstances in which dogs bite and fight that won't be addressed simply by taking control and removing stressors from their lives. It always helps, but isn't necessarily the whole solution on its own. But before we examine what the solutions may be, we need to talk about kit.

### Dog training kit & stooge dogs

By "kit" I mean all the bells and whistles, including those that are sold to ~~gullible~~ impressionable dog owners as being, "*The only tool you'll ever need*". I would call it paraphernalia if I could spell it, but it comprises of all the muzzles, leads, harnesses, collars, coats, shoes, hats, umbrellas, dangly things, jingly things, wiggly things, electric things, vapour and spray things, whistles, bells, throwing things, squeaky things, screechy things and some things that do stuff I haven't even thought of.

Whilst some of these bits and bobs can help you handle your dog, none of them are guaranteed to stop your dog biting and fighting. So how to separate the wheat from the chaff? Well, for starters don't even consider using anything that supresses or punishes because it might increase stress and make the problem worse.

You'll probably have used treats already so you will know that you need the appropriate treat for the circumstance. Personally I don't think that bought-in treats are particularly useful and tend to stick to tasty/smelly human food, such as cheese or cooked chicken skin. Whatever you and your dog choose, you will need a highly salient treat when training in high arousal situations.

171

Kit such as collars, head collars and harnesses are down to personal preference and should be used to provide gentle guidance to help your dog make the right decision. If you feel comfortable using a particular head collar, perhaps with a double ended lead attached to a harness or neck collar, it could give you improved control over your dog's movements. This could be important if you are working on the edge of your dog's capabilities, in the same way that we can use a house-line to ensure appropriate behaviour. Harnesses, collars and leads should be well fitted and comfortable for both you and the dog. Avoid anything that might dig in or cause friction burns if it is pulled through your hands.

To muzzle or not to muzzle? No easy answers because it depends upon the individual circumstances and how confident and competent the handler feels. No dog should be left on their own muzzled and, as the whole point of changing behaviour is to train in a controlled situation whilst avoiding the stimulus at all other times, any muzzle will only be needed under direct supervision. Therefore the only risk should be to people who are working with the dog, and they should be able to predict and avoid any bites anyway. You also have to ask yourself the question, "*If we can only work with the dog when he is muzzled, is he safe at other times*?"

My preference is not to muzzle if I can possibly get away without one. The only sure circumstance would be if he was redirecting his aggression towards his handler in training. In that case we would lose the options of any toy play as a reward, because the muzzle takes too long to take off and back on again, but we could still use food rewards if we cut out a hole to post treats or squeeze cheese-in-a-tube through a basket-type muzzle.

I don't use a fabric muzzle that is supposed to close the mouth because they never do; dogs can still give a nasty nip with their incisors. The basket-type allows breathing, panting, lip-licking and yawning, all of which can be important to a dog in a stressful situation.

The two final considerations for muzzles are that dogs have to be trained to wear one as a positive experience and, having served its purpose, it will probably have to be withdrawn from the training at some point. The first requires time and effort and the second is a potential danger point, as handlers think the aggression is over when the dog is merely entering the next phase of training.

A muzzle warns other dog owners that your dog is not safe to approach? Yes, it can do, but I don't believe that dog-owning obligations stop there. Yes, other owners can be a pain if they let their dog leap all over yours, but by the same token you have an obligation not to allow your dog to rip it apart. You should be able to walk away without a fight breaking out. If you do muzzle your dog and the muzzle comes off in a fight, you'll have a heck of a job convincing a court that your dog wasn't aggressive. And if he's aggressive, he must have been the instigator, mustn't he?

Work out the risk; decide if you really need to muzzle. If you do, that's fine, but if you don't there are head collars that provide increased control and allow playing and treating, that may be more appropriate.

Whatever kit you decide on, make sure that it is well fitted and won't fail at a crucial moment, and don't just slap it on and hope for the best. Condition your dog to enjoy wearing or using it well before you need it.

## Stooge dogs

A stooge dog is one that helps you and your dog with your training. Ideally you need a placid, non-reactive dog that will not be worried by your dog's reaction if it all goes wrong. Professional trainers often use them, but they also know the value of one. Constantly exposing a dog to fighters is not good for his emotional balance, regardless of whether they get close enough to engage, so stooges have to be handled sensitively and with consideration. If you have access to such a dog and handler, then brilliant! But you can't just grab the nearest pet.

Because stooges are very difficult to find, you need other options available when another dog needs to be introduced into your training programme. One is to use a realistic toy dog that a helper can manipulate at a distance. Trust me, your dog will not be able to tell the difference.

I have a realistic toy Jack Russell Terrier, imaginatively named "Jack", who I animate by trotting him along on his lead. At the same time I have a recording of a JRT barking on my phone that I can play. At more than ten yards most dogs can't tell Jack isn't real. If you are not confident in your ability or you can't tell your dog's reaction distance, a toy is the best and safest way to test yourself. Get it right with the toy and you will feel more confident progressing to a real dog.

Alternatively, as you are _always_ going to be working _below the threshold_ at which your dog even looks slightly askance, there is no reason why you can't use other dogs at a distance, provided you are careful. Arranging for friends to help is always good practice, but random dogs in the park can be used without anyone knowing. Done properly, no-one will never know that your dog has a problem, or that you are using them as an aversive stimulus at a very low-level of exposure. But there is a very important condition: you must _never_ expose them to any kind of negative reaction from your dog.

In the park, walk back and forth far enough from the path so that your dog can see passing dogs, but not so close that he will react and voila! many different but completely unaware stooge dogs that won't be affected by your desensitising and counter conditioning process.

This kind of parallel walking to far-away dogs is very useful because you can control the distance, allowing you to remain below the threshold for the behaviour and, as you will see, the distance reduces over time as your dog becomes less reactive. Likewise you can walk *behind* other dog-walkers, not in a secret stalking kind of way, but far enough not to cause either your or their dog any concern.

Again, you are also in control of the distance, and if you are in control of the distance, you are in control of your dog's behaviour. Too much and you can back off, too little progress and you can catch up a bit. Dogs either walking away or parallel, rather than heading straight towards each other, are always less stimulating. Control of the circumstances gives you control of your dog's behaviour. Simple. But don't start just yet…

## What dogs want

Okay, you're all set up to start your training to change your dog's behaviour. You've assessed the risk, reduced the stress and changed your dog's relationship; you are in control in most areas of your dog's life, you've trained "sit", "go to bed" and an "attention" request until you are blue in the face, you play at least one appropriate game, you've increased the value and number of rewards, conditioned any kit you are going to use and set up any add-ons, like stooges.

Your next task is to read your dog's mind. You need to find out what it is that he wants; why he is biting and fighting. And I'm going to make it easy for you, because what they almost all want is relief or excitement. They don't want a food treat, or a toy, or to be told how clever they are, although we will use those later. They either want the thing to stop so they can access the feeling of relief that rewards and perpetuates their aggressive behaviour, or they want the excitement of the challenge. They want that "*Pheeee-e-e-e-w-w!*" moment where all the tension and conflict drains away, or that "*Yip-pee-ee-ee!*" pumped-up moment of thrill.

The relief obviously applies to the dogs that are propelled over the tipping point by fear and frustration and, although it seems counter-

175

intuitive for dogs whose driving emotion is fun, it still applies for those dogs that have developed "fun" through fear and frustration. Take away the annoyance, the original anger or worry, and we can divert the dog to finding their fun elsewhere.

The exception is where pure predatory behaviour is the cause, because there is, and has never been, an underlying fear or frustration. Consequently there is no negative aspect of the behaviour and the dog does not experience any relief. These most-dangerous of dogs are characterised by unpredictability and inflicting extreme injuries, or even death. Predatory chasing, like searching, stalking or any other aspect of predatory behaviour can be diverted and contained, but predation to the extent that the dog attacks another dog or person, unless extremely predictable, and therefore avoidable, is very dangerous to deal with, simply because the aim of it is to kill.

Society does not usually allow dogs that prey on people to live. There are no dogs that have killed a human being alive in the UK today. Every one that ever transgressed has been destroyed. Dogs that prey on other dogs must be managed every time they see one. Whilst there is no evidence that dogs that prey on other dogs ever transfer that to people, it is not desirable to allow them to come into contact with any other dogs. They cannot be allowed to do it even once more. There is no knowing what the next trigger might be and for that reason there is no training that can exclude it. Only management is appropriate.

For dogs that prey on other animals, which we could consider more normal dog behaviour than preying on their own species, training can and should help. It is the abnormality of an adequately socialised dog turning social interaction into unpredictable predatory killing that causes the danger.

In short, a dog that preys on cats every time it sees one is normal predictable behaviour and can be trained because of that predictability. A dog that unpredictably preys on other dogs cannot be

176

trained because of the abnormality and unpredictability. A dog that predictably preys on a category of other dogs, for example big dogs preying on smaller ones, might be able to be trained if the behaviour remains predictable. I have never come across a dog that *predictably* preys on all other dogs.

To deal with predatory behaviour towards other species, as opposed to preying on other dogs, please see my book *"Stop!" How to control predatory chasing in dogs*.

The *"Yippee!"* moment is also desired by dogs biting in play, caused by either a lack of learned bite-strength-inhibition, or over-exuberant breed-specific behaviour. In both these cases the dog's intention is simply to have fun..

Predation and play access positive emotions, but otherwise we know that when our dogs are biting and fighting they are doing so to make the problem go away.

## What we want

What we want is not quite as important as what our dog wants in terms of changing the behaviour, but we should know what our aim is before we start to train, then we know when we've succeeded.

So what *do* we want? Obviously we want our dog to stop biting and fighting, but *not* doing something, is not a behaviour we can train. We need to state our aims in terms of something that our dog *can* do. We don't negatively ask for our dog *not* to bite or fight, we ask our dog to positively do something else.

Therefore we can't train our dog *not* to bite the Mayhem twins, but we can train him to take himself off to his bed when the Mayhem twins arrive, to keep out of their way, which prevents him from biting them. We can't initially train our dog *not* to bite our own dear ankle-biter, who has just started to crawl, every time she moves towards him, but we can train him to come to us to tell us he is worried by her. We can't train our dog not to fight with other dogs, but we can train him to come away to us before a fight starts.

What you want is crucial to the success of your training plan and determines your method, both in terms of how you go about it and how achievable success is likely to be. Do you want your dog to simply tolerate being in the same room as the Mayhems without growling and snarling, or do you want him to love their cuddles and finger-in-eye-pokings? Do you want your dog to walk away from dogs in the park, or do you want him to love being jumped on by the world's friendliest Boxer?

In both cases the former is much more achievable, in much less time and with much less effort, than the latter. That's not to say that the latter might not be achievable in some cases, but it won't be in all. In almost every case the amount of time and effort required for the former will determine whether you even attempt the latter, but you will also be able to get a pretty good idea from your assessment.

For dogs that have multiple issues of biting and fighting in different circumstances you will of course have an aim for each circumstance. Make a list of each circumstance and write against it what your desired outcome is.

So, what do you want for, and from, your dog? State your ultimate aims but don't worry, because they can change as training develops. They are aims, not commandments.

### Nearly ready!

Let's say you've plumped for the minimum that you need to change the biting and fighting, then, when you've achieved that, you can use it to build on from there.

You wouldn't know it from all the handbooks, unique protocols, methods and therapies, but there is only really one way to do it, and that is to present each problem at a level below which it stimulates the aggressive response from your dog, and then show her a way out of that doesn't involve aggression. And repeat, increasing the level at which the stimulus is presented as the dog learns the alternative response, until it is acceptable.

These principles are not new; the scientific investigation of the psychology of specific fears goes back a hundred years, and they have been successfully used on humans since then. What is new is the burgeoning number of dogs that that need our help in this way. All you have to do is apply the principles properly.

As you do, you must continue to control the current circumstances minutely. For dogs that are fearful their food may be taken away, you must prevent people approaching them whilst they are eating until you set up your training. For dogs that are fearful of visitors you must absolutely prevent them coming into contact with callers until you are at the right training stage. For dogs that are growling at your dearest ankle-biter you must control your tot's access to them for now. For dogs that are fighting dogs in your own home, you must keep them apart, and for dogs that are fighting other non-household dogs you have to prevent them getting to one.

In every case you have to pre-empt and prevent, to temporarily make the problem go away until you can present it under controlled conditions, because controlled conditions are the secret to your success.

# Chapter 10
# Biting and Fighting

Finally (phew!) this chapter gives examples of how to address different instances of biting and fighting but, before we look at them, I need to emphasise the need for safety and then round-up where you should be before you start. If you can't keep safe and don't have the preparation so far, you are setting yourself up to fail.

## Safety

It is absolutely imperative that you do not put any dog, other person or yourself in any danger whilst training. You should know the danger your dog poses from your assessment of his previous behaviour and if that is not acceptable you have a decision you must make. I would never encourage anyone to work with a dog that may potentially cause an unacceptable level of danger.

Each person also knows their own level of competence and should only work within it. If you have worked through this book and achieved all the goals we've set for getting this far, then you should have the ability to take the training on. If at any stage you feel that you haven't been up to it, for reasons of time, commitment, coordination, ability or any other, you probably need professional help. It is not a disgrace to ask for help. There is no reason why you should be an expert dog trainer. Some skills are just beyond some of us. I'm slowly beginning to realise I may not be the next Robbie Williams, even though I think I sound quite good in the shower.

Likewise, some dogs are just easier to work with than others. If your dog is responding well and you feel confident, keep going. If not, seek out qualified professional help. I used to service my own car, change the oil and coolant, clean out the carburettor, adjust the spark plugs and timing, until the cars I bought were beyond my understanding; then I had to admit I didn't have the ability and sought professional help.

When training you may not put your dog into the position where he may come into biting or fighting contact with a dog or person not involved with the training. Neither can you use people, or their dogs, if they don't understand and yet say they are prepared to accept the risks involved. "Not understanding the risks involved" includes the idiots who approach you in the park saying, "*Oh, don't worry, he won't bite me*" or, "*It's Okay, my dog just wants to play.*"

You must stay away from them until your dog is safe. The law is very clear on that; if your dog injures or puts anyone in fear of injury in a public place (at the time of writing a proposed new law extends that to private places as well) you have a dog that is dangerously out of control and are guilty of an offence under the Dangerous Dogs Act 1991. By fighting other dogs, you and your dog may fall foul of the 1871 Dogs Act, too. You can't borrow the public or their dogs to train yours if there is the slightest possibility your dog will show any kind of aggressive response towards them.

For dogs that threaten children, you are likely to want to use children in your training. Make sure that you have absolute control of the situation. Whilst it should go without saying that you should never, ever, leave dogs alone with children, you also have a responsibility for what you are teaching the children who are helping to train your dog.

Without scaring the living daylights out of them, primarily teach children that this is a special dog that doesn't understand them, but also that it is only ever alright to approach any dog with an adult's permission. They must always ask. Teach them that they can call the dog to them, but never pursue him if he doesn't come. If you are in the advanced stages of teaching your dog to enjoy being petted by children, consider that you are also teaching the child how to pet a dog. Avoid any kind of close facial contact, hugging or any other cuddling that confines the dog. This is your responsibility. A lifetime's facial disfigurement is not worth the risk of getting it wrong.

The responsibility for safety is yours. Not mine, not this book's, not your helper's, not the dog that didn't react how you expected her to and caused yours to attack her. Yours alone.

## The round-up

If you think you are ready to start, here is your check-list of things you should have completed if you want a chance of succeeding. You should have:

1. Accounted for your dog's sex, neuter status, breed, innate tendencies and upbringing.
2. Learned a degree of canine communication skills.
3. Assessed your dog's history of biting and fighting to determine the risk he poses in the future, and acted upon that information.
4. Assessed the development of the biting and fighting so you know where it came from, its motivation and how it is perpetuated.
5. Prevented your dog from continuing to reinforce the biting and fighting.
6. Adjusted your relationship with your dog to maximum effect.
7. Identified and removed any untoward stressors from your dog's life.
8. Trained "attention", "sit" and "bed" – properly.
9. Used breed preferences to add a toy-reward, and trained it.
10. Defined your aims for each biting/fighting incident - realistically, taking into account your capabilities and the difficulty of the dog as determined in 4 above.
11. Ensured you are able to guarantee the safety of everyone concerned in training.
12. Considered professional help.

As I've said, if you have done all that, your dog's inappropriate biting and fighting may have disappeared. Their perceived need to use this extreme form of communication may no longer be necessary. If you have succeeded through doing all those things you will understand your dog and be able to communicate with him more than you have ever done before.

## Methods

In the examples that follow you will find basic ways of teaching dogs that biting and fighting is not necessary in even the most provocative circumstances. They can be used in any situations, but not in isolation. If you've picked up the book and flicked straight to here because you are champing at the bit to get going with your dog, go back and read from the start, because you won't have the underpinning knowledge of what you should be doing.

With solid groundwork in place you have much more chance of effecting permanent change. If you wade in without that you are less likely to achieve the desired result and risk making the problem worse, through repeating the biting and fighting strategies.

The following are the basics. There are a number of other methods that professionals can and will use in circumstances that they think are appropriate. They are not wrong, but they often take considerably more expertise and skill than the average owner has, even one who has read and implemented the advice in this book up to this point. There are also stacks of add-ons that might be of some help in some circumstances but not in others, and I want the training that follows to be accessible to as many owners as possible, so everyone has the chance to change their dog's behaviour if they need to. I don't want owners to have to sift through a list, applying some aspects and discarding others.

The good news is that there is no reason why the basics, if applied consistently, should not be effective for all dogs and owners.

I have made the principles as simple as I can, to enhance understanding and application for both dog and owner. A few simple but effective steps may take slightly more time, but are easier to implement and more likely to lead to success than a complicated programme, or one that needs extra-ordinary skills.

So, by all means add to the methods if you think it will help, but don't miss anything out because they are pared down to the minimum.

Because I can't specify every single circumstance in which dogs bite and fight, I'm going to use the most frequent ones as examples and let you take your own problem from there. There may be combinations of motivations and emotional states in some dogs, and I suggest that you take the strongest and work with that first, but in every case our plan will follow the same pattern of changing behaviour:

* Background, in which we examine what specific preparation and understanding we need to help us succeed for this exact problem.
* Training Alternative, in which we determine and train an alternative response for the dog, out of context.
* Control, in which we examine problem-specific safety measures and methods of control.
* Context, in which we apply the new training to the biting and fighting behaviour in context.

Which gives us the catchy little acronym of "BTACC". Just what we need, another label that just rolls off the tongue. No? Maybe you're right, let's just do some dog training, starting with the most frequently reported problem.

### Dogs that fear close contact with unfamiliar dogs

Background

This is the biggest group of dogs that fight, almost a quarter of cases referred to the Association of Pet Behaviour Counsellors, so you're not alone. It is usually caused by either a lack of appropriate social referencing, one or more specific aversive experiences, or both. The

184

prognosis for successful resolution, taking into account the generic factors in Chapter 7, is better for dogs that are well socialised and have fewer and more recent aversive experiences.

Realistically, dogs that are very under-socialised are unlikely to greet every new dog without stress, and the aim for them is probably to get them to trust you enough for you to ask them to rely on you to solve their problems for them.

For the dogs that have only recently developed fighting as a strategy due to a single aversive experience, it is far more likely that they will be able to re-integrate into canine society. The rest will fall somewhere between these two extremes. If you are in any doubt where your dog sits on this scale, start by taking control for him, and test by allowing cautious re-introduction to a toy stooge dog.

The initial steps are to determine what kind of dog(s) distress your dog, and the distance at which it is possible to see them without tipping him into aggression. Make a scale of aversion, starting with the least feared, that causes only the mildest reaction, such as a lifting of one ear and one eye, and ends with the most severe reaction of full blown havoc. This is known as a stimulus hierarchy for desensitisation and in human fears can start with imagining the feared object.

Obviously we can't work within the dog's imagination, so we start with the actual stimulus that provokes the least reaction. You might start with *seeing a small dog 200 yards away, facing away* (your stooge), and work through the degrees of severity up to *a large dog running at us growling five yards away*. In between you will manipulate the variables, such as, *small dog 200 yards away, facing towards us; large dog 200 yards away facing away; small dog 150 yards away facing away.*

Make a numbered list that you can tick-off when you achieve each one. You may never get to the scariest stimulus, but settling for your chosen alternative reaction to *large dog walking towards us ten yards away* might be the best anyone can hope to achieve. Be realistic, based on your dog's previous behaviour and your assessment of the possibilities for change.

## Training Alternative

You need to decide what alternative behaviour you would prefer from your dog. Some protocols suggest shaping your dog's behaviour by reinforcing any kind of deferential or non-combative behaviour, perhaps through removing the stooge dog when your dog looks away or relaxes slightly. This reinforcement of lower level behaviours is entirely appropriate if you have the skills to implement it accurately, and in particular is excellent for teaching dogs that lack social communication skills, rewarding them with the very thing they want, the removal of the aversive stimulus (proximity of the dog), as your own dog makes the right decision. You will need a skilled stooge dog and handler and to be well versed in the application of the protocol. If you are offered this opportunity by a skilled practitioner, jump at it.

Without the skilled practitioner and stooge dog, take control for your own dog, and ask him to focus on you instead of the other dog. Don't train him to sit or lie down, as these more vulnerable positions hamper his ability to walk away, and you are going to show him that he can simply walk away from potential trouble when he needs to.

The attention signal you have trained ("*Wat-sis?*") needs to be 100% rock solid, and followed by a "come away" signal - in dog training parlance, a recall. Your options for rewarding these alternative behaviours should also be firmly in place: food treats, high praise and toy-play, all with a high-value owner.

## Control

Safety and control are vital, particularly as we are venturing out into a public place. You should already have places you walk your dog that have a low density of other dogs, and you can use them, unless your dog is so reactive that he reacts immediately at the sight of another dog. In that case you must find a private place and either a toy-stooge or a friend with a non-reactive stooge.

As you will be working at huge distances your dog should not have a great effect on your friend's dog, but you should bear their emotions in mind as well. Don't stress your stooge. This is most important as you don't want to be ruining another dog whilst helping yours.

Start with your own dog very close to you on a lead and the stooge/toy a long way in the distance. Once you have the desired behaviour on a short lead, you can make some progress by allowing your dog to make decisions.

You must never at this stage let your dog run free, but attaching a long line provides the ideal compromise of allowing him the freedom to make choices, always maintaining physical control to ensure they are ultimately the correct ones.

A long line can be a purpose-bought one, a lunge-rein, climbing rope or strong washing line, depending upon the size and strength of your dog. Attach it comfortably to your dog, to a wide strong neck collar or harness, never to a head collar.

Consider safety and comfort for your dog. Long-necked dogs are always better on a harness; some say all dogs are. Also consider that you will be holding the line if things go pear-shaped and will need to keep on holding it, so something comfortable will be softer on your hands. If you are using a muzzle or a head collar, make sure it is conditioned and fitted properly before you start training. The last thing you need is your dog fighting the kit.

Context
In this case, the training and the context are the same. If you were to simply expose your dog to the lowest level of stimulus on your list and

nothing else happened, it would be pure desensitisation, and take forever. If you add in something positive you will also be counter-conditioning, which is making something good happen when the aversive stimulus appears. A combination of desensitisation and counter-conditioning is a very potent way of changing behaviour.

There is a threshold at which dogs tip into fighting. It will differ slightly from day to day, dog to dog and circumstance to circumstance. The secret to success with training an alternative emotional response is always to work below that threshold.

Take your dog to the appointed place where your training is set up, with all control measures applied, and arrange for your helper and chosen stooge/toy to appear at the required distance. Mobile phones are very useful for communicating between you and your helper.

When your dog cocks an eye or ear at the lowest level on the hierarchy of aversive stimuli, before he shows even the lowest level of concern, call your attention signal "*Wat-sis?*" and reward him for looking at you by running in the opposite direction to the stooge and heaping on your preferred reward, either food-treats, lavish praise or a toy-game. Well done. Your first step to changing your dog's fighting behaviour is successfully completed.

The next step is to do it again. And again. And again, progressing to the next level on your hierarchy and to a long line. The next X number of steps is the road to showing your dog he can choose to come away from another dog and at the same time allowing him to start further away from you as the stimulus-dog comes ever closer. There should never be the chance of coming into contact with the other dog as you always have the opportunity to walk away if necessary.

You can mix and match with the toy, the stooge and dogs in the environment (both parallel-walking and following), varying distances, but most importantly never allowing your dog to tip into the aggressive response. This is your responsibility because you control the training. If you aren't able to control the circumstances, for example if there are too many random dogs milling about in your training area, abandon ship for now and set it up again later.

When you get to the stage where your dog only reacts to dogs that come very close, you may choose to use dogs so far away in the environment that they will not even be aware that you are borrowing them. BUT, you may not subject any dog to aggression from your dog. Ever.

Practice repeatedly looking at the far-away dog, "*Wat-sis?*" come away with you and reward, until it becomes engrained as the default position whenever another dog appears, whatever the distance.

Always set up the circumstances for success. Be aware that like the rest of us he will have good days and bad days when he will be less or more reactive, and take account of that. Be prepared to go back to a previous success level and don't push on too fast. If you get it wrong you strengthen the old fighting response and set back your progress.

The number of sessions and exposures within each session is always governed by what your dog can cope with, but a rule of thumb would be a couple of sessions per day with three or four exposures within those sessions. If he can't cope with that, you will rapidly become aware of his distress and you need to back off. Schedule training in your regular walks; intersperse the training exposures with games and free-sniffing time.

Pretty soon when your dog sees another dog he will look to you for guidance. If he is calm and not looking stressed you can provide feedback in the form of low-level praise, "*Good boy, very clever*" and walk on. If he looks like he might need some help to lower his stress level, give a, "come away" request and reward with one of your options. Always err on the side of caution, you can't do much harm by over-rewarding good behaviour.

189

Tick off your hierarchy of aversion as you work through the list. One single representation of each probably won't be enough for you to progress to the next, and slight variations in the actual exposures help your dog to generalise the circumstances, so a few at each level are likely to be more beneficial than trying to race through them all.

Whilst it appears that you are rewarding with one or more of your three options, his real reward is the feeling of relief that he avoided the fear and conflict. This feeling of relief will drive the new behaviour of "coming away to you" when his stress levels rise.

By monitoring him you can decide how much help he needs every time. Progressively he will allow dogs closer to him as he is now able to cope without having to fight, but, and it is another massive BUT, you must keep him safe or he will lose faith in his new strategy. If you ever allow him to be beaten up he will be set back horribly. Your responsibility again, so don't let it happen.

This is the stage at which the under-socialised and the recently-attacked diverge. The under-socialised may well have gone as far as they can, and if you want to stop at teaching him to come away to you when he is stressed by another dog, that's fine. Many people do.

However, if your dog has previously been happy to play with others, you can work on getting back to that. It will take more time and extra monitoring, and you must always be there to judge the best time to ask him to come away. That could be on first contact, or it could be after a good old sniff and bit of posturing. But at this stage keep him on the long line.

This has two advantages. Firstly it is a security blanket for him; he knows you are in control and can rescue him if you need to. Secondly you can actually get him away unscathed if you make a mistake. If it looks like it is about to blow up, run away backwards with slight pressure on the line, calling "*Wat-sis?*", and he will follow you out of trouble.

190

Only when you are completely confident that he will follow you without the line should you discard it. By then you will be happy that he can keep himself out of conflict.

## Dogs frustrated at not being able to make close contact with other dogs

### Background

Dogs that are frustrated at not being able to make close contact with other dogs get angry at their inability to control the situation, which causes them to show an aggressive response, usually to the other dog, but also sometimes towards the owner who is holding them back.

Your dog may want to play with the other, or she may want to run up to intimidate the other dog because she is frightened. There can also be a combination effect where if your dog is allowed to run up to the other, it depends on how the other dog reacts. If the other dog isn't worried by a dog running at her, it may turn into play, but if she is worried she may give off "go away" signals that make your dog afraid and it could turn into a fight. These are the "unpredictable" ones that play with some dogs but fight with others. They are not unpredictable, they just depend on the other dog's reaction.

For our purposes, of changing the fighting behaviour towards other dogs and also biting the handler from frustration, it doesn't much matter if the exact motivation is straight frustration or fear + frustration because we are going to change it in the same way, by taking it under control.

You need to have all the groundwork in place, with particular emphasis on the relationship change, which reduces frustration, an attention signal, a "come away" signal and a solid "sit".

The dogs for whom no part of this behaviour is motivated by fear are the ones most likely to resolve without any changes other than the background measures. Improving their relationship with their owner and their response to requests, increasing calm behaviour and consequently reducing frustration generally, is quite often enough to stop her throwing a tantrum because she can't go and play with every dog she meets. The fear-tinged ones need slightly more work.

## Training Alternative

For frustrated dogs you need two alternatives. The first is the same as in the pure fear dogs, a "come away" request that you reward heavily. However you also need to allow your frustrated dog to meet and greet other dogs appropriately, and to do that you need her to be calm when she actually gets there, so you need to teach a signal for calm behaviour that you can reward with increased proximity to the other dog.

This is easier than it appears because you already have a signal for attention and another for the "sit". Putting those together into a "sit and look at me" allows you to reward with calm praise and moving towards the other dog. Practice "sit and look at me" out of the context of other dogs, but in the locations where you might meet one, for example out on walks.

## Control

To prevent your dog directing her frustration onto the handler you must have a solid relationship foundation before considering attempting this training. She also will not bite you because you are working below the threshold for the behaviour, well away from the tipping point.

Eventually you may progress to a long line, but initially you will need to work with your dog on a secure lead attached to a wide flat neck collar or a body harness.

Your stooge dog is equally as important and to be protected as before, and a toy-stooge is a very good start point as you hone your own skills. Because you are going to allow your dog to move closer to the stooge as a reward for calm behaviour you cannot use dogs you randomly find in the environment.

Using a dog with which your own dog is familiar, and friendly, is the step after a toy. Only when you have trained your dog to walk calmly up to all the steady dogs you count amongst your friends can you start to use unknown dogs. Of course the upside to this behaviour is that is likely to be more extreme towards dogs that yours knows, because they are known to be fun to play with. Unknown dogs are likely to be less attractive. So, when you've made significant progress with your friends' dogs, unfamiliar dogs should be a piece of cake.

## Context

Again, set up your training bouts so you have full control of the circumstances. Have a friend appear trotting toy dog Jack at a distance beyond which your dog would normally react and begin to walk towards her. Jack should come into sight then stand still, although with slight animation to keep him real.

The moment your dog pulls on the lead towards Jack, before you get any fighting-type behaviour, ask for "sit and look at you". Reward this with lots of low-level calm praise and when your dog is a smidgeon calmer walk towards Jack again.

If your dog does not calm down even slightly, give a "come away to me" request and walk a few steps backwards, before asking for the calm sit again. This is an emergency strategy because you have moved past the threshold for the frustrated behaviour, and not something that should be factored into the training repeatedly.

Very quickly reward any degree of calmness by walking towards Jack. It is quite likely that your dog will start to look at you as you walk forwards, and this should be rewarded with lots of praise so long as she stays calm. Any fear of Jack that surfaces should be dealt with through the "come away", rewarded with the increased distance and your chosen very high value reward.

Your most difficult task is to discriminate between excited frustration and fear, which may surface in the same dog at different times. Frustration is most likely when the dog is a long way off, and fear is most likely as you get closer. Excited frustration is controlled by asking for calm attention to you, with the calm being rewarded by moving towards Jack. Fear is controlled by asking your dog to come away, the reward being the increase in distance from Jack and your treats/praise/toy-game.

The big clue is the presence of excitement. Frustrated dogs that want to get closer look excited and display a variety of bouncy forward postures with a fast waving tail. Fearful dogs try to make themselves look bigger and more scary, maybe with laid back or flicking ears and some anxious expressions such as lip-licking and yawning, and a slower-waving tail. Pilo-erection, the raising of the hairs along the spine, is a dead-giveaway for fear.

Frustration/fear is the most difficult of the combinations of motivations for fighting other dogs, as initially your dog wants to meet/greet/play with the other dog, but as they approach the fear takes over. Manipulating your dog accordingly, taking control of the emotion underlying each motivation, allows you to provide the release to reward alternative appropriate behaviours for each.

This is a dance where you move towards Jack when your dog is calm, dealing with the frustration, and move away to deal with the fear. If it is simply fear you need only work with the training described in the previous section. If it is solely play-frustration only use the *reward calmness with approach* training.

Practise in different locations with Jack and quite quickly your dog will start to check in with you whilst walking more calmly towards him. Only then can you use a friend's dog. Because you've upped the stakes you will have to work harder, probably inserting more sit-calms, but always reward any calmness with forward movement. Of course this depends on a very sympathetic and well-controlled stooge dog. If you have no doggy friends or suitable stooge dog, you will probably have to look for help from a qualified professional.

Walking between your dog and the other can block her sight-line and encourage her to look at you. Don't expect *too* much calmness on the first few attempts, but reward what you can. The idea is to make progress in small increments, not to demand absolute and utter calm immediately. Don't include too much delay, as that in itself may increase frustration, which is exactly what you are trying to reduce.

Once you have reached the other dog you are likely to have to teach calmer greeting and play behaviours. You can do that by allowing appropriate contact, but walking your dog away when she gets too excited and goes over the top. It will help if the other dog is also able to walk away at that point, as that is how yours should have learned appropriate greeting/play as a puppy. Inappropriate behaviour means the interaction ends. If that causes frustration, call her away and reward compliance with high value treats/praise/toy-games to end the session.

Progress to other dogs, starting with parallel-walking and following where appropriate, and use the walk-up approach each time. Eventually you will be sufficiently confident in your dog to let her think she is free to make decisions on a long line. Always reward your end-of-contact come away request, and occasionally, especially if she is getting close to over-the-top, call her away, ask for calm and allow her back again as the reward.

Because you are teaching your dog appropriate canine interaction, which is itself rewarding, she will choose to inhibit her own behaviour and gain her reward of social contact for doing so. All you ever do is guide her in the right direction.

## Dogs having fun fighting unfamiliar dogs

### Background

These are the dogs that have usually started from a fear base and developed to a positive emotion as the relief at resolving the fear combines with the buzz of victory.

The current motivation for these dogs is to engage in combat and vanquish the foe, and their reward is the huge thrill they get during and afterwards. Especially in the combative breeds the fighting is fuelled by the neurochemicals of reward.

Dogs that appear to be having fun fighting unfamiliar dogs actually are having fun. Because this behaviour takes repetition to develop, unlike fear or frustration which can spontaneously arise, we have allowed it to get this far. Boy, have we let him down.

Fun-fighters actually seek out other dogs rather than avoiding them, and there will be no fear-type body language exhibited. Although I say "unfamiliar" dogs, the possibility that they regularly engage with the same dogs also can't be ruled out. By unfamiliar I therefore mean "dogs with which they are not regular friends".

There may even be elements of predatory searching and stalking, but when the attack takes place it will be loud and intimidating, not silent and deadly, as is predation. It will often include roaring and wrestling, shoulder-barging and fang-fencing, although many of these overtly social motor patterns may well be omitted in in the dog-fighting breeds.

If you are in any doubt if it is predatory or fun-fighting in a dog-fighting breed, it is far more likely to be fun-fighting; the breed does what it says on the tin.

Our options for change are limited by the fact that this is now a sought-after emotional state for the dog. He is therefore not seeking to avoid the confrontation as the fear-fighters and even most frustration-fighters would prefer to do. Rewarding him by removing the stimulus is not an option, any more than allowing him to get closer would be.

Your only possible way forward then is to provide him with a reward greater than fighting the other dog, and this is where all your background relationship change and increasing the value of rewards is at its most valuable. It is all you have.

There is also the possibility that he will be frustrated if he is held back from engaging in combat, but again your relationship and basic training should be enough to contain that, if not deal with it altogether.

## Training Alternative

The only alternative you have to him focussing on the other dog is a "Wat-sis?" and "come-away" request, massively rewarded with stacks of toy play. He wants fun, so you have to give him an alternative source of fun. Any kind of toy-play is your alternative behaviour, but you must be in control of it. Fetch is favourite, but you may want to look back to teaching Terrier-types a retrieve and tug game on page 166.

## Control

Control is massively important. You must have physical control of your dog, so firstly the lead and then the long line are once more your friends. If you make a mistake and tip him over the threshold he is likely to charge towards the other dog. You must have a substantial line that will not hurt either him or you if he does. Attach it to a wide flat collar or a secure body harness.

## Context

Go back to the fear-fighting section and re-read it. This is even simpler because there is no intention of ever letting your dog get close enough to another to start a fight. You will always call him away. On the plus side you can practice it at home in your own garden with a toy dog.

On the basis that you should always try to reward your dog with what he wanted out of the inappropriate behaviour, if he was looking for fun, give him a fun game (a few may prefer food treats, so it is always worth testing).

Starting with your own dog on a lead, practice calling him away from Jack for an extremely exciting game. You have to be more exciting than the previous behaviour, so ramp it up. All progress is determined by the attractiveness of the stimulus compared to your own attractiveness (no, not that kind of attractiveness - lose the high heels and lipstick). The stimulus is the other dog. Jack may be the least attractive as a small, motionless, silent, dog, facing the other way at distance. Call your dog when he is still by your side and then reward with play.

Everything else is manipulation of the variables. Animate Jack, reduce the distance between Jack and your dog and increase the distance between your dog and yourself by using the long line. Proportionality of the distances is important.

There is likely to be a distance from you that your dog will not respond. The lure of the stimulus trumps your attractiveness. For many dogs this is about halfway, when he is equidistant from you and the other dog, no matter what the actual yardage is, for example:

You_ _ _ _ _ _ _ _ _ _ _ _ _ _Dog_ _ _ _ _ _ _ _ _ _ _ _ _Jack

is the same as

You_ Dog_ Jack

With training you can improve those distances in your favour, but only up to a point. There will always be a relative distance at which he will prefer the other dog regardless of what you say or do. Your job is to practice, without ever getting it wrong so you lose control, moving the tipping point towards the other dog. You are basically training the best recall in the world.

You start at:

You_ Dog_ _ _ _ _ _ _ _ _ _ _ _ _ _ _ _ _ _ _ _ _ _ _ _ _ _ _ _ _ _ _ Jack

and move towards

You_ _ _ _ _ _ _ _ _ _ _ _ _ _ _ _ _ _ _ _ _ _ _ _ _ _ _ Dog_ _ Jack

Practice calling him back at times when there is no other dog present, so his reaction to your call is not to first scan the horizon for dog. When you are confident with Jack in a variety of locations, move on to friends' dogs and/or park dogs walking parallel or following, but start at a greater distance for safety and always confined by at least the long line.

Can it ever be safe to let him off the long line? Yes, it can be, but you have to be confident that you can maintain control and never be surprised by a strange dog coming round the corner. You are in control. You are to blame if it goes wrong. You decide if you want to take the risk.

Your final aim is to train him to prefer your game, so that when he sees another dog he runs to you because he knows the sight of another dog predicts the possibility of a game with you. Over time you can take the level of the game down from the maximum excitement you will initially have to use, but the possibility of a game should always exist.

## Dogs that fight familiar dogs within the home
### Background

As you can see, I've strayed from my intention to describe the behaviour through what the dog is feeling, and gone for a straight observable description of what is happening. This is because when dogs fight in the home it usually stems from only one reason, that of resource protection.

Unfortunately it is difficult to state with any certainty whether that is through fear of the loss of the resource, frustration at being unable to gain or retain access to the resource, or a combination of both. It could develop into a fear of the other dog on sight because of previous aversive encounters and could be between two or more dogs.

The resource in question could be anything from a person, food, water, another dog, sleeping place, exercise, toys, to the right to mate (even there is no other mate-able dog present).

However, and this is the good part, whatever the motivation, to control fighting in the home there is only one solution. Well, actually, two solutions, but the other is to re-home at least one of the dogs to a single dog household, which isn't really dog training or behaviour modification.

We've already noted that the more alike dogs are the more likely they are to prefer the same things, which can lead to conflict. Litter sisters seem to be the most difficult, followed by mother/daughter and litter brothers. Dogs of totally different breeds and sexes would be at the other end of the spectrum.

The hormones in entire (not neutered) dogs and bitches seem to fire up competition in same-sex fights. Bitches coming into season can be grumpy in defence of resources because, in a natural state, keeping and holding resources gives a bitch a better chance of bringing up her pups successfully.

Another bitch is seen as a competitor for resources and quite often the hormonal bitch is not satisfied until the other is driven away. Confined to a family home this cannot happen and they become locked into a cycle where neither can escape the fighting. Obviously neutering is the solution if caught early enough, but by the time that happens the fighting can have developed into a fear/frustration battle.

Bitch wars can be devastating and result in the death of one of the fighters. I once saw a bitch that simply wanted her grandmother dead. She also lived with her mother and sister, both of who ran for cover when they saw her coming and deferred every resource to her, but Grandma was a bit doddery and didn't move away fast enough for the bitch. She took umbrage and attacked. The only solution was to re-home the bitch because we couldn't risk one more attack that would probably have killed grandma.

Dog wars, on the other hand, usually start over a fight for a single resource such as a toy, a bone or attention, then can either dwindle as one of the dogs decides to defer, which is less likely if they both value the resource highly, or escalate as neither is prepared to back down.

Caught early enough, and if both dogs are castrated to remove a source of testosterone-fuelled competition, they may simmer down enough to train an alternative behaviour.

Unfortunately, with any breed and sex of dog it is possible to see competition for resources escalate out of hand, and the sooner you intervene with guidance for them, the better.

For the sake of simplicity of understanding I've written this for two fighting dogs, but the same principles apply if there are more, you just need more individual beds and more eyes to watch them.

Training Alternative

The alternative in this case is always to go sit on their respective beds, not as a punishment as in the case of errant children sitting on opposite ends of the sofa, but to give them a viable way of backing down from the fight.

People will tell you to always back up the winning dog; to take his or her side. However, do you really want the other to be perpetually cowed? What kind of way is that to live your life?

No, any fighting is always wrong, no matter who started it. Both dogs get sent to their beds, not as a time-out, not as a punishment, not as a place to, "*Think about what they have done*", but as a reward for not fighting, or at least as a reward for breaking off immediately they were asked.

Of course, this means that you must teach an attention signal and it should by now go without saying that you need to have a firm grip on your relationship with each dog, but most of all your "go to bed" request must be so rewarding that they happily skip there each time.

You should place the beds far enough apart that they cannot start fighting there, and then teach them to go to their own bed individually. When each is rock solid on their own, introduce both together. You can use one signal for both dogs, as both are going to their own bed every time. Make sure that you teach them to stay until released, but there's no harm in using a slowly-consumed treat to reinforce it.

Control

Of course control is as vital as always, and you should not leave the dogs together on their own as you have no control over them if you or another responsible adult are not there to monitor them. You may consider a house-line, the younger brother of the long-line, if you do not have complete confidence in you own ability to part them when you are present, but don't leave it on them when you go out.

When left alone they should be parted for safety and, if you are not able to monitor them even when you are there, you should think about partitioning the house, perhaps with baby-gates to prevent another battle breaking out. The partitioning should be temporary as the intention should be to get the dogs back to living together, if not in absolute harmony, then at least in tolerance of each other.

If you know what makes them kick off, for example a big raw juicy bone, or both going through the door together, then avoid the stimulus, although admittedly some stimuli are easier to remove than others.

## Context

Once you have completed the training, you can allow the dogs back together again, under direct supervision.

The context is simplicity itself. Introduce the trigger at a low level, perhaps knocking on the table rather than waiting until someone randomly knocks at the door, and then send both dogs to their respective beds for their earned reward. Of course some triggers can be removed and stay removed, there is no need for a dog to have a raw bone ever again, and some are easier to manipulate, but the more you can identify and present at a low then increasing level, the easier it is to train "go to bed" as an alternative to fighting.

But what if the trigger is actually the presence of the other dog, or even the owner? Same process. Present it at a low level and encourage calm behaviour. Practically this means that you are going to go through a reintroduction process that is under your control.

Moveable beds are good for this. Remember when you taught the "go to bed" you could decide what you used so long as it was identifiable to the dog? The best choice for these dogs would be a piece of blanket or fleece that you can move about the house.

As you are dealing with two dogs, you will probably initially need another person to help as well. With both dogs on a lead sit one on her bed at one end of the house, room or sofa, depending on the size of the dog and severity of the problem, and the other on her bed at the other end, and ask for calm. You've pre-trained this so it should be fairly easy. Next time move the beds and the dogs closer to each other. Rewarding with very calm but heart-felt praise and stroking or food treats is probably better than a toy-game, which will get them excited.

You and your helper will still be in-between the dogs as you bring them and the beds closer. Before you get too close for comfort take the dogs back to the original start point and yourselves to the outer side of the dogs, still on a lead. This is a crucial stage because now the dogs are looking at each other directly and you must monitor them closely for signs of unease, before you can decide to move them closer again. Take your time over this.

When you have the beds next to each other with dogs sitting or lying calmly on them, remove the beds to their permanent position and repeat the whole process of bringing the dogs closer on the lead, but without the comfort of the beds. If they become uneasy, send them to their beds to calm them down. In this way they learn that if they are not happy with the other dog they can take themselves off to their bed to get out of the situation.

Once you've retrained this level of tolerance you can start to allow the dogs some degree of freedom again, not forgetting the house-line if you need it. Keep a very beady eye on them. Look for the precursors to their fighting and interrupt before they start. That sideways look, that little throaty not-quite-growl, that slight stiffening. If you see any of those off to bed with both dogs to earn their reward for not fighting.

If you know what the initiators are, such as attention from you, or a knock at the door, you can introduce them at a low level and reward the dogs for not reacting. If one dog appears to be "bullying" the other, still send both to their beds. You are not punishing them, just showing them better behaviour.

It can be extremely difficult for people to determine exactly why dogs are intolerant of each other because the perceived slight may not have even been noticed by us. The first growl is not necessarily from the instigator. Lots of things we may not have noticed, such as staring, body blocking or other intimidation may have been going on before that.

Eventually you might allow growling back into the communication again, especially if they are growling and walking away to their bed, and both dogs understand that it is not a signal to start fighting, but one to move away.

And that's it. It depends upon you being vigilant and in complete control, but if it had been easy you would have cracked it already. Knuckle down and watch them like a hawk. The price of failure is at least re-homing one dog.

## Dogs that fear close contact with familiar children

### Background

I've split this category into adults and children in consideration of the disproportionate number of bites that children suffer from our pets.

A dog has three untaught options for dealing with the presence of people they find threatening: hide, move away or social communication. Lower levels of canine threat-reducing social communication such as head turning, lip-licking, body postures and yawning are rarely understood by people for what they are, and are even less likely to be understood by a toddler. Higher levels of communication though, such as snapping and biting, inevitably remove the threat.

Most parents don't have a problem with their dog and baby until the baby starts to become mobile. Then baby seems irresistibly drawn towards the dog and they relentlessly crawl or shuffle towards him. Continually moving towards another dog is one of the ways that dogs bully other dogs; constantly invading their space and never allowing them to settle. From the dog's point of view this little monster, who up to now hasn't bothered the dog at all, within the space of a few weeks develops into an incessant bully. The dog moves out of the way, then moves again and again as each time the bully changes tack, continually crawling at him. Sometimes he may literally be caught napping and if that happens the monster grabs a tiny handful of skin, hair, tail or ear, and nips or pulls. It hurts and makes him more worried about being approached.

Children are therefore most likely to fall foul of the dissonance in communication between humans and canines. Without prior learning, dogs find being hugged, cuddled and confined, and face to face contact, threatening. When they find themselves in that position they frequently aren't able to hide or move away. Biting is too often the result. Unfortunately, because it is often the nearest part, it is the face that is bitten.

But there's also a lack of canine understanding of what a baby/toddler/child actually is. Dogs brought up exclusively or mainly with adults do not comprehend the completely different young human body language. In fact, unless exposed to it sympathetically, dogs often don't understand any form of "non-standard" human body movements, such as exaggerated limps or walking with sticks.

All of my police dogs found drunks slightly threatening simply from the staggering gait and over-effusive movements. They also learned that quite often drunks mean trouble and came to expect it from them. A police dog can spot a drunk a mile off.

Human youngsters use non-standard human adult body language. Babies cry, squeak, chortle and gurgle, and wave their arms and legs uncoordinatedly. When they start to crawl they obviously move on all fours. Toddlers and upwards stagger, make jerky movements, jump up and down, and run around unpredictably. They act impulsively and emit high pitched shrieks.

Whilst this atypical human behaviour can be worrying for dogs, increasing threat and distress through lack of understanding, there is also the possibility that it may stimulate predatory behaviour. There is a large body of thought that considers most attacks on babies by dogs to be predatory. I'm not so sure all are, but why take the risk? Don't ever leave a dog alone in the same room as a baby or child.

## Training Alternative

The alternative isn't "not biting" because that is not a positive thing that you can teach a dog to do. You have to come up with a trainable alternative behaviour and the "go to bed" is yet again very appropriate. A retrieve with a drop of the toy on the floor will come in handy later and should form part of your training package, as should Learn to Earn.

However, the positioning of the bed needs careful thought, because not only do you have to train the dog to go there, you also have to eventually train the child *not* to go there. The bed is the dog's sanctuary, place of safety and refuge from any children. What the dog needs is to get away from the child. Show him he can do that without biting and he has an escape route.

The positioning of the bed is vital because the responsible adult should be able to see dog, bed and child at any one time. Simple mathematics tells us that you either need three independent eyes or to keep the dog, bed and child within one view.

For those with persistent children it may be necessary to construct a barrier, such as a safety gate or fireguard, with only a small entrance for the dog. This gives the dog a greater feeling of den security and allows you to explain to the child that under no circumstances should they go the other side of the fireguard, into the dog's space. Be inventive - I once saw a client with just this problem and we made the Staffy a den behind the sofa. The only access was over the back of the sofa. One small leap for the bouncy Staffy, and the child couldn't reach him.

Once he's been taught to go to his bed he can happily skip off there to avoid the child. The clever parent who sees him do that will make sure that baby does not follow. When baby has her nap, or is in her play-pen, he can come back out and enjoy some quality time.

All this is fine for preventing, controlling and containing the problem, but baby and dog are probably going to have to live their lives in close proximity for a number of years to come, and there is no reason why they can't get on together.

There are some great resources for introducing children to dogs, The Blue Dog is good http://www.thebluedog.org/en/ and you can look for other reputable organisations for further in-depth study, but for those who have left it too late and allowed conflict to develop, we already know how to introduce a worrying stimulus to a dog: desensitise and counter-condition.

## Control

Control is always your responsibility and both child and dog need to be monitored. Controlling the dog is relatively easy, he will avoid problems where possible, and more so when he knows to go to his bed to get out of the way. Never force your dog to participate in any training with the child if he would prefer not to. He should always approach you and the child, never the other way round. If he feels that he approached of his own free will, he can also walk away if he needs to.

There should be no need for house-lines or muzzles. If you think they are necessary the situation is too dangerous for your child, in which case you need to back off and start from a reduction of the stimulus - perhaps with the dog held on a lead at the far side of the room from the child sitting on another adult's knee. Your previously re-jigged Learn to Earn relationship places you firmly in control of the situation, with your dog expecting you to provide guidance.

## Context

Any dog that has shown any kind of proactive *or defensive* social communication towards a child will benefit from desensitisation and counter conditioning in the home environment, because he is communicating his fear. No one should want a dog to be afraid of children; it can never lead to a good outcome.

Sit quietly with the child and call your dog over. Treats can be an added attraction and reward for calmness. All that is necessary in the first instance is for the child to be present whilst you reward the dog. If your dog is too worried to approach, you can toss treats to him.

Progress to increasing the stimulus as his tolerance increases, for example, get the child to sing him a song. When your dog is ready you could allow the child to stroke him as you treat him. Depending on the child and dog you could consider placing a treat on the palm of her hand to offer to him. Eventually you should be able to call him over and allow the child to stroke him. Impress upon the child that she should only do that when you are there.

You can also use toy-games to desensitise and counter condition. Children love to throw things for dogs to fetch back, but make sure that there is no conflict over giving them up. Your dog should already have been taught to drop toys on the ground on request, and of course rewarded with another throw. If you are in any doubt as to how your dog may respond, re-train it out of context yourself and then insert the child into the training.

Your praise, coupled with food treats and appropriate games from the child, always with the option of trotting off to his bed if he needs to, change the dog's perception of interaction with children from a negative to a positive one.

Don't expect this training to generalise from one child to many. Adult dogs will always need to treat each child as a potential threat until they prove otherwise. Just because your dog is now fine with your daughter, she will not necessarily be with her friends, neighbours and any other children he may come into contact with. You can introduce new children to him in the same way, and it will probably take less time each time you go through the process, but expect him to be at least wary and treat him accordingly.

## Dogs that fear close contact with familiar adults

<u>Background</u>

The majority of bites towards any family members arise from fear: either fear of resource loss, which will be dealt with later, or fear of the interaction the person is attempting to carry out.

Adults are less subject than children to the communication disparity between the two species, but equally guilty of failing to understand that what they are doing is threatening to the dog. This most often manifests itself in forms of contact, but can be any stimulus that the dog worries about.

Ways of touching the dog are the most obvious, but approaches that predict an aversive stimulus can also trigger a fear-bite. For example, if a dog is hurt when being groomed, even approaching her with a comb may trigger the fear and a snap or bite.

Less obvious is the "over the head" dog that is fine with being touched except when a hand goes over her head, when she bites. This often develops from the hand taking her collar to prevent her from doing something, or to take her out of the room. The collar-grab becomes aversive and generalises to other circumstances. Now she won't let anyone take her by the collar and snaps any time a hand goes over her head, because that's the last thing she sees before it grabs her collar.

In the days when it was a popular form of punishment, scruffing, taking the dog by the scruff of the neck and shaking it, also pushed dogs into biting hands over the head. (It was thought to be an appropriate form of punishment because, "*That's what the bitch does to puppies to discipline them*". I sometimes wonder if the people who propose these strange and barbaric practices have ever seen a dog before. Bitches do not discipline puppies by scruffing them.)

Other forms of punishment, such as smacking, rolling over and holding down also encourage dogs to defend themselves by biting, but so can innocent forms of contact that have accidentally hurt the dog.

## Control

I've taken this category out of turn because it does not signify control of the dog here, but your own self-control. Your dog will only fear-bite a familiar person if she is afraid. The clue is in the name. Therefore if you leave the dog alone she won't bite. If you don't know what it is that is making her bite, stop initiating whatever physical contact you have with her. Do not approach her, but always ask her to come to you. If she doesn't come, don't make her. You can lure her with a treat and reward her for coming in the short term, until you have re-educated yourself.

## Training Alternative in Context

The training required to change the behaviour depends on what is causing the biting, but it all comes back to good old desensitisation and counter conditioning. Unlike other training this cannot happen out of context before inserting it into real life, because it is always in context. "Tolerating reaching over the head" can only be taught in the context of reaching over the head, but taking away, or reducing, some aspects of the composite stimulus may help you with reducing the overall action to a level acceptable to the dog.

The basic training we covered should all be in place, together with the relationship changes, before you attempt anything new.

Because context is everything, it is difficult for me to recommend the exact training you will need, but perhaps a few examples will allow you to formulate a training plan applicable to your exact situation.

Example 1: your dog is so afraid of a family member that she growls every time he comes in the room and lunge-bites if he tries to talk or reach towards her. There could be several reasons for the build-up of this fear, from a concerted campaign of teasing the dog, to once accidentally treading on her tail.

In this case the person should lower his stimulus value as much as possible; don't look at, speak to or attempt to move or reach towards the dog. At the same time he should gently drop a very high value food treat in the dog's direction, free of charge. The dog doesn't have to do anything in order to earn it. You are simply changing the perception of the dog as the person appears from outright fear to the anticipation of a pleasant outcome of food arriving.

It will help to increase the value of the food and if the dog is hungry, but something like warm chicken skin is useful because the smell is highly salient. The dog recognises and responds to it immediately.

A few pieces of chicken each time the person enters the room is a good start and once the dog gets over his outright hostility and starts to anticipate a treat the person can start to look, first out of the corner of his eye, then more directly, and offer the food from his hand.

Asking more, such as a quiet "sit" and petting of the top of her head can only be dictated by the dog's progress. Some will come round quickly and others will take longer. Never push too fast and always err on the side of caution, keeping the dog comfortable and relaxed.

Eventually you will reach the next stage, which is used to deal with the fear of direct contact...

Example 2: this dog is afraid of hands that go over his head and bites when they do. The fear has developed in one of the ways described in the Background section above. Take a warm chicken skin treat and sit with your dog sitting facing you. Show him the treat and allow him to lick at it in your hand. At the same time stroke the side of his face or under his chin with your other hand, then release the treat for him. Take another treat, but do not allow him to lick it. Stroke his face, chin and chest, then reward with the treat. Take another treat.

As you start to stroke his shoulders, make sure your hand approaches from the side and do not stray towards the neck. If he shows any sign of stiffening, wider or narrower eyes or nervous glancing at you, stop stroking there, wander your hand back to a place where he is comfortable, stroke there and finish.

You can do this four to six times a day for five minutes at a time. If you are following on from example 1 above, don't start with the problem person, but someone else. The problem person should be in the room and sit closer and closer to the dog and trainer. After the dog is comfortable with the problem person being close as the trainer strokes him all over, they can take over, but starting from the beginning again.

Generalise the training with different people and in different places, but always watch for your dog showing the slightest discomfort and back away before pushing him into using overt aggression. He will bite if you get it wrong.

If he fears his collar felt, or his neck gripped, just to continue the change in perception you can include those stimuli in the training, starting gently then building up to the full stimulus. But I fail to see why you'd ever want to grab his collar or scruff in the future, and if you do it will set your training back again.

Example 3: Some dogs fear being groomed and will snap at a hand that holds a comb or brush. In this final example you follow the same principles as the previous two, but include the grooming kit in the process. If your dog has a very aversive association with the grooming tools you have, you may need new ones. They shouldn't hurt you know. There are many combs, brushes and other tools especially made for sensitive-skinned dogs. Have a look at yours and if you wouldn't use it on yourself, think about replacing it.

Whilst a dog is capable of recognising a grooming brush it may also help him to get over his fear if the old brush is replaced. A brush may be a brush, but if it isn't *that* brush it might not be quite as scary.

Start with the brush lying on the floor beside him as you treat him. Progress to holding it in your hand whilst you treat him. Place it back on the floor and work through the touch training in Example 2. Then work through it again using your fingers as a brush. Then work through grooming with your fingers, with the brush in your hand, but not using it. Providing treats at variable intervals will keep him tolerant.

Eventually you will be able to bring the brush into the equation, but on no account hurt him, or you are back to square one. Start on less sensitive areas until he is happy, then move on to the more ticklish ones, but be careful. Keep looking for the tell-tale stiffening, head turning, nervous glancing and other signs that he is not happy, and finish on a good place.

It isn't possible to cover *every* circumstance where a dog is fearful of contact with a familiar person, but these examples should give you an idea of where to start if your dog has this problem.

## Dogs that bite people when frustrated

Background

There are undoubtedly dogs that lack inhibition and become frustrated when prevented from doing whatever it is that they want do. That frustration can become so extreme that it causes them to bite their owner. The identifying feature of this aggression is that there will be some kind of resource that the dog desperately wants to access, and is being prevented from doing so. It is unusual to find pure frustration without there being some element of fear, but it can happen.

Examples would be a police dog that really wants to bite football supporters and instead bites the leg of her handler, or a greyhound that really wants to chase a running cat and bites her owner who is holding the lead.

Less serious instances include dogs that grab and rag the lead when they are held back from other dogs, and dogs that attack the boundary fence that separates them from the person they are trying to drive away. As you can see, the people are almost incidental - the frustration is driving the biting and the people just happen to be in the way. If there is any suggestion of fear, you must train for that as well.

## Training Alternative

The big training task here is to get your relationship right, so Learn to Earn is paramount. If you are in control, you take the sting out of the need to bite *you*. Although there still may be a need to bite, that inhibition too should be reduced through the structured relationship. Your dog will feel at ease with herself, more fulfilled and consequently less subject to frustration.

You may also need to redirect the biting onto an appropriate toy, should it surface during training in context, so training a toy-game with a "leave" will also help. Where the original stimulus is driving the frustration, breaking focus on it with an attention signal prevents it becoming so arousing she can't help herself.

Finally, if there is an obvious underlying cause, and there almost always is, that should be dealt with as a separate issue. For example, the dog that attacks the fence can be dealt with by way of the methods in fear/frustration of unfamiliar people, and in the case of the greyhound and cat, where frustration is caused by an inability to perform predatory behaviour, there's a book I may have mentioned…

## Control

You will already have physical control because it is the barrier that is contributing to the frustration (the lead or fence that holds her back). The control you require is her self-control, which you can help her to achieve by training initially out of context and then applying the same principles in context.

<u>Context</u>
Dogs that bite their owners when held back should be provided with the lowest level of the initiating stimulus as possible, then asked to pay attention to their owner and rewarded with toy-play. In effect it is rewarding the dog for not paying attention to the initiating stimulus, which reduces the frustration and prevents him from reaching the arousal level that tips him into biting.

The context is invariably the underlying cause and if you have dealt with that, for example controlling barking at unfamiliar people or the desire to chase cats, then the need to redirect frustrated behaviour will disappear. Adding in the attention signal and reward of praise, play and/or treats will ensure that you maintain control of the situation each time it arises. On the basis of replacing like behaviours with like, using toy play as the preferred reward places something in his mouth that isn't you.

## **Dogs that fear or are frustrated by the loss of resources (not-food or people)**

<u>Background</u>
The reason that I define this as "fear or frustrated" is that it is difficult to know where one stops and the other starts. If I really want to hold on to something, I can be afraid that someone is coming to take it from me. If I believe that I'm going to lose out to someone else I become frustrated at my inability to control the situation to my liking.

Very often what starts out as fear of the loss turns to frustration, which causes anger. So now the bite is less like a fearful quick snap and retreat and more like an angry attempt to make the challenge go away. Dogs unable to secure resources they consider to be important become angry at people who try to take them away.

Whilst it stems from a fear of the loss, the ultimate anger drives a much more concerted attack.

But what "resources"? Simply, a resource is anything the dog values, and could be as varied as a comfortable sleeping spot, her own toy or a "stolen" item of yours; food and people are considered as resources separately, later.

As is often the case there may well be a genetic predisposition driving the behaviour, and dogs that lack impulse control are most prone to frustration. The second genetic predisposition that may drive resource-control is that of the breed. Many breeds have been specially developed to find holding something in their mouth to be highly valuable.

The retrieving breeds (Spaniels, Labradors, Golden and other Retrievers, Poodles, the European Hunt-Point-Retrievers) are all rewarded with a brain-chemical boost to their contentment when they pick up and hold something, because it is part of their breed-specific behaviour.

It is easy to see how, if a behaviour is highly valued, being prevented from accessing that behaviour and the nice feelings that it engenders could be aversive. In short if she is enjoying the feeling so much and you try to take it away, she may feel angry.

The next thing we need to consider is that all dogs are subject to challenges that cause them distress and, as we saw with Jim the Beagle in Chapter 5, one of the ways to cope with that distress, and return to emotional balance, is to secure access to a resource that makes them feel good.

Any dog can choose any coping strategy, such as lying curled up on the sofa as Jim did, or cuddling up to something that smells of their Mum, or chewing something solid. Many dogs are also directed by their breed-specific behaviours.

Consider then a Spaniel that is subject to challenges that cause her considerable distress. She could choose to cope with that distress by "stealing" an item of Mum's clothing to cuddle up to. It is no coincidence that the most "stolen" clothing items are the smelliest: underwear and footwear.

As a breed that enjoys something in her mouth, she may well also hold on to the knickers. And as she's distressed she may find herself chewing. So now she has three ways of making herself feel better that rely on the briefs: the comforting, cuddly smell of Mum, the breed specific relaxation of holding something in her mouth, and their chewability.

How do you think she feels when you reach under the table to take them from her? Happy, or not happy? She's depending upon these bloomers to keep her head straight. She feels the fear of the loss of emotional balance again, and frustration at her inability to hold on to something she values so much. And towards you? Resentment and anger. Little wonder she plucks up the courage to tell you to back off.

It doesn't even have to be that complex. Think of the first warm sunny day of the year. The sun is streaming through the window onto your bed, where your elderly pet hound stretches out, oblivious to the fact that you've just changed the white linen quilt-cover. She is in bliss, not a care in the world. Outraged at the mucky old mutt, you storm into the room and tell her to get off. She lifts one eye, then ignores you because this is far too comfortable a spot. Even more annoyed that she's ignoring you, you reach to turf her off.

She bites you because she is not prepared to lose her comfort. Her frustration at you, the challenge to her emotional balance, tips over into anger. She tells you to back off.

Biting in these circumstances can be exacerbated when people have punished their dog. Punishing a dog increases her fear of you. If she can predict times when you punish her, such as when she is under

218

the table chewing your underwear or lying on the bed, she becomes afraid at your approach. What she can't do is project that backwards. She knows you punish her for lying under the table chewing your pants, but she can't make the association when she feels the need to take your pants in the first place. Punishing a dog for "stealing" doesn't address the underlying problem and can cause a breakdown in your relationship that causes her to fear and possibly bite you.

By the way, "stealing" is in inverted commas because dishonesty is a human construct. So far as dogs are concerned, anything not currently in your actual possession is there for the taking. You can teach them not to appropriate individual items, but that is a learned rule, not a concept. Dogs can't *steal* because they can't understand the concept, they can only "steal".

Training Alternative

The above examples are really about who owns what, and who has the right to ask the other to give something up or move. Only if your dog has the idea that they can challenge your decisions will they bite in these circumstances. A simple relationship shift as described in Learn to Earn is required.

However it is worth noting that outrage is rarely a useful emotion in which to communicate with a dog. Had the encounter been handled differently, perhaps by exchanging something for the knickers or offering an incentive to get off the bed, the outcome could have been very different.

For dogs that challenge over a resource, no matter what the motivation, the solution has to be to offer the dog an alternative way of achieving the result they want/need/desire. This means training them out of context in an alternative behaviour, for reward.

For dogs that refuse to get off the sofa, train them to jump on to the sofa and then back off again. Practice: on the sofa, stay, then off the sofa. On the sofa only gets a reward of mild praise, but off the sofa bags the bigger reward of massive praise, game or high value treats.

This of course is another situation where a "go to bed" request will solve the problem. Keep your treat pot near to the bed and when you want her off the sofa, wander in that direction and reward her for following.

Dogs that "steal" items that are not theirs, or guard items that belong to them, such as toys, should be taught from scratch a word that means "*If you give me that you will get something better in return*". "*Leave*" is quite popular, but if it has been used to death, change it for a new word. If you are not using it for anything else, "*Wat-sis?*" will work.

You can teach a "*Leave*" by placing a small low value food treat in one hand and then as you say the word, produce a high value food treat from behind your back in the other. Progress to placing the low value treat on the floor and when she happily leaves that in expectation of something better, change it for a higher value one. Manipulate distances as well as values. Things closer to her have higher attainability than those closer to you. Finally you should get to the stage where you can throw a high value treat across the floor, say the word and she will walk away from it in expectation of something even better from you. Now she really knows what the word means.

If it is toys she values, and snarls at the thought of giving one up, teach her using the two-toy game, where you take two identical toys, give her one and animate the one you have to give it more value. Hiding a detached squeaker in your own hand makes her think that the one you have is always squeaky. Never compete, just have more fun on your own than she is having.

Dogs that value your possessions to the extent that they "steal" them (please also see the *Frustrated by the loss of people* section, later) can be given old scented clothes in their bed, if it is safe to do so.

Chewers can be given more appropriate things to chew; take your pick from the many chew-toys on the market.

If she values food treats more, the "go to bed" with treat-pot may persuade her to give up her treasure, but the underlying principle is that she should always think that you have something that is more valuable than whatever she has. You are a Fairy Godmother, after all!

## Control

A house-line may make you feel safer if you are dealing with a dog that has engaged in conflict with you for some time. Refusals to accede to your requests to move from a place can be countered by asking once only for the trained alternative behaviour ("on the floor" or "go to bed") then backed-up by taking hold of the far end of the line and walking away. Never walk towards her. No competition, no aggravation, just a fait accompli.

The best control you can have though is in the relationship change that means your dog looks to provide what you want in order to get the good things in life.

## Context

The training should always take place as training (short bouts several times a day) until the words are learned and the behaviour is fixed in that context. Then you can transfer it into the previous contexts of inappropriate behaviour, using the same words and rewards. Always take great care to balance her emotions, by providing all the necessary support for her, especially if you are taking away from her a resource that she relied upon. Either replace the resource with something more appropriate, or find an alternative way of helping her cope.

Punishment is not appropriate in these circumstances because it has the potential to make the problem worse. The worst case I saw involved a working Cocker that had been punished for picking up and carrying about household items - anything left around she could fit in her mouth. She was told off and had her nose smacked, not brutally, just a tap to, "*Tell her she was a bad girl*". In an astounding example of anthropomorphism she had also had her toys taken away as punishment. She had nothing left to hold. By the time I saw her she was catching sunrays and shadows on the kitchen floor, lying with them between her paws and growling and snarling at her owners when they went near, because she feared the tap on the nose and the loss of her only toy. We gave her a teddy bear, taught her to swop it for a retrieve game and did some touch and approach training to deal with her fear of people. The bear became her security blanket, a treasured possession that nobody ever needed to take from her.

## Dogs that fear or are frustrated by the loss of food

Background

All current dogs are descended from ancestral pye dogs, pariahs that scavenged on the edge of society. The majority of dogs still are pye dogs (estimated at 85% worldwide) and our western pet dogs' not-too-distant ancestors lived a life where they did not know where or when their next meal was coming from.

Although this is obviously a successful adaptive lifestyle, we have not taken into account the inherent predispositions that go with it when developing our modern breeds. Dogs are a species of scavengers. For a species of scavengers, food is a valuable resource and it is understandable that dogs defend it.

Hunger is determined in the brain through hormonal feedback between the stomach and the hypothalamus. It is your brain that tells you when you are hungry. It also tells you when you are not. However, some breeds of dogs and individuals within those breeds seem to be hungrier than others, and will eat to bursting point. Labradors are a case in mind, but there are individuals of other breeds too.

222

The question that bothers me slightly, is: if these dogs eat anything edible, and some things that are not, at any opportunity, even if it is low value food and they have just eaten a large meal, does that mean they constantly feel hungry? I find it difficult to conclude that they don't. Otherwise why do they act like that? The purpose of the feeling of hunger is to stimulate us to eat. Constantly being on the lookout for anything edible suggests that the driving emotion behind the behaviour is hunger. I know what it is like to be hungry, and it isn't pleasant. I don't know what it is like to be *always* hungry, but I bet it even less pleasant. I bet a dog that is always hungry places huge value on food.

That said, it is extremely rare for dogs to actively challenge for food that is already in the possession of another, whether that be another dog or person. In dog terms it seems that with regard to food, possession is 100% of the law. If it is mine, it is mine and you cannot take it away.

Biting and fighting over food that is either not yet claimed, or is in the dog's possession and being defended, is one of the most persistent forms of aggression. This is particularly so when it has been practiced for some time, as we examined the case of Bobby in Chapter 2. It very often starts in the communal feeding bowl of tiny puppies as each defends his patch.

Guarding very high value food, such as meaty bones, is normal dog behaviour. Most will pick up a bone and move away as a person approaches, or keep still and hang on to it by mouth or paws, but if your dog proactively attempts to control his access to a valuable bone through snapping or biting, you have two options. The first is to go through the process described as teaching a "leave" above, and the second is to stop providing him with meaty bones. As it is difficult to persuade him that you have something better to offer him than the bone he already has, most people go for the latter. It also needs much less training.

The other form of development is when for no good reason people take food away from their dog. Don't forget, dogs consider any food in their possession to be theirs. You give up any rights to it when you hand it over. You do not get to take it back again. In dog terms, how would that make sense?

Taking food from a dog may not encourage defensive biting in the future, depending upon the temperament of the dog and the value he places on food, but likewise it may.

If we look upon it from the point of view of your relationship with your dog, you provide his food conditional upon calm, appropriate behaviour. That means he has earned it, as in Learn to *Earn*. If you then take it away again, it is the same as you going to work for a month, being paid and then your boss randomly taking a portion from your bank account, "*Just to show he can*". Would you enjoy that as your card is being refused in Tesco? Neither does your dog.

If you give food to your dog it is his. Don't ask for it back. However, if your dog has just reached social maturity and has always been defensive over his meals, he may start to be more proactive in that defence and start to growl when people go close, like Bobby did in our earlier example. Then you might want to do something about it.

Training Alternative

Again, the alternative is never just "not growling" but a change of emotion in the dog from the worrying expectation of a challenge, to one of the anticipation of a pleasant thing happening.

You can do this in several ways depending upon how severe the problem is. The simplest is to have a supply of high value food that you can toss into his bowl as you pass, like we did with Bobby. You would need to feed a boring low value dog food, such as simple dried complete all-in-one kibble, to highlight the difference between the two.

This is a good strategy if you can get near enough to his bowl without an adverse reaction.

If you can't, remember that possession is everything and dogs can't defend what they don't possess. On that basis measure out your dog's food portion into a container on top of a table, and place his bowl on the floor. Again, you will need to feed a dried kibble type food. Drop one piece of kibble into his bowl and it will be eaten in a second. Follow it with another and another and you will find that you are sitting next to your dog whilst he eats, without him growling at you. Occasionally say his name and when he looks at you, hand-feed him a high value treat.

When he is happily looking at you when you say his name, drop a piece of kibble into his bowl, say his name and, if he leaves it to look at you, treat him from your hand. He has left his bowl for you.

You can now drop three pieces of kibble into his bowl, then a small handful, which he will spend more time eating. If at any time he goes back to growling, go back a stage and feed fewer pieces at a time.

There are variations on this theme that you can play with if you so choose, for example you could place two bowls on the floor and train him to go between the two by judiciously throwing a high value treat into the one he isn't feeding from.

However the next progression is back to placing the quarter-full bowl on the floor and occasionally dropping high value treats as you pass. Then the half-full bowl, then the full bowl. Always monitor and never push too far at a time. Realistically, if your dog has been practising the aggression for a long time this could take six months. Taking great care and more time is never wasted.

Control

Other than a sound Learn to Earn, there is little in the way of control that is useful here. Children should be kept out of the way unless

225

participating in the training under supervision. In this context, control is all about your management of the circumstances.

To increase training opportunities and reduce his hunger, which in turn reduces the value of food, you might consider feeding four to six small meals each day rather than one or two bigger ones.

## Context
There is no way that dealing with dogs that bite over food is not in context. Once your relationship has been straightened out, the training is always done in the context of food.

## **Dogs that fear or are frustrated by the loss of people**
### Background
People are undoubtedly a resource for dogs. Lots of good things emanate from us. They also attach to us very strongly, to the extent that some dogs find it difficult to cope without us. When we discussed a dog's maintenance set of coping strategies that support emotional balance in Chapter 5, we included proximity to a significant attachment figure. Being close to Mum or Dad allows you to cope with life's challenges.

It therefore follows that the opposite, being parted from Mum or Dad, subjects you to extra distress. For the dogs that depend too much on just proximity to their attachment figure, being removed from them signals they are in for a harrowing time. Anything that predicts that her person is being taken away becomes aversive and to be avoided or fought.

Many, many dogs suffer from distress when separated from a significant attachment figure and do not attempt to deal with it through confrontation and biting. I have a great deal of sympathy for these dogs because we've bred them to be dependent upon us and then expect them to cope on their own. There are ways to help them but unfortunately we can't cover everything in our limited space and must confine ourselves to those that have developed an aggressive response to what is obviously an aversive situation.

This could be the removal of the person him or herself. Some dogs will fight the person they love to stop them going out of the door without them. They will stand in front of the door and bar the way, growling, and even bite and tug their leg to prevent them exiting. They will jump into the car and sit there with bared teeth, daring their person to try to remove them.

Or it could be the removal of all attention or a specific kind of attention by the person. This can happen when the telephone rings, which is a signal that no attention is going to be available until the call is over, or when the theme tune to your favourite soap concludes the programme, which signals that the dog is no longer able to sit on your knee as you get up to put the kettle on.

Or it could be biting directed at another person, a family member or a stranger, who approaches "her" person, signalling a possible loss of potential attention. Dogs will push themselves in between cuddling partners to defend their access to "their" person, and snap and snarl at people who approach on the street for the same reason. "She's not yours, she's mine! Now, go away!"

Do not make the mistake that little Fluffles is protecting you because she thinks you are under some sort of threat from the kisses of your boyfriend or from the girl handing you a discount leaflet in the street. Little Fluffles is protecting her property (you) for herself. She thinks that she owns you in the same way she owns the food in her bowl and her squeaky rubber bone.

There are two strings to the development of this type of jealous behaviour. The first is an over-dependence on one person and the second is an unrealistic expectation of what the dog is able to control. Together they can cause an aggressive response.

Let's take the first. We know that over-dependence on a single individual is as a result of not having sufficient other good things in her life, and can also be supported by a lack of adequate social referencing. A lack of socialisation could also contribute to the fear felt when approached by another person and the perception of a safe base from which to repel them.

An overly-dependent dog typically follows "her" person everywhere around the house; maybe she won't even allow her person to close the door to the lavatory without creating pandemonium. Even when her person is going about their normal predictable household chores, she will follow them. Owners can't get up to make a cup of tea, as they do every evening at eight o'clock, without her following them into the kitchen and back. She likes to be resting on or very close to her person, often touching them. This allows her to feel secure that they can't move without her knowing. She may push her way onto her person's knee or like to rest her head on their feet. I've seen some lying across their person's shoulders like a stole. These are not the normal snuggles that dogs carelessly give their owners, but are driven by anxiety that contact could be lost.

Owners of course often don't recognise this clinginess for what it is and enjoy the attention from their dog - up until it causes *them* a problem. It is an interesting aspect of human nurturing needs that some people enjoy owning a dog that is so dependent upon them that she can't cope without them. The functions that dogs fulfil for humans are many and varied.

Many overly-dependent dogs go through their life without showing any inclination to biting, and the behaviour in itself, although it can be stressful for the dog, isn't necessarily problematic for the owner. You could describe these dogs as being needy. Others find the potential loss of access so aversive it causes them to growl as a

228

reflection of the negative emotion when the person moves from under them.

As we saw in Chapter 6, when we looked at Resource Holding Potential, the other aspect that can contribute to protecting people as a resource is that of control. Who controls who and what? Or more accurately, who *thinks* they are *entitled* to control who and what?

Dogs that depend on a person to maintain their emotional balance value attention very highly. For some, it can become a necessity in their lives:

attention = comfort

lack of attention = lack of comfort

lack of comfort = distress

Consequently any time she loses access to attention she becomes distressed and has to seek attention. Therefore she has to make sure that she can get attention at any time.

This vicious circle can drive dogs to find ways of trying to control their access to their person's attention. They fear the loss of attention because that causes them distress so they manipulate their owners to ensure it is always on tap.

Owner inconsistency (butter-side-up/down toast) means that they sometimes have to persist very strongly, which can cause frustration when they fail. This provokes anger which can cause them to bite in order to deal with the fear of the loss of attention compounded by their frustration at not being able to control their access to it.

When we looked at RHP we saw that we can inadvertently give dogs the impression that they are able to gain our attention whenever they want. When dogs are used to controlling their access to resources even temporary failure to do so can cause them to up the stakes and use aggression.

Not all dogs react like this and many find less confrontational ways of dealing with their access to their owners, but in a small number of cases over-dependence combined with a perceived ability to control their owner causes them to bite.

Training Alternative

Because there are two factors driving the biting we need to address them separately. Firstly let's deal with over-dependence.

The basic training will already have helped because you have increased reward values and trained a calm "sit on bed". Increasing the value of other people will also help where possible. Involve other family members in the walking, playing and feeding of your dog.

Provide self-play toys, particularly food-toys where she can expend some time and energy in focussing on enjoying a game that doesn't involve a person. Even something as simple as a chew can provide a pleasurable interval for her.

You can improve the value of her bed as a place of comfort and safety by making it comfortable, and you might consider temporarily providing her with cloths of your own scent to cuddle when you are not available.

Cut an old sheet into three. Place one piece in the bottom of your bed overnight. The next day place that piece in her bed and the second piece overnight in your bed. The next day take the sheet from her bed and wash it, replace it with the one from your bed and place the third piece in your bed. Continue to rotate the pieces so she has a fresh you-smell every day.

There are prescription-only medications that you might consider, for which you should consult a specialist veterinary behaviourist. Alternatively or in tandem you might also consider pheromone therapy, food supplements or herbal remedies. I suggest that if you have reached this stage you need the advice of a professional behaviourist to guide you through the minefield of commercialism that drives the sales of products, many of which have not been double blind placebo tested and may have little scientific validity.

Training advice for owners of dogs that have inadvertently been given control of aspects of their human to an inappropriate extent is easy to give but harder to implement. It consists of the relationship change in Learn to Earn.

From now on you micro-manage your own interactions with your pet. You maintain consistency in your approach and help her understand that all the good things in life are there, conditional on appropriate behaviour. Pre-empt any situations in which you have previously deferred to her and substitute a request for more appropriate behaviour.

Before she jumps on your knee, ask her to sit and be calm for a moment. If she tries to compete (grabbing the toast?) ask her to pay you attention and reward that look with heart-felt praise... and then hand the toast to her. By all means ask her onto your knee for a cuddle, but conditional on calmly waiting until she is asked.

Move one of her day-beds to the sofa next to where you sit, just out of touching distance. Train her to go and stay there and reward staying there with stroking and petting. You are rewarding the slight distance from you with the very thing she values highly. Extend the training to staying on her bed as you walk out of the room and back again. Just one second at first, but building up over time so she doesn't notice how long it is.

A useful tool in the training box is a signal for no attention. It can be anything you like so long as it is tangible. Some people like to use a towel draped over a door handle or a special item placed on a coffee-table.

It doesn't have to be anything fancy, but it does need to be salient, because when it comes out you do not pay your dog any attention. You do not look, speak to or touch your dog. She does not exist for the three minutes the signal is there. Then you take the signal away and interact with her as normal again. She learns that temporarily there is no attention on tap, but it will come back.

Any item will do and I have heard of all manner of things, but the one I like the most is a big clockwork alarm clock. It is very salient to her because it is big and noisy, and it reminds you of the time elapsed before you take it off.

Because this is training you can do it several times a day, and you should increase the times up to the point at which, when your dog sees the signal come out, she goes and lies down by herself because there is nothing happening. This is not licence to deprive your dog of attention, just a way of her learning that a lack of it is not aversive.

You can also build up the time she is left alone by walking out of the back door and coming back in the front. You are training her that although you leave, you also come back. Walk out, wait for three seconds and come back in. If she can cope with that it is only a question of extending the time. Do not make a big fuss of her for five minutes before you leave. You do not want to highlight the difference between your presence and your absence. Wait until she is calm before you greet her on returning, rewarding calmness with the attention she seeks.

We have been basically talking about desensitising and counter conditioning to a loss of attention from a significant attachment figure. If your dog has other issues surrounding loss of attention you need to be flexible in your approach to the same principles.

If she kicks off at the sound of the telephone, arrange for her to be sitting on her bed and stay there whilst it rings only twice, and then reward her. Increase it to three rings, then four and so on. Use your mobile to ring your home phone, or record the ring so you can play it back at a low level. Be inventive.

If she squeezes between you and growls at your partner when you are snuggling up together, send her to a nearby bed to calm down, maybe with a stuffed food-toy for company. You won't be cuddling for that long, will you? Pre-plan it as proper training so she settles down beforehand and you don't have to wait until she growls. I know, I'm an old romantic aren't I? Wine, chocolates, lights down low, soft music, dog-chew...

If done properly, by taking each step in small stages and providing guidance in the correct behaviour before frustration builds, this training shows your dog that it is not necessary to over-depend on an individual and there is therefore no need to try to control access to you. This takes away the conflict and the potential for biting with it.

## Control
Control in this case isn't about physical control of your dog, but controlling her expectations through your actions and guidance. Always look to pre-empt any inappropriate behaviour and substitute it with guidance towards behaviour you can reward.

## Context
There is some absolute training in this that can be taken out of context, such as presenting the stimulus at a low level and counter conditioning it to a rewarding outcome, but the nature of desensitisation and counter conditioning is that it more and more represents the stimulus in context as the dog learns the alternative emotional response. You are always working towards context from the start, you've just broken it down into smaller, more achievable, chunks.

## Dogs that fear close contact with unfamiliar people
### Background
Normal adult animal behaviour is to avoid any strangers, but immature (child, puppy, kitten, calf) behaviour is to approach anyone without fear.

The young of many species are more approachable than the adults. As dogs retain many of the characteristics of a canine juvenile into adulthood, we must expect them to retain a degree of puppy friendliness. Some continue to wiggle their way towards any people they happen to meet throughout their lives, but most don't. Most have their circle of human friends and can take or leave strangers. Of course once they get to know the strangers, they join their circle of friends.

There are two reasons that dogs can fear unfamiliar people. The first is lack of social referencing at a sufficiently early age, and the second is one or more specific aversive incident(s) with that person or type of people. Of course if a dog lacks socialisation it is easier for them to perceive a specific aversive incident from a person. Scary people are even scarier if you're scared of people to start with.

By far the most common reason is lack of social referencing, although people are very keen to invent the back-story for rescue dogs: *"He trembles when he gets anywhere near children, and I'm sure he would bite them if they came close enough, so it is obvious he has been hurt by children in the past."* Perhaps it is easier to blame errant children for the dog's animosity rather than ascribe his malicious intent to a lack of understanding on his part, but it is rarely the case.

"Type" of people has quite a wide meaning, from the different sexes, children, people that walk with sticks, people wearing hoods, people in uniforms; almost any common feature that can be identified by the dog.

The guarding breeds or those deemed "*suspicious of strangers*" easily drop into this category through their breed dispositions, although they may disguise the fear with breed specific behaviour, coming forward apparently confidently rather than showing overtly fearful body language.

Biting unfamiliar people may not manifest itself until the dog reaches social maturity, even though the origins lie in lack of early socialisation or an aversive event when young. This is the time when a dog changes from using deferential puppy behaviour to deal with threats (hiding behind your legs, squirming, grinning and wiggling, rolling over on his back and urinating) to more proactive adult behaviour. *"I'm grown-up now and don't have to settle for being scared any more. I can make you go away"*. This abrupt change in styles of dealing with fear takes many owners by surprise as they had not noticed that the puppy was actually afraid. They just assumed he was being silly as he tucked his tail, hid, wriggled and wet himself.

Remember also that there is good evidence for a second sensitive period for learning about social behaviour at around puberty. With all those hormones whizzing round and the change from puppy to adult behaviour patterns it is little wonder that dogs can need some help in how to relate to people as an adult, rather than as a puppy.

Naturally, if pup has had little social experience whilst young, the second sensitive period increases their vulnerability to developing social fears at precisely the time that they are changing to adult ways of dealing with them. A frightened pup that hides behind legs can grow up into a biting dog with no other change than the passing of days.

Adult dogs that have been well socialised as pups can also develop fears of strangers, from either a specific incident, such as being spooked by a man with a brolly suddenly appearing in the twilight, or by a withdrawal from society followed by a reintroduction. Social referencing has to continue throughout the dog's life for it to remain effective; withdraw it and you need a sensitive reintroduction.

There are two circumstances in which dogs can meet unfamiliar people: if they are out and find a stranger in their path, or if they are at home and the stranger comes to them. In both cases the original motivation is fear but, because the motivation develops differently, when dealing with it we should split the two into home and away. Of course, if your dog is exhibiting aggression towards unfamiliar people in both circumstances you will have to implement both.

Regardless of the way in which your dog has developed the fear of unfamiliar people that is now causing him to want to bite, your basic training package of "sit", "pay attention", "go to bed" and Learn to Earn once again comes to your rescue.

## Away from Home
### Training Alternative

When away from home proactive aggression is likely to be less extreme and only when the unfamiliar person is very close. Because of the opportunities to get out of the stranger's way when out and about, dogs are much less likely to show aggression than when they are on what they consider to be their own territory.

For aggression to people when away from home you need to train a strong "pay attention" request ("*Wat-sis?*") out of context until it is perfect and a "come-to-me" request, often called a recall. For both of those you will need to increase your own value through the use of a suitable reward. This will either be lavish praise, food treats, or an exciting game, or maybe combinations of all three at various times.

By now you should also know that for your dog to pay you any kind of attention at any time, you need to make sure your relationship is balanced, hence you also need "Learn to Earn". This training is very similar to that for dogs that fear unfamiliar dogs, so please re-read that section.

## Control Away from Home

Being confined to a lead may make the reaction worse as the dog has no option to escape. Remember the three "pre-programmed" canine strategies: hide, move away or make the scary thing go away? I'm not suggesting you should just let him loose, but you need to be aware that confinement could make him more reactive.

236

Being off-lead gives your dog more options to avoid the stranger and consequently control his own fear. Unfortunately it doesn't give you any control of him if it all goes pear-shaped. The compromise, once your training moves beyond being on a close lead, is that long-line again. This allows him to think that he is in a position to make decisions, and indeed he can do so, so long as it is the right one: to come away. If he doesn't come away and starts to set himself up, you can enforce the right decision, walking him quietly away, without compromising safety.

Muzzling or not is your choice, but it reduces your options for treating and playing. Your dog should not be close enough to any other person to be a danger to them and should not re-direct towards you if you have your relationship in kilter and are working below the threshold at which he feels it necessary to bite.

Context Away from Home

This process is no different from the one for fear of other dogs. You have trained your "pay attention" request and can now start to introduce the feared stimulus at a distance. Using a toy-stooge isn't really an option, but you could use a friend suitably disguised as a "type" if that is applicable. For example if your dog reacts to men in hoodies, you could use your friend in a hoodie at a distance. It depends upon the type of person your dog fears as to how suitable setting it up might be but, as ever, be inventive.

If you can't find a suitable stooge, you are left with using people at large in the environment. You must never, ever, place any person in fear during your training. If you do, you are breaking the law. However, as you should always be working below the reaction threshold, this should not present a problem. People won't even know you are there, let alone engaged in dog training.

Take your dog to the training place, which may be anywhere and everywhere, but give some consideration to the necessity to keep the stimulus at a distance that does not arouse the proactive aggression. You need to encounter the people farther away than his reaction distance so you maintain his distress within workable levels.

When he looks at the kind of person that previously made him kick-off, ask, "*Wat-sis?*" excitedly and walk away to reward in your chosen manner. And repeat. And repeat in another place with another person. And keep on repeating, rewarding coming away to you until he starts to volunteer the behaviour.

When he does that of his own accord, move to the long-line to give him the impression that he is making his own decision, whilst you retain the option to encourage him to make the right one.

It is then just a matter of varying the stimulus (different people) and the distances, bearing in mind that he will have good and bad days because stress is variable and cumulative. By this time you are working on his distance from you and proximity to the people. The nearer to you and further from the person he is, the easier he will be to call away. Conversely, the nearer he is to them, and further from you, will make guiding him more difficult.

If you want to stop there and be the owner of a dog that chooses to come away from unfamiliar people, always with the potential to require some guidance from you on his bad days, that's fine. Lots of people, including me, think that it is not necessary for dogs to approach unfamiliar people or unfamiliar people to approach dogs.

If you want your dog to be approached and maybe petted by strangers, you will have to add on some more training, which you cannot do without stooges because you are continuing the process of desensitisation and counter conditioning by bringing the feared stimulus even closer.

In practice this means once you are able to walk past on oncoming person of the type to whom he would previously react, whilst giving and receiving a cheery "*Good morning!*" without any reaction from your dog other than a look at you, you can up the stakes.

As your previously primed stooge approaches ask your dog to sit. As you've trained it so well he will immediately plonk his bum on the floor and look at you. Give praise for a job well done and as you are doing so your stooge should give a jovial "*Hello*", keep walking slowly past and drop a high value treat at your dog's feet.

The "*Hello*" should be timed to attract his attention so he sees the treat being dropped. Because your relationship allows him to take treats with your permission, you should give him the go ahead to take it.

You will need to repeat this several times over several days with several people for it to be effective. You might consider a sympathetic dog training class if you can't find the stooges.

Initially the stooge should be very low-key, not looking at, reaching for or speaking to the dog, but over time as he begins to see people as a positive, with the potential for a good experience, they can become less restrained. They can stop for a while and talk to you, taking the opportunity to withhold the treat until he reaches towards them, then offering it from their hand. He should always make the move towards them, never them towards him.

Eventually your dog will view people as source of positive emotions (the anticipation of a treat) and will seek out interaction with them. Be careful. If you overdo it he will want to run up to every new person to inspect them for food and you will have exchanged a biter for a mugger - mugging people for treats. Keep practising calling him back so you can guide him away from people who it is not appropriate to approach. Balance the training between approaching people when you allow him and ignoring people when you don't.

If you want to go even further and train him to enjoy being petted by strangers, you need to add on the touch-training explained in the *Fear of familiar people* section, starting with friends again, then moving on to less familiar people.

## Home
### Training Alternative

This will require more effort in the initial training, and mainly uses the "go to bed" request. People shout at their dogs to be quiet, but usually the dog has little understanding of what the words mean. Rather than yelling at a dog, it is far better to give him something else to do. Train a rock-solid "go to bed" request so he knows exactly what it means and can be sent there from anywhere in the house at any time.

The positioning of the bed is also significant. If he is not actually attacking visitors, but makes a lot of noise, the bed should be positioned so he has a view of the door, reducing any frustration he might otherwise feel at not being able to see who the visitor is.

Now start to introduce parts of the composite "visitor experience". Rap on the table and send your dog to bed. He will bark because he is responding to a stimulus like the knock at the door but, because it is not the exact noise, his response will be less. That means he is more likely to follow your request for him to go to his bed. If he does not, take the stimulus down a peg or two by tapping even more quietly. If people ring your doorbell rather than knock, record it on your phone and play it back very quietly. Whatever the stimulus is, it needs to be presented on cue by you at a level where your dog remains (just) under your control.

Once he is quiet, reward him with a high value treat from the treat-pot above the bed. Train five or six knocks several times a day. Pretty soon your dog will use the tapping as a cue for going to bed to wait for a treat by himself. Take the training up a notch by knocking on the inside of the door or increasing the volume on the recording of the bell, and so on until you are properly knocking on the door with your dog under full control.

Once you have the required control with the full knocking on the door stimulus, you need another person. All family members should be taking part anyway, because it may be necessary for them to control the dog too. A familiar person should allow your dog to watch them walk out of the door, leaving it ajar, and see them knocking on it. The dog will still bark because he is responding to the stimulus, and you have made it more like the visitor experience. The knocker should then come in, send the dog to bed if he hasn't already gone, and treat him when he is quiet.

You can progress that to the whole visitor experience by the familiar person going out of the back door without the dog seeing, and then knocking on the front door. You can send the dog to bed before answering the door, and the "visitor" can reward him for sitting quietly on his bed.

For dogs that actually attempt to or succeed in biting people who come to the door there is a control refinement that you also need to factor in.

## Control at Home

If your dog has shown the slightest sign of advancing upon a person who has come to your door with the intention of biting them, he must not be allowed in contact with any person that comes to the house. This is not just a suggested option, it is absolutely imperative for the safety of visitors and delivery people. Likewise he should not be given free run of the garden because visitors and delivery people have a right to walk up to your front door unmolested. A **Beware of the Dog** sign is not sufficient to get you off the hook; you are still culpable.

The most simple control factor would be to place your dog in a secure room that does not have access to the doorway. Do not try to jump straight to the "sit on bed" training because it won't work in the face of the full stimulus. You need an interim control measure.

If your visitor is simply delivering something and leaving, you may decide that excluding your dog to a different room is all you need. No training, just control. That's absolutely fine if that's all you want.

However, if you want your dog to get used to visitors coming into the house, you need to introduce him to them. For safety's sake he should be on a lead, and you can practice this as an extension of the family's sit-on-bed training above. Once the familiar person comes in the house the dog is placed on a lead and sits with you whilst the pretend visitor tosses him treats. This sets the scene for the combined control/training required for real visitors.

Whilst going through the process of training the sit-on-bed out of context, the dog should be excluded from the doorway and the room into which real visitors are brought. When a real visitor arrives, place the dog in another room and leave him there as you seat the visitor. It is good practice to ask visitors to phone ahead to let you know when to expect them, and to let them know that you will be putting the dog away and may take a few extra minutes to answer the door.

When your visitor is seated, and your dog has calmed down in the other room, you can start the introduction training in context.

Context

Give your real visitor a pot of treats, then go and fetch your dog from the exclusion room. Make sure he is on the lead and that you have full control of him, so he can't approach the visitor. Bring him into the room and sit with him away from the visitor. This is where you bless the hours spent training him to sit.

The visitor should toss him a treat. A big smelly treat has more chance of getting through to him if he is highly aroused, but it should be small enough to be gone in one gulp. The first treat will calm him slightly, and change his emotional expectation of the visitor. They are now less frightening and more attractive. The following two or three treats will confirm his view that this person is actually alright.

At the point at which he relaxes and you can see the fear dropping away, you can allow him to approach the visitor to take the next treat from their hand. After that, probably on consecutive visits, you are getting into the touch training outlined in *Fear of familiar people* earlier.

Be aware that people sitting down tossing him treats are less scary than people who stand up to leave (or for any other reason), and that he may reach threshold again when they do that. Call him to you and place him on the lead again before they move.

There are interim stages between this and the full control of sending him to bed to wait for a complete stranger to toss him a treat, and you will have to play each one by ear. He will likely favour some people over others and take more time to get to know some. Each brand new person should start from scratch, because you can never be too safe.

For houses and dogs that are suitable for it, you might consider placing him behind a baby-gate rather than excluding him in another room altogether, where a real visitor can toss him a treat over the top of it as they pass. A handy treat-pot by the door allows visitors to prepare to greet him with a treat as soon as they come in.

A long-ish house-line attached to his collar gives you some control as you traverse from total exclusion to the sit-on-bed.

Setting up the visitor-training is always a good idea. Plan your visitors in advance and what you are going to do to progress your training each time. Does he know this visitor? Can we skip putting him in another room and go straight for the bed, possibly with the added safety of the house-line in case he doesn't respond as asked? Might it be worth asking the visitor to bring a big smelly treat for immediate delivery as they walk in the door?

Slowly over time you will change your dog's expectation of people who come to the door from one of fear to one of anticipation of a nice thing happening. Initially the hope is for a food treat, but eventually the pleasant interaction with the visitor will replace that as his fear subsides.

If your dog is one of the ones that have gone beyond overt fear and is looking forward to the competition – the chance to chase someone away from the door – the basic principles are the same. You will just be changing his expectation from one of aroused competition to one of relaxed interaction. The techniques of taking away the opportunity to perform the behaviour to prevent further reinforcement, followed by reintroducing and gradually increasing small parts of the composite stimulus under control, as you reward the alternative behaviour, are exactly the same.

## Dogs that bite people through fun

### Background

There are two reasons that dogs bite people in fun. The first is that they haven't learned not to and the second is that they get carried away. Of course, as you'd expect, "both" is also an option.

Puppies have a lot to learn if they are going to grow up to be well-balanced adult dogs, and one of their early lessons is bite-inhibition. They learn it in the most efficient way possible from their siblings.

It is a natural behaviour for puppies and even adult dogs to use their mouths in play with other dogs and unsurprisingly they transfer that type of play to people too.

Play-biting is very common in young puppies as they explore the world and their fellows. Anyone who has spent any time with puppies will have been variously nipped, chewed and ragged by needle-sharp teeth. When puppies play nipping with each other, it hurts. Their teeth are disproportionately sharp for delicate ears and tails.

When one pup bites another too hard the bitten pup squeals and stops the game, with a slightly sulky look on his face. The biting pup learns that if she bites this hard the game stops. It is operant negative punishment, the removal of a pleasant experience contingent on the stimulus; a very effective way to learn. It doesn't take many "*Ouch!*" moments for pups to learn that biting hard makes the fun stop, so they inhibit their bites to an acceptable level.

Naturally, there are a myriad of things that can go wrong with this process. They might have a controlling Mum who doesn't allow rough play; some breeds enjoy body contact more than others; they might be exceptionally tolerant of pain, or they may be extremely intolerant of pain, so the puppy never learns that there is an acceptable low level of play-bite.

Or we may find a human factor included; a macho-man who likes to play rough with puppies and encourages them to bite him, or, without realising it, pushes the rough play too hard for the pup, who then learns to retaliate hard. Or a singleton pup, or a pup that prefers to play with older more tolerant dogs in the household… or… as I said, many things can go wrong and, if they do, our pup doesn't learn that biting too hard isn't acceptable.

If your dog hasn't learned bite-inhibition as a pup she will use her teeth too often and it will hurt. She will bite hard from the start of play, as it is normal play behaviour for them. She doesn't know any different.

The dogs that get carried away are slightly different, because they have learned at least some bite inhibition. The combative breeds are most commonly represented in this group because the type of play in which a dog likes to indulge is dictated by their breed specific behaviour. What tends to happen is that stroking turns into ruffling and then into push and shove, then into wrestling, then rough-housing and before you know it she has got hold of the sleeve of your best cardigan and is tugging with all her might. This is slightly better than the alternative of tugging on your arm, as cardigans don't bleed.

This usually happens after she has been playing for a while and you have upped the stakes. She is pushed beyond her ability to control her own arousal, and her breed instincts take over. You will see an almost glazed quality to her eyes and the skin underneath her white patches of hair may turn pink. Although she is enjoying it and gets a massive buzz from it, she can't actually help herself at this stage. You've gone too far.

Other breeds can get locked into their breed specific play behaviour as well, in the same way that I mentioned our Collie gets carried away playing football, but whatever form it takes in your dog, the same principles apply.

Training Alternative
In the case of both reasons, the obvious thing to do is stop playing with her like that. I say it is obvious but people keep doing it, despite the cuts and bruises.

The second step is to focus on object play, rather than social combative play. In short, play "fetch" not "fight". Your first training objective is therefore the retrieve. If you want to teach it via the tug-rope-toy in Chapter 8, that is fine, but do it carefully.

It will be easier to divert her play into objects rather than parts of people if your relationship has a sound basis, so implementing a

Learn to Earn is also a must. A Learn to Earn relationship gives her the understanding that when you say, "*Please stop*", you mean it, and there is no alternative.

Finally a, "go to bed" provides a pleasant alternative to inappropriate play, where she can earn a satisfying treat or chew-toy based reward.

## Control

There isn't a great deal of control involved, other than to avoid the play that causes the biting behaviour, covered in Context below.

## Context

For dogs that lack bite inhibition, if she initiates the play that usually results in biting and you cannot divert her into retrieving an object, you squeal like you are hurt and immediately stop the play. Walk away and refuse eye contact. If you can manage a slightly sulky look on your face, so much the better. Then you ask her to go to her bed to calm down. Once she is calm you can invite her back to play retrieve with the toy.

Like another puppy, you take away the play when she bites and reintroduce it when she is calm again, but to encourage the calm behaviour you have an option to prompt it that other pups don't have, by sending her to her bed. Your process works in the same way that she should have naturally learned as a puppy, but with added consideration that reduces frustration.

For dogs that get carried away, you use the same process, but don't need to stop the play until the point a little before she loses the plot. So long as you can keep play below the tipping point for the inappropriate behaviour, by selectively withdrawing the opportunity to play (stop, walk away, refuse eye contact, sulk), you can keep her within appropriate levels of arousal. The crucial part is that you must never let her get above the tipping point because that's where she loses self-control and you will not be able to get through to her, so err on the side of caution and stop well before that.

Ask her to go to bed to encourage her to calm down, as a positive move to earn a reward, and, when the time is right, re-start play at an appropriate level. The more practiced that you become at interpreting her mood, the easier it will be to ease off before you need to stop altogether and play her mood up and down, but never too far.

Eventually she will learn that the best play happens when she controls herself. Ultimately you will gain the only dog-training control worth having, which is her own self-control.

# Chapter 11
# When It All Goes Wrong

To train a dog successfully to modify his behaviour away from biting and fighting it is necessary to remain below the ceiling of arousal that causes him to flip, and in an ideal world no dog would exceed that threshold. But they do.

In every case where a dog bites someone they shouldn't, a person has made a mistake. It might be the person that put the dog in that position, such as when delivery people are confronted by a dog, or the person who was bitten, but a mistake has been made. In an ideal world, mistakes would never happen. But they do.

So far this book has been all about how to keep your dog below the threshold and how to avoid making mistakes, but it would be wrong of me not to acknowledge that the world is less than ideal. There wouldn't need to be a book at all if dogs never bit nor fought.

So I have to include a chapter on what to do when it all goes wrong. What to do if you are confronted with a dog that appears to want to bite you, or with a dog that actually engages with you or another dog. Now, the advice that follows is not aimed at the professionals whose work can bring them into conflict with dogs, because they have their own procedures and equipment, but at the average person in the street who may come into contact with dogs in everyday life.

Most dogs do not want to bite you and are looking for a way out of the situation. It is therefore a mistake to take a fighting initiative; after all, they are better armed than we are. You may take on a dog in a fight and even beat it, but you are unlikely to escape unscathed.

Professionals who frequently deal with dangerous dogs spend all our time and energy keeping them below threshold. If we have to push them towards threshold to see how dangerous they are, we do it gently and under control. If we are bitten, we have made a mistake.

Never employ a dog trainer who carries many dog-bite scars - they have made many mistakes. I've never been bitten in seven years assessing allegedly dangerous dogs or pit bull types. I've been muzzle-bumped once (although he hit me five times on the torso) when working as a pet behaviour counsellor in the owner's home, in over ten years. I was unintentionally bitten no more than half a dozen times in twenty-six years working as a police dog handler and instructor, although I calculate I took well over fifty thousand intentional bites in training. I don't think they are bad averages.

Having just written all that I am confidently expecting that by tempting fate I shall be mauled any day in the very near future.

My point is that it is possible to avoid dog bites, even when you think they intend to bite you. There are several circumstances in which you might find yourself in conflict with dogs, almost invariably because they think you are a threat in some way but, whatever they are, you have two main priorities: the first is to prevent the dog coming into physical contact with you and the second is to persuade him to back off, to let you escape.

## Contact indoors

If a dog can't touch you, it can't bite you. The first step in any contact with a dog that threatens you in any circumstances, whether it is your own dog at home or a dog you have never met before, maybe encountered on a country walk on your holidays, is to stop. Stop whatever you are doing and stand stock still.

Now think. Think what it is you might have done to make this dog see you as a threat. If he is your own dog at home, you must be doing something. Are you approaching him when he has a bone or other valued object? Does he think you are going to tell him off or otherwise punish him? Is he in pain? Have you surprised him by tip-toeing in late at night without putting the light on? Are you drunk? Or

250

both? Have you tugged his hair with a comb? Stood on his foot? Are you having a barney with your partner? Throwing things? Are you stepping over him? Are you standing in his bed to show him your dominance? Are you holding him down or rolling him over? Are you eating from his bowl? Cleaning his teeth? Cutting his nails? Grabbing his collar or scruff? Kissing and cuddling him?

Yes, some amusing ones, but all circumstances I have known a dog to bite their owner. It does not matter what it is, but whatever you are doing, stop. It gives you both time to think and reflect on the best course of action.

If your dog is stiff and growling, but does not make any move towards you, he may be content that you have backed off. However he may not allow you to approach him without becoming more defensive again. You may be able to break the deadlock by changing his emotion with a positive expectation, such as going for a walk or eating. If he is not actually prepared to attack, but will not allow approach, try to snap him out of the standoff by picking up his lead and, in a cheery voice, offering to take him for a walk. Alternatively, pick up his food bowl and rattle biscuits into it, or open his treat-pot or a tin of dog-food.

By giving him opportunities not to be aggressive, he can back off or remain static but calming down at any point, but if he doesn't, then straighten yourself into a defensive stance.

This is with your feet shoulder's width apart, and your leading foot half a foot's length in front of the back foot. Your weight should be evenly balanced and your arms slightly in front of your body, bent at the elbow. Your hands should be facing forward in a placatory gesture, towards the dog. Saying, "*Woo-o-a-h*", like cowboys do to stop their horses but much softer and lower in tone, followed by, "*It's ok, go-o-o-d dog*" in a friendly voice, shows him you mean no harm.

This stance allows you to back away slowly by shifting your weight onto your back foot, without making sudden movements that may arouse an attack. Keeping your hands open and towards him lets him see *you* are not moving to attack, but at the same time allows you to make a defensive block to fend off an attack by him.

This should take no more than two seconds and whilst you are doing it look around you, without taking your attention from him. Don't stare straight at his face, but keep your eyes monitoring his whole body. You are looking for movements that suggest he is gathering himself, but also at the room layout for your avenues of escape and options for defence.

He is initially likely to be fairly rigid, so any muscle or facial movements will be very apparent. Any bunching of the muscles, particularly in the back legs, may indicate an imminent lunge at you. Softening of the front legs indicates a withdrawal.

If he lunges you have a split second to react, but if you are prepared you can shift your weight onto your back leg and quickly step your leading leg backwards, immediately moving yourself a body-width away. This means that when he lunges he will not reach you with his intended maximum force.

Do not attempt to catch hold of him, but continue the movement of what was your leading leg, but is now your back foot, swinging it behind you by pivoting on your standing leg. Because this turns you sideways on to him, you will be able to use one or both hands to push the side of his head and shoulder, directing his momentum past you, as you continue to move in the opposite direction. Although this is wordy to describe, it should happen in one fluid movement.

Now utilise whatever you identified earlier as your best option for defence or escape. Whilst you were looking at him to weigh up his intentions, you were also looking out of the corner of your eye at the room layout. Now is the time to increase distance between you. You can either pick up a kitchen chair to hold in front of you, step behind an armchair, or exit the door, closing it behind you. At the least, pick up a cushion or briefcase or something else that will block another attack.

Retreat away from him without turning your back. Stay sideways on, to retain the ability to block, fend and move again as you head for your escape route. If you can reach it in one step, go as quickly as you can. If you need more time, back away slowly whilst watching him again.

For small dogs at floor level it is your legs that are in most danger and you will not be able to reach to fend off with your hands. Keep the original posture, but if he lunges raise the sole of your front foot towards him. Do not kick as he is faster than you and may duck under it, which gives him the initiative. Neither do you want your foot caught in his jaws as this could topple you. A broad foot-sole facing towards him gives him nothing to bite at. Of course you will need to drop your foot to walk backwards, but you can progress through a series of single steps with your foot raised in protection each time - skip-hopping backwards.

The goal is to avoid being bitten at all costs by moving away, talking quietly and fending him off with your hands, feet or any structures in the room. Getting behind something on your way to the door gives you further protection, but do not hem yourself into a corner; you always need to get out. Tables, chairs and like furniture move, so drag them with you, keeping him on the opposite side as you leave.

Always keep half-sideways on to him, never turning your back as you block, fend and move. It is vital that you stay on your feet, so move slowly and don't trip. If you do go to ground, roll up into a ball, tucking your knees into your stomach and with your arms covering your head and neck, protecting vulnerable parts and offering nothing to grip.

Most dogs will not press home an attack and just be glad that you are not threatening them anymore. If you are on the floor they may approach and sniff you before wandering away. Once they are no longer threatening get slowly to your knees then your feet, watching all the time, and try to leave as before.

If you fail to fend him off, he may bite and release, or he may make repeated lunges and snaps, in which case continue to try to block, fend and depart. Smaller dogs may grab trousers and hold on, which is better than biting your leg. If you can walk towards your exit with them still gripping then do so. Keeping the pressure on by pulling gently against the grip encourages them to keep hold. If they keep hold of your trousers, they are not biting you.

If you are going out of a door, close it on your trousers, so that it forces the little dog to let go. Your trouser leg becomes momentarily trapped in the door, but you can open slightly to release it. If there is no door to exit, you can either out-wait him until he releases of his own accord,  or trap your trouser-leg between a solid object and something else, for example by pushing two chairs together or pushing a cushion against a sofa, making a trouser-leg sandwich with him on the other side. If nothing else is available and you must get loose, force an object down your leg towards him so that when he releases his next bite will be at the object - bread-board, washing basket, footstool, magazine rack...? Variations of all of these will also work for a larger dog that has hold of clothing.

Small dogs' bites can be painful if he makes contact, but most release quickly. As soon as you are able, block, fend and depart.

If a larger dog bites and holds, it could be life-threatening and although I always recommend not hurting the dog if you possibly can, there may come a time where it is your only means of escape. The reason for not hurting the dog is not just for his welfare, but because once you get into combat where pain is involved, he may become enraged and it may make the attack even worse.

This kind of determined bite and hold is extremely rare, but is more frequently seen in the dog-fighting types, and the reason that pit bull terrier types top the fatality list. There is a myth that such dogs possess a distinctive feature that allows them to lock their jaws. This is not the case, although they do have extremely strong musculature that gives a very hard grip. It is the motivation that gives the dog the locked-on appearance, where they will take immense punishment but retain their grip - the fighting dog persistence and determination not to give in.

There are options open to prepared professionals to release a biting dog, such as purpose-made dog deterrents, water-jets and a blast from a water or $CO_2$ fire extinguisher, but none of these always work, and are not often to hand when you are being attacked.

Options for hurting a dog into releasing a bite concentrate on his vulnerable areas: throat, eyes and stomach/genitals. Choking a dog out of consciousness can be done by twisting his collar either by hand or by thrusting something through and twisting it round. If you have the strength it is possible to grip the windpipe at the top of his throat, under his jaw, and squeeze until he passes out. Gouging his eye sockets and squeezing or kicking his genitals will cause him the most pain you can - although as I have said this may be counter-productive if it makes him more angry. However, at this stage you are fighting for your life and who am I to tell you not to try anything you like?

If you feel you need to hit him over the head with a chair, or ram a table-leg down his throat, or some other intuitive fighting tactic no one else has thought of, in order to save your own life, then who can criticise? Certainly not me, sitting here in the cold light of day.

I have seen reports that poking a pencil, pen or your finger into his rectum will make a dog release his grip, but I have also been told of occasions when that has not worked. In fact there is no single thing that is guaranteed to work. Even Tasers, electric stun-guns used by police officers, sometimes fail to make proper contact, and bullets can miss.

What I can say is that the sooner you can get back to block, fend and move, the safer you will be.

## Contact outdoors

Coming into contact with a strange dog outdoors follows the same process of physically protecting yourself and reducing the threat to the dog so they stop the attack.

People out cycling, jogging or walking can misinterpret an approaching dog; many just want to check you out as you pass through their patch. If you stand still she might just sniff you and wander away again. Don't try to interact by reaching out to pat or stroke her, although there is no harm in saying something innocuous such as, *"Hello puppy"*. Dogs usually think that "puppy" was the first name that was given to them, and the word usually has good associations. People vary rarely use it in a negative way, so it is a good word to use to address an unknown dog.

If you are approached by a dog that is growling and snarling, as opposed to giving a few barks, she may be a threat to you. Stay calm and follow the advice for indoor contact. Do not try to shoo her away, hit or kick her, as that only confirms her opinion that you are a threat. If you are cycling, dismount and place the bike between you and her, then slowly walk away, keeping her on the other side. Do not try to speed away as this will encourage her to bite, and make sure you are out of her interest range before you remount.

On foot your options for blocking her with furniture are fewer than indoors, but make use of whatever street-furniture is there, such as a lamppost, bench, or litter-bin.

Outdoors you will have to travel further to escape, which means you will have to watch her for longer. Again, don't stare at her but turn your head slightly to one side and downwards. Watch her very carefully out of the corner of your eye. It will also be more difficult to prevent her moving round behind you, so keep moving gently to present a half side/front view of your body.

Fortunately she is not likely to pursue you very far. Keep walking and talking up to the point at which the dog loses interest in you. Try to place more solid objects between you, for example move from lamppost to litterbin and hold something in front of you, such as your briefcase, bag or coat. If you must get past the dog, try to circle round her, keeping at least the original distance between you.

Do not scream or yell. If you know there are people within hearing distance, call to them for help. Stay on your feet and do not corner yourself. Continue to walk slowly away, backwards or sideways, looking down and sideways, talking reassuringly, fending off if necessary and aiming to place solid objects between you as you leave.

If you are bitten, the guidance is the same as for indoors, but bite and holds are even more rare from dogs you meet in the street.

## Separating fighting dogs

Intervening in dog fights is dangerous. People are often bitten when they put their hands in between fighting dogs. The dogs either don't actually know they are biting people, or when the red mist descends they see anyone that touches them as a threat and react accordingly.

But we can't just let them get on with it can we? Well, we shouldn't if we can break it up, but neither should we place ourselves in danger. I've seen many court cases where the two dogs fighting have both come out unscathed, but the intervening person has been badly bitten.

If left to sort it out themselves, most dog fights turn out to be handbags-at-ten-paces encounters; all bluff, bluster and noise, with little or no actual injuries. Usually the fear/frustration combination means they want the other to back down, but are too afraid to actually make them do it.

Sure they snarl, lunge and barge, but with the equipment dogs have, each fight should be fatal. It doesn't take a great deal of effort to rip out a throat. I guess we should thank the social inhibition processes inherited from their ancestors for the fact that in most cases they simply don't want to do much damage.

Most dog fights look like mayhem, but are generally little more than exaggerated posturing. However, they look ferocious and people certainly don't want their dog involved, so they try to break it up.

There are several ways that are less dangerous than putting your hand in between them. If they are both your dogs you may be in a position to throw a bucket of water over them, or shock them with a blast from the garden hose. These are the staples of staff when breaking up dog-fights in kennels, along with purpose-made sprays or noise deterrents. An alternative indoors is to throw a blanket over the fighters, adapted outdoors to throwing your coat over them - but expect it to be ripped in the process. Is a ripped coat a better or worse outcome than a ripped hand? An infected ripped hand? An infected ripped hand that swells up like a balloon for a month on antibiotics? Your choice.

Away from home you could hit one of the fighters with your bag or lead, but not with the metal parts, and aim for the shoulders to inflict less injury. It wouldn't do to injure a dog when they were each going to walk away unscathed before your intervention. Usually it is the other dog you hit, not your own, but that is just human spite and bias. Unfortunately you are at risk of the other dog turning on you if you get involved, although I have also known people being bitten by their own dogs as they've intervened to try to help them. Red mist again.

More hands-on if they are really in gear and won't part, loop your lead around under your dog's withers, around her waist just in front of her back legs, then lift her back legs off the ground and away from the fight, until she breaks off. Slightly more dangerous would be to loop your own hands around the same place and pick her up. She is likely to turn on you, but you then have the option to throw her away from both you and the other dog, and she should land on her feet without injury. You can try the finger/object up the rectum, but as I said it won't always work. In any case, I always take my own pen when visiting rescue centres to avoid having to borrow one to write with.

Most dogs are looking to disengage if they get the chance and are happy to be broken up, but the odd one will come at your dog again. Standing between them with the sole of your foot up to block the protagonist, whilst backing or circling away as in *Contact indoors*, is the safest option.

For the sake of safety, any dog bites you sustain should be seen by a qualified medical professional, as many become infected, and you must check that you have up-to-date tetanus immunity.

Despite what appears to be a dire chapter, dogs causing severe injuries is still relatively rare, and most dog bites and fights are comparatively minor affairs. In 2011 there were an estimated eight million dogs in the UK, in 27 million households. At just over six thousand serious bites that's one in every 1,300 dogs or one in each 4,500 homes.

Whilst every bite is a cause for concern, you are very unlikely to be badly injured by a dog, and now that you know how to avoid being bitten, the odds for you personally are even less. Remember, every time a dog bites a person, somebody has made a mistake. Don't make mistakes and you stand much less chance of being bitten.

# Chapter 12
## Over to You

If you follow the advice in the preceding chapters through to its conclusion you will keep yourself safer but you won't cure your dog from biting and fighting. You will not cure him because biting and fighting is not a disease, it is a normal behaviour that is happening in circumstances in which we would rather it didn't. It is a mismatch in expectation; a misinterpretation of communication; a lack of understanding.

In our case we are failing to get through to our pet, and in your dog's case he is trying to cope the best he can in the circumstances. He never set out to be a bad dog, any more than we would set out to be an inadequate owner.

No dog will ever lose the capacity to bite and fight, but what we should aim to do is to keep the circumstances in which he feels it is necessary to an absolute minimum; none at all if possible. But it is down to you, not to him. You have to show him that he can do it. You have to guide him to make the right decisions. And you *can* do it, but it takes time and effort.

Dog training and behaviour modification is like that. It needs commitment, understanding and communication. It takes time on a daily basis, when you'd rather not go out for the third time because it is tippling down and your coat is still wet from the last time. And it takes time on an extended basis, when you are beginning to question your training programme because you don't seem to have made any progress for three weeks. But, if you have a biter or fighter, he's made his choice, and if you don't make the effort to change it, no one else will, least of all him.

I haven't told you everything there is to know about dogs that bite and fight because I don't know everything. Be wary of people who say they do. The more I find out about dog behaviour, the more I realise how little we actually know about our pets.

If I was to try to tell you everything that is known, I would need to write an individual account of every single dog, because there are tiny refinements that will help each one on an individual basis. There are little ways of hastening teaching the "go to bed" request for some dogs by luring or tossing treats; ways of turning the head of a dog away from the aversive stimulus at exactly the right time to enhance the alternative behaviour and provide the reward of that relief.

You could write a book on just the different ways to teach a dog to pay attention to you, or a retrieve-play-game. If they haven't done already, somebody probably will.

Learn to Earn too can be applied to minutely fit each individual because each individual's requirements are just that – individual. Yes, they might seem to be similar to others and in some cases might actually have some overlap with other dogs' requirements, but when you really get to know your dog you start to understand their uniqueness. It is that uniqueness that makes them special to us, but which can also sometimes cause them difficulties in relating to our world.

What you have now are the essentials; an understanding of the basic underlying emotions that drive biting and fighting dogs, and the rudimentary tools to address them. If you change the emotion, you change the need for the behaviour. If you change the need for the behaviour, you can change the behaviour to one you prefer.

You have basic protocols for each situation in which dogs bite and fight, but only the fundamentals. To be any more specific would be overcomplicating and providing some advice that works for some dogs and not for others.

When it comes to dogs there are never any one-size-fits-all solutions, but the basic protocols are a platform on which to refine, fine-tune, adapt and improve them to fit individual dogs and their owners. And to do that you don't need any more than what you now know, plus imagination and flexibility.

I would say, "*Good luck*", but you don't need luck now, just time and patience. So, take your time and be patient with your dog and with yourself, and you will both get to where you want to be in the end, with a dog that doesn't feel the need to bite or fight.

# Appendix

# Learn to Earn: Is Nothing in Life Free?

*An evaluation of the use of resource control programmes in modifying dog behaviour.*

Mat Ward BSc MVS CCAB www.petbehavioursorted.com

David Ryan PG dip (CABC) CCAB www.dog-secrets.co.uk

The concept of controlling a dog's access to resources in order to improve their behaviour has for many years been a core component of many behaviourists' treatment programmes. "Learn to Earn" is one term among many that is used as a label for this concept. It lends itself to adaptation and exists in many guises, such as "Nothing In Life Is Free" (NILIF), "Say Please Programme", and "Integrated Compliance Training" (ICT).

Used at its best, Learn to Earn is a vital addition to many behaviour modification programmes. However, if the mechanism behind the concept is misunderstood, and it is implemented inappropriately, it can impact negatively on dogs and their guardians. In particular, the pervading but misplaced preoccupation with "dominance" and "pack leadership" has meant that the mechanism underpinning resource control programmes has been misattributed to "status" or "rank" reduction, which can result in ineffectual or harmful implementations of Learn to Earn. This article aims to clarify the rationale and effective application of the Learn to Earn concept, and outline how its use can improve both the welfare and behaviour of pet dogs.

## What is Learn to Earn?
Learn to Earn is simply the day to day control of resources that a dog values, to teach them that looking to people for direction is worthwhile. It increases the predictability of a dog's life, enables them to obtain

important resources in an appropriate way, and teaches dogs to exercise impulse control. The more enlightened illustrations compare it to teaching a dog good manners, using "lifestyle rewards", or teaching a dog to work <u>with</u> the owner to get the things they want. Learn to Earn works by establishing leadership via controlled resource *facilitation* rather than through resource *restriction*.

### The Core Objectives of Learn to Earn

Learn to Earn is about teaching a dog that *the most successful way to obtain the good things in life is to respond to specific directions from people.* It is about changing a dog's perception of their owners as pushovers, or handbrakes, into guiding facilitators.

Teaching a dog to automatically offer a sit for resources is a great first step, but not as powerful as a dog thinking, "How does he want me to behave so that he will facilitate my access to the ...?".

It is a mind-set where the dog thinks "How can I *work with* my human to get what I want?" rather than, "What do I have to do to *prevent her stopping me* doing what I want?" or even worse, "What action *makes* her do what I want?"[1]

### Resources

A resource is something a dog needs or desires. It is something that a dog will be happy to expend time and effort in acquiring. It could be as simple as an item of food, or as complex as the ability to get out of the door so they can get into the car so they aren't left alone as the owner leaves to go shopping. A resource is something valuable to a dog.

In a generic Learn to Earn programme resources are often broken down into categories such as: food; toys/games; and attention. While this is a simplistic approach, it can help owners to focus on what their dog values.

---

[1] These cognitive narratives are used for explanatory purposes, they may not represent accurately the cognitive processes occurring with dogs.

What is regarded as food is mostly obvious, but includes things dogs value as food but we don't. Toys/games again include the obvious, but also breed specific behaviour such as herding, chasing, biting/holding/shaking, and even things such as rummaging about in a hedgerow. Attention is contact from people, including petting, being talked to, and eye contact. There are many other valuable resources that don't necessarily fit neatly into a category, such as social interaction with other dogs, and access to comfort such as lying on the sofa or in front of the fire.

Each dog will place different values on different resources. For example a Border Collie may place massive value on the opportunity to chase a ball, and less value on food. But this balance is flexible, so if the Collie is hungry the opportunity to chase a ball might be relegated to second place.

Control

Many of the resources that dogs value are of little concern to us humans. For example, we may throw a ball whenever it is dropped onto our lap by our dog, stroke them whenever they shove their nose under our hand, or allow them to eat food dropped on the floor without permission.

It should be emphasised that none of these things are necessarily problematic or should by default be avoided by the owner, we do not need to worry that dogs are trying to control us in order to achieve "pack leadership" or "high status", dogs are simply doing what works to get them the good stuff in life. However, if a dog has a history of successfully controlling many situations that are of no concern to an owner, their interactional expectations *may* increase the possibility of inappropriate attempts to achieve what they desire. Unfettered access to resources can also result in dogs who do not view requests from their owners as meaningful, as these requests often serve to restrict access to resources rather than facilitate access. Finally, unfettered access to resources can result in dogs who lack impulse control and are more likely to become frustrated when expectations of control and access are not met. This frustration can result in escalations of intrusive or inappropriate behaviour, and in a small proportion of dogs may even bubble over into a loss of emotional control and aggression.

Therefore, to resolve many problem behaviours it can be advantageous to alter the dog's interactional expectations by taking control of resources that do not necessarily constitute part of the problem behaviour.

## Motivation – not intimidation

Learn to Earn emphasises that thoughtful rather than forceful control of resources is both an effective and compassionate way to control a dog. Pet dogs have limited opportunities to control their own lives, and benefit from guidance to ensure that their attempts to fulfil their desires are consistent with human expectations.

Learn to Earn is about using *motivation* rather than *intimidation* to control dogs. If a dog achieves access to many of the resources they desire by following the directions of their human, life becomes more harmonious for both dog and human. The owner gets a dog that is more responsive to instructions as the dog begins to see these as *opportunities* to fulfil their desires, rather than something that might compete with or restrict access to resources. From the dog's perspective things improve as they begin to have a consistent way in which to obtain the things they value – *looking to their owner for direction*. This can greatly reduce the daily frustration experienced by a dog, which has significant benefits for both dog and owner. The effects of a Learn to Earn programme are also desirable from a welfare perspective, as the motivation to behave appropriately stems from a desire to obtain the good things in life, rather than a desire to avoid pain, fear, or intimidation.

## Awareness of a dog's requirements and emotional sensitivities

Fulfilling the motivational needs of a dog is important to prevent emotional problems such as profound frustration, conflict, or anxiety. Controlled facilitation of the mental, physical, and social desires of a dog forms the core of an effective Learn to Earn programme. Seeking opportunities to facilitate the desires of a dog, rather than restricting them is very important.

Dogs' requirements for access to resources differ between every individual, and within each individual over time. It is therefore impossible to lay down hard and fast rules for fulfilling a dog's requirements, but a skilled behaviourist is able to make value judgements based on a dog's breed or type, current lifestyle, personality, and emotional sensitivities.

## Practical application of Learn to Earn

One of the criticisms of Learn to Earn is that any withholding of resources can cause anxiety and frustration. But if a dog is provided with clear, achievable behavioural alternatives to obtain what they desire, anxiety and frustration is seldom a problem. An important initial step when introducing a Learn to Earn programme is to train acceptable behavioural alternatives out of context, and only then cue them in situations where a dog desires something that their owner controls. Reinforcement for inappropriate behaviour and lack of compliance is stopped, while delivery of the resource occurs if the dog behaves appropriately or responds to a request. During this training process a dog should not be taken beyond the point at which arousal and frustration makes learning difficult, but over time the situations where requests are made before a dog obtains what they desire is broadened. As there is clarity as to the behaviour that "works", frustration is reduced rather than exacerbated. Over time a dog becomes more likely to exert self-control in order to achieve things in their life that they value.

Examples of this process include:

- Opening of the front door at the start of a walk may be delayed until a dog moves to their bed on request.
- A dog is not allowed up onto the couch for a cuddle if they jump up of their own accord, but they are invited up if they respond to a quiet "sit" request given once.
- A dog may be kept on lead and prevented from getting to other dogs they want to play with while they continue to pull towards the other dogs, but allowed off-lead to play once they "down".
- Midway through a tug game with a rope a "drop" request is quietly given, and the rope brought in to the owner's legs so it is "dead" and boring, the owner than waits until the dog decides to let go, and the rope is immediately presented for the dog to play with again.

A key part of this process is that *the dog makes the decision* to respond to a quietly spoken request given once, rather than being forced to do so. For example, simply holding a dog back from the door and walking out first teaches a dog virtually nothing (other than to pull and compete physically with their owner). But asking them to sit and stay while the owner opens the door and moves outside is an excellent exercise in impulse control.

It is important to note that a Learn to Earn programme should NOT advocate that *all* resources are controlled *all* of the time, but that situations where a resource can be controlled by an owner are *opportunities* to become a meaningful facilitator. There is nothing wrong with allowing a dog to obtain resources for free some of the time, as long as their behaviour is acceptable. *Some things in life should be free!* For example, at the start of a walk it is perfectly acceptable to sometimes open the door and allow a dog to walk out without doing anything to "earn" it (as long as they are polite)!

Being proactive with the programme rather than reactive

It is important to note that the focus of a Learn to Earn programme should not be to always wait until a dog wants something before making a request. Initiative needs to be taken to identify the things that a dog loves, and look for opportunities to provide these resources if the dog behaves appropriately or responds to a request. Learn to Earn should be about helping a dog achieve what they desire rather than the draconian control of everything that they show interest in.

Should affection be free?

Many dogs learn from a young age that intrusive behaviour is the most effective way to obtain interaction with people. One common recommendation to deal with dogs that jump up, bark, or mouth, is to simply ignore such attention-seeking behaviour. However, dogs that have received reinforcement for their own attention-seeking initiatives tend to be very persistent, and can increase the intensity of their responses if their behaviour is simply ignored. This often results in occasional reinforcement of some kind from their owners. Simply removing attention also provides no guidance for the dog as to what behaviour might be more successful. As a result, attempts to ignore dogs for attention seeking can often result in the development of *more* persistent, proactive, and intrusive attention-seeking strategies, and a continuation of perceived control on the part of the dog.

In a Learn to Earn programme it is important to ensure that undesirable attention-seeking behaviour is not reinforced, but it is even more important for owners to *take the initiative* to identify and reward a dog with interaction when they behave appropriately or respond to a request. To state that attention-seeking should be ignored in a Learn to

269

Earn programme is valid to some extent, but a vast over-simplification which, if implemented dogmatically, can backfire for both owner and dog. *Cuddles can, and should be free some of the time, as long as a dog is behaving politely.*

## A warning about inadvertent chaining of behaviours

It is important not to respond to inappropriate attempts to obtain resources by then cueing a behaviour followed by provision of the resource. This can result in inadvertent reinforcement of inappropriate behaviour. For example: a dog barks because they want a ball to be thrown – the dog is then asked to "sit" – the dog sits – the ball is thrown. This chain of events reinforces the dog for barking. The "sit" cue essentially acts as a positive reinforcer for barking because it is a very good predictor of impending access to the ball. Pre-empting the inappropriate barking by providing guidance with the 'sit' request before it happens, or at least once the dog stops barking, would prevent inadvertent reinforcement of such barking.

## Conclusion

Because it is a popular and catchy phrase, the term "Learn to Earn" has been adopted and interpreted in different ways by different people, which adds to some disparity of opinion regarding the concept. Its association with misguided attempts at "pack leadership" and "rank-reduction" further muddies the waters.

However, if the mechanism behind the concept of Learn to Earn is understood, and the focus of the programme is on *facilitating* access to resources rather than *restricting* access, it is the most compassionate and effective method of controlling dogs, and is in the interests of both dogs and their owners. It can and should be applied by every dog guardian who wants to work *with* their dog, rather than *against* them to establish desirable behaviour.

Printed in Great Britain
by Amazon.co.uk, Ltd.,
Marston Gate.